Pro Smartphone Cross-Platform Development

iPhone, BlackBerry, Windows Mobile, and Android Development and Distribution

**Sarah Allen,
Vidal Graupera,
Lee Lundrigan**

Apress®

Pro Smartphone Cross-Platform Development: iPhone, Blackberry, Windows Mobile and Android Development and Distribution

ISBN-13 (pbk): 978-1-4302-2868-4

ISBN-13 (electronic): 978-1-4302-2869-1

Printed and bound in the United States of America

President and Publisher: Paul Manning
Lead Editor: Mark Beckner, Ewan Buckingham
Technical Reviewer: Fabio Claudio Ferracchiati
Editorial Board: Steve Anglin, Mark Beckner, Ewan Buckingham, Gary Cornell, Jonathan Gennick, Jonathan Hassell, Michelle Lowman, Matthew Moodie, Duncan Parkes, Jeffrey Pepper, Frank Pohlmann, Douglas Pundick, Ben Renow-Clarke, Dominic Shakeshaft, Matt Wade, Tom Welsh
Coordinating Editor: Jim Markham
Copy Editor: Ralph Moore
Compositor: MacPS, LLC
Indexer: BIM Indexing & Proofreading Services
Artist: April Milne
Cover Designer: Anna Ishchenko

Distributed to the book trade worldwide by Springer Science+Business Media, LLC., 233 Spring Street, 6th Floor, New York, NY 10013. Phone 1-800-SPRINGER, fax (201) 348-4505, e-mail orders-ny@springer-sbm.com, or visit www.springeronline.com.

For information on translations, please e-mail rights@apress.com, or visit www.apress.com.

Apress and friends of ED books may be purchased in bulk for academic, corporate, or promotional use. eBook versions and licenses are also available for most titles. For more information, reference our Special Bulk Sales–eBook Licensing web page at www.apress.com/info/bulksales.

The source code for this book is available to readers at www.apress.com. You will need to answer questions pertaining to this book in order to successfully download the code.

To Bruce and Jack Allen for their love and support.
—Sarah Allen

To my loving wife, Tara, and my children Maggie, Grace, James, and Kathleen.
—Vidal Graupera

Contents at a Glance

Contents v

Foreword x

About the Authors xii

Contributors xiii

About the Technical Reviewer xiv

Acknowledgments xiv

Introduction xv

Chapter 1: The Smartphone is the New PC 1

Part 1: Platform Development and Distribution 15

Chapter 2: iPhone 17

Chapter 3: Android 35

Chapter 4: BlackBerry 51

Chapter 5: Windows Mobile 65

Part 2: Cross-Platform Native Frameworks 81

Chapter 6: Rhodes 83

Chapter 7: RhoSync 113

Chapter 8: PhoneGap 131

Chapter 9: Titanium Mobile 153

Part 3: HTML Interfaces 161

Chapter 10: Mobile HTML and CSS 163

Chapter 11: iWebKit 183

Chapter 12: Animated UI with jQTouch 207

Chapter 13: Sencha Touch 225

Chapter 14: BlackBerry HTML UI 235

Appendix: Cascading Style Sheets 247

Index 255

Contents

Contents at a Glance iv

Foreword x

About the Authors xii

Contributors xiii

About the Technical Reviewer xiv

Acknowledgments xiv

Introduction xv

Chapter 1: The Smartphone is the New PC 1

Application Marketplace 2
    Increase in Mobile Usage and Trend Toward Smartphones 2
What is a Smartphone? 4
    Smartphone Landscape 4
    Cross-Platform Frameworks 5
    The Branded Experience of Mobile Applications 6
Web Techniques 10
Cross-Platform Frameworks 10
About this Book 13

Part 1: Platform Development and Distribution 15

Chapter 2: iPhone 17

Introducing Xcode 17
iPhone Development Standard Practices 18
Building a Simple iPhone app 18
    Create the Xcode Project 19
    Create the Interface 20
Installing the App on the Device 29
    Finding Your Device ID 31
    Create the Provisioning Profile 32
    Install the Provisioning Profile 32
    Install and Run on the Device 32

■ **Chapter 3: Android** **35**

Android Development..36

    Setting Up The Development Environment With Eclipse......................36

    Building a Simple Android Application...39

    Simple Application Using Android WebView....................................46

Building for an Android Device..48

Distribution on the Web..50

Android Market...50

■ **Chapter 4: BlackBerry** **51**

BlackBerry Platform..51

Set Up for Classic Java Development..52

Building a Simple BlackBerry Application...53

    Create the Eclipse Project...53

    Create the Interface...55

    Code Explained...57

    Build and Test the Application...58

    Simple User Interface Application Using a Label, Text Field, and Button.......58

    Code Explained...60

    Simple Application Using BlackBerry Browser Field.............................61

■ **Chapter 5: Windows Mobile** **65**

Setting Up for Windows Mobile 6.5 Development....................................66

Building a Simple Windows Mobile App...67

    Creating a Smart Device Project...67

    Setting Up Base Functionality...68

    Deploying and Test your Application..72

    Fleshing Out the Application...73

Packaging and Distributing Your App...76

    Adding a CAB Project to the Solution...77

    Customizing Your Product Name..77

    Adding the Application to the CAB Project..78

    Creating an Application Shortcut..78

    Adding a Registry Entry...78

    Building and Deploying the CAB File..78

    Installing the CAB File...79

Distributing Your Application...80

Part 2: Cross-Platform Native Frameworks..................................... **81**

■ **Chapter 6: Rhodes** **83**

Development Architecture...84

Runtime Architecture..85

    Device Capabilities and Native UI Elements......................................86

Database (Rhom)...86

Threading...87

Differences Between Rhodes and Rails..88

Creating a Rhodes App..88

    Installation and Setup...88

Building a Rhodes Application..89

Running the Application...91
    Running on the iPhone..93
    Running on Android 94
    Running on BlackBerry 94
    Running on Windows Mobile 6 95
Generating a Model...95
Debugging Tips 100
    iPhone...100
    BlackBerry 101
    Android 101
Rhodes Device Capabilities..101
Contacts Example 103
Camera Example 106
Geolocation and Mapping Example...108
    Creating the application 109

▨ **Chapter 7: RhoSync** **113**
How the Sync Server Works 114
    Data Storage: Why Triples? 114
RhoSync Source Adapters 115
Initialize 116
Authenticating with Web Services: Login and Logoff 116
Retrieving Data: Query and Sync 117
    Query 117
    Sync 119
Submitting Data: Create, Update, and Delete 119
    Create 119
    Update...120
    Delete..120
User Authentication 121
Product Inventory Example 122
    Creating Your Application on RhoHub 122
    Creating Your Application on a Local RhoSync Server..127
    Debugging RhoSync Source Adapters 130
    Testing Your Application 130

▨ **Chapter 8: PhoneGap** **131**
Getting Started with PhoneGap...133
    Sample Application 134
    Android 136
    BlackBerry 137
    PhoneGap Simulator 138
Writing Hello World in PhoneGap 139
Writing a PhoneGap Application..141
Contacts Example 146
    Contact Example Code Explained 149
Camera Example 150
    Camera Example Code Explained 152

■ **Chapter 9: Titanium Mobile** **153**

Getting Started 153

    Writing Hello World 155

    Building for Device..157

    Titanium Mobile Device Capabilities..157

    Camera Example..158

■ **Part 3: HTML Interfaces** **161**

■ **Chapter 10: Mobile HTML and CSS** **163**

Platform Overview 163

    iOS for iPhone, iPad, iPod Touch..164

    Android 164

    BlackBerry 165

    Windows Mobile 165

Common Patterns 165

    Screen-Based Approach 165

    Navigation 166

    UI Widgets 169

    Check Boxes 169

    Selection Boxes 171

    Text Boxes 173

    Text Areas 174

    Radio Buttons 175

    Additional Components 177

    WebKit Web Views 178

■ **Chapter 11: iWebKit** **183**

Working With the iWebKit Framework 184

    A Few Words of Caution..185

    Required Header 186

    Body 186

    Organizing Data with Lists 187

Navigation 194

Forms 196

Landscape Mode..200

Phone Integration..200

Integrating iWebKit in Mobile Applications 201

    Creating a Native iPhone Application with iWebKit in Objective C............201

    Create an Application..203

    Add iWebKit Framework to Application Layout Template......................204

    Setting up PhoneGap for iWebKit..205

■ **Chapter 12: Animated UI with jQTouch**.. **207**

Getting Started with jQTouch..208

    Running Example Code 208

    Creating a Simple jQTouch Application..209

Adding Screens..211

    Loading Additional Screens with Ajax..212

    Cancel, Back, and Browser History..214

Other Buttons 215
jQTouch Initialization Options 215
    Basic Views 217
    Customizing Your jQTouch Applications 218
    Animations 218
    Navigation Bar (aka the Toolbar) 218
    Customizing Your Views with Themes 221
    Integration with Rhodes 222
    Integration with PhoneGap 222

■**Chapter 13: Sencha Touch** **225**
Getting Started 225
Adding HTML Text with a Panel 228
Adding Components 231
Creating Interactivity 232

■**Chapter 14: BlackBerry HTML UI** **235**
BlackBerry Browser UI Controls 236
BlackBerry 4.2 Browser Control 237
    Fonts 239
    Frames 241
    JavaScript 241
    Rhodes Tip for Dynamic Layout 242
BlackBerry 4.6 Browser Control 244
Display and User Interaction 244
Development Environment 245

■**Appendix: Cascading Style Sheets** **247**
The Cascading in Style Sheets 247
CSS Syntax 248
Comments 249
Identifying Elements with ID and Class 249
Common Patterns 250
Common CSS Attributes (Display: block verses inline) 251

■**Index** **255**

Foreword

The year 2010 is an exciting time for those of us who have worked in and around the mobile industry since before the, now, decade-old 21st century. Some have referred to this year as "The Year of the Mobile Developer." It's true that, following the creation of frictionless paths to market through Apple's App Store, Google's Android Market, and the other handset or OS app stores, developers and brands alike are pursuing a market previously limited in reach. The options of distribution of applications until recently included carrier decks, handset portals, third-party channels such as Motricity, or even one's own web site.

Carriers once dominated and controlled which applications were allowed to reach eager end users via their portals—picking winners and losers by the weight of their business development and testing processes. Distribution via carriers has been difficult and costly, requiring direct relationships with carriers. Each carrier required a new business development effort and a different set of requirements for OSes and handsets supported, along with a unique testing process. Handset portals also required major effort from business development and also required joining expensive developer programs. The third-party and web-site options for distribution were easier but required individual marketing effort by developers, and the process for users to install downloaded apps on their own was a barrier for widespread adoption. Until recently, these challenges in the business of mobile development limited experimentation and innovation by all but a few hardy souls or the largest brands with the budgets to support it. Enter Apple's App Store.

The Apple App Store not only provided a path to market, but also, a dramatic change in marketing position for developers. Apple established the new industry standard with the "There's an App for That" campaign. Suddenly, instead of choosing a device for its hardware specs, end users considered what they could do with a phone beyond make calls and send text messages. The value of a device, now, has become its ability to run lots of applications. The iPhone didn't initially include an App Store. End users drove this innovation, as is often the case. Early adopters of the iPhone broke open the OS and began to extend it's capabilities with apps, but Apple was quick enough to leverage the iTunes connection for delivering $.99 songs to delivering $.99 applications.

The app store trend didn't and couldn't have happened without the availability of more capable devices. Nokia punctuated the importance of a new class of handset commonly referred to as smartphones in 2007 by calling their advanced handsets "Multimedia Computers." Smartphone as computers has become a more common analogy as smartphones grew in processing and storage capability. The steady increase of smartphone marketshare hit an inflection point in 2008 by crossing the magical 20% penetration rate in both the UK and the US. Historically, any technology mainstreams at the 20% penetration level, which has clearly been demonstrated by experience since 2008. According to Morgan Stanley analyst Mary Meeker, the rest of the world (ROW) will reach 20% smartphone penetration in 2012.

It is in this context of explosive growth in smartphone marketshare, a frictionless path to market through device and OS app stores, and a viable business model that the authors take us to the next step—cross-platform development. Cross-platform frameworks are still in the early stages of technology evolution, but the timing is perfect for developers to add cross-platform frameworks to their tool box.

This is especially true for web developers and those serving brands that benefit most from the tradeoffs between wide distribution and deep integration.

In Part 1, the authors provide a survey of the top development and distribution options consisting of mainly handset and OS vendors including the iPhone, Android, BlackBerry, and Windows Mobile. Part 2 follows by introducing emerging cross-platform solutions covering both proprietary and open source frameworks with an emphasis on building native applications. And finally in Part 3, the authors address techniques for using HTML to create a native look-and-feel for web applications and services.

A key thread throughout the book is recognition that mobile development is a business endeavor and opportunity. There is a presentation of how-to instructions and code samples that will be useful to those just getting started with mobile development, but the audience that will benefit most from the pragmatic vision of the authors are professional developers and agencies. Certainly, many web developers are pursuing mobile development because it's a good decision to grow their business and if their clients aren't already requesting mobile applications, they will soon.

The book isn't targeted at developers of gaming apps. While gaming is a leading category for all app stores, it's one of those categories that benefits most from deep integration into the OS or device. Cross-platform frameworks aren't likely to be the best solution for games. Productivity apps, branded apps, and some communications services such as social networking apps will benefit from using the tools and techniques covered in the book.

Several of the tools presented in the book are currently leading this emerging category. We are in the early days of cross-platform use on mobile devices. Of the estimated 17 million software developers worldwide, according to Motorola as quoted in Forbes, around 4 million of them are developing for mobile. While Rhodes, Appcelerator, and PhoneGap have been used to deliver applications via the Apple App Store, the total number of developers using these frameworks is in the low six figures. Like the early days of the web, and to some extent, still, experimentation is vital to moving the ecosystem forward. This book is an important contribution to that effort.

Debi Jones
Editor In Chief
Telefonica Developer Programs

About the Authors

 **Sarah Allen** leads Blazing Cloud, a San Francisco consulting firm that specializes in developing leading-edge mobile and web applications. She is also co-founder and CTO of Mightyverse, a mobile startup focused on helping people communicate across languages and cultures. In both technical and leadership roles, Sarah has been developing commercial software since 1990 when she co-founded CoSA (the Company of Science & Art), which originated After Effects. She began focusing on Internet software as an engineer on Macromedia's Shockwave team in 1995. She led the development of the Shockwave Multiuser Server, and later the Flash Media Server and Flash video. An industry veteran who has also worked at Adobe, Aldus, Apple, and Laszlo Systems, Sarah was named one of the top 25 women of the Web by SF WoW (San Francisco Women of the Web) in 1998.

Website: blazingcloud.net
Personal Blog: www.ultrasaurus.com
Twitter: @ultrasaurus

 **Vidal Graupera** has been developing award-winning mobile applications starting as far back as the Apple Newton in 1993. He founded and ran a successful software company that developed more than a dozen consumer applications on a variety of mobile platforms over a period of ten years. Vidal holds engineering degrees from Carnegie Melon University and the University of Southern CA, and an MBA from Santa Clara University. Vidal currently consults with clients on developing web and mobile applications.

Website: vdggroup.com
Personal Website: www.vidalgraupera.com
Twitter: @vgraupera

 **Lee Lundrigan**, a founding engineer at Blazing Cloud, develops mobile applications using cross-platfrom frameworks on four platforms and Objective-C on the iPhone and iPad. He is an expert in CSS and HTML and also has experience creating dynamic UI in JavaScript. He has developed cross-browser CSS and HTML to run on iPhone, Android, BlackBerry, and Windows Mobile.

Website: blazingcloud.net
Personal Blog: www.macboypro.com

Contributors

Lorien Henry-Wilkins, lead iOS developer at Blazing Cloud, is an expert in iOS development and has created both iPad and iPhone applications. She also has written natively for Android. Her background is UI development in Javascript, HTML and OpenLaszlo. She created svg2vml, an open source javascript library for cross-browser vector graphic drawing, which still helps make the world safe from IE.

Michelle Lupei is an independent consultant focusing on symbiotic design, with a specialization in creating location-aware and social media driven products designed to engage users while embracing the three pillars of sustainable development — social, environmental, and fiscal responsibility. After obtaining degrees in Evolutionary Biology and Linguistic Anthropology from the University of Illinois, Michelle eventually found her own niche as a user experience designer and software engineer focusing on mobile and web applications. More information about Michelle's experience and her current projects can be found at www.michellelupei.com.

Pablo Kang has over 15 years of software development experience ranging from native code and mobile development to scalable server technology to Web application. For the past five years, Pablo has focused on dynamic web UI development at Laszlo Systems, Share Grove, and most recently at Blazing Cloud. He is an expert at CSS, HTML, JavaScript, and OpenLaszlo.

About the Technical Reviewer

Fabio Claudio Ferracchiati is a prolific writer on cutting-edge technologies. Fabio has contributed to more than a dozen books on .NET, C#, Visual Basic, and ASP.NET. He is a .NET Microsoft Certified Solution Developer (MCSD) and lives in Rome, Italy.

Acknowledgments

The authors received enthusiastic support from many of the creators of the software discussed herein. We would like to extend our thanks for technical review and enthusiastic support from the Rhomobile team: Adam Blum, Lars Burgess, Brian Moore, Evgeny Vovchenko, and Vladimir Tarasov; Brian LeRoux from Nitobi, David Richey and Jeff Haynie from Appcellerator; and Ed Spencer from Sencha. We also want to acknowledge Rupa Eichenberger's significant contribution to early technical reviews; Nola Stowe for initial work on the Android chapter; and Sarah Mei for her work on Rhodes geolocation. Jim Oser, Bruce Allen, and David Temkin each had a substantive impact in reviewing specific chapters.

Introduction

Developing mobile applications can be tricky business. Mobile developers need to use platform-specific tools and APIs and write code in different languages on different platforms. It is often hard to understand what it takes to develop and distribute an application for a specific device without actually building one. Each platform has different processes and requirements for membership in developer programs and documentation for different parts of the development process are often scattered and hard to piece together. Therefore, we have divided the book into three main topics: Platform Development and Distribution, Cross-Platform Native Frameworks, and HTML Interfaces.

Part 1: Platform Development and Distribution

In Chapters 1–5, we provide an overview of four platforms: iOS, for building iPhone, iPad, and iPod Touch applications; the Android open source platform, created by Google; Research in Motion's BlackBerry platform; and Windows Mobile from Microsoft. Each chapter follows the same outline:

- Building a Simple Hello World
- Running in the Simulator
- Adding a Browser Control
- Building for the Device
- Distribution Options and Requirements

This common outline allows for comparison across the operating systems and provides a feel for the patterns of the development process. If you decide to pursue native application development using only the vendor SDK, you will need a lot more details than any single chapter can provide, but this should provide the right amount of information to kick-off some experimentation or help make a decision about which platforms to pursue.

It is inevitable that developers create ways to share code across plaforms when CPU power is fast enough and there is sufficient memory to support some kind of abstraction and demand fuels faster time to market. We saw this with cross-platform desktop frameworks that emerged in the 1990s, and now with cross-platform mobile frameworks.

Part 2: Cross-Platform Native Frameworks

Chapters 6–9 provide an overview and examples of applications written in three popular native frameworks. In categorizing as a "native framework," we selected software that allows a common development approach across platforms but that build to an application that is indistinguishable by a user from one built with native code (as described in Part 1). Note that to build using these frameworks, you will still need the vendor SDK described in Part 1 and use vendor-specific techniques for code signing and distributions.

There are two chapters on the Rhomobile platform, one for the client-side Rhodes and one for the RhoSync server framwork. Rhodes is covered in more depth than the other two platforms: Titanium Mobile and PhoneGap. Rhodes is at version 2 at this writing, Titanium v1.2 and PhoneGap 0.9. As with the rest of the book, these chapters are designed to provide a feel for what it is like to develop for each platform, to kick-start some experimentation, and aid in deciding what platform to spend more time with.

Part 3: HTML Interfaces

You can use the technique of adding a browser control in combination with the HTML and CSS patterns and frameworks presented in Chapters 10–14.

To develop a mobile application user interface, a mobile developer must typically learn a platform-specific language and SDK. This can become quite cumbersome if you need your application to run on more than one platform. Fortunately, there is an alternative; all smartphone platforms today include a browser control component (also known as a web view) that a developer can embed in their application that will allow them to write some or all of their app in HTML, CSS, and JavaScript.

Leveraging HTML and CSS for mobile application UI gets even better with the introduction of the mobile WebKit browser. WebKit is an open source browser engine originally created by Apple. WebKit introduces a partial implemention of HTML5 and CSS3 with full support for HTML4 and partial implementation CSS2. Note that as of this writing, HTML5 and CSS3 are still in "working draft;" however, these emerging standards have been aggressively adopted by multiple web browsers and the latest versions of WebKit-based browsers include most HTML5 and CSS3 features. The WebKit mobile browser is currently the native browser for iPhone/iPod Touch/iPad, Android, Palm, and many Symbian phones. BlackBerry plans to catch up with its own WebKit-based browser, recently demonstrated at Mobile World Congress in February 2010. Windows Mobile ships with an IE-based browser, which includes a better implementation of CSS1 and 2 compared with BlackBerry, but still has limitations. It is possible, though sometimes challenging, to build cross-platform UI in HTML and CSS that works across WebKit, mobile IE, and BlackBerry broswers. The most challenging part is differing levels of support for current HTML and CSS standards.

Chapter 1

The Smartphone is the New PC

The mobile phone is the new personal computer. The desktop computer is not going away, but the smartphone market is growing fast. Phones are being used as computers by more people and for more purposes. Smartphones are generally cheaper than computers, more convenient because of their portability, and often more useful with the context provided by geolocation.

Already there are more mobile phones than computers connected to the Internet. While a minority of those phones would be considered smartphones, we're seeing a fast-moving landscape where today's high-end phones become next year's mid-range or even low-end phones. With profits from applications growing, we'll see continued subsidies of the hardware and operating systems by manufacturers and carriers, keeping new phones cheap or free.

We're seeing a change in how people use computers. Desktop applications that we use most frequently are centered around communications, rather than the more traditional personal computer task of document creation. In the business world, we file expense reports, approve decisions, or comment on proposals. As consumers, we read reviews, send short notes to friends, and share photos. E-mail is the killer app of the late 20th century, not the word processor or spreadsheet. Both in the business world and in our personal lives, these communication-centered tasks translate effectively into mobile applications.

As smartphones gain widespread adoption, the desktop computer will be relegated to the specialist and elite professional, much as the mini-computer and supercomputer are today. Many of the routine tasks we currently perform on a desktop or laptop, we will be able to accomplish on a smartphone. More importantly, new applications will meet the needs of people who don't use a computer today. Software development will shift toward mobile development as the majority of people who use computers will use them indirectly through a mobile phone. The center of gravity of the software industry will be mobilized.

Application Marketplace

In September 2009, Apple announced that more than two billion applications had been downloaded from its App Store. With more than 100,000 applications available, Apple has transformed the mobile phone market by dramatically increasing consumer spending on applications and successfully shifting independent developer mindshare toward mobile application development. By the end of 2009, Google Android's open platform was reported to have over 20,000 apps in the Android Market online store.[1]

Mobile applications are not new. Even in the late 90s, mobile development was considered to be a hot market. While there were independent application developers and most of the high-end phones supported the installation of applications, the process of application install was awkward and most end users did not add applications to their phone. Examples of early smartphone and PDA devices from this era included the Apple Newton Message Pad, Palm Pilot, Handspring (and later Palm) Treo, Windows Pocket PC, and others. Almost all mobile developers worked directly or indirectly for the carriers.

The iPhone revitalized the landscape for mobile application development. Apple created an easy-to-use interface for purchasing and installing third-party applications, and more importantly, promoted that capability to their users and prospective customers.

Smartphone operating systems actively innovate to keep up with advances in hardware and ease development with improved tools and APIs. As we've seen with the iPhone App Store, often the most significant innovations are not purely technical. The App Store reduced barriers to application development by providing easy access to distribution. Unsurprisingly, people develop more apps when there is an accessible market and distribution channel. Google's App Market, Blackberry App World, and Windows Marketplace for Mobile are likely to drive the success of existing applications for those operating systems and draw new developers as well.

Increase in Mobile Usage and Trend Toward Smartphones

Six in 10 people around the world now have cell-phone subscriptions, according to a 2009 UN Report,[2] which surpasses the quarter of the world's population with a computer at home. Smartphones are still a small minority of mobile phones, but growth is strong and the numbers are particularly interesting when compared to computer sales. Mobile Handset DesignLine reports that smartphones represent 14% of global device sales, but Gartner projections note that smartphone shipments will overtake unit

---

[1] http://www.techworld.com.au/article/330111/android_market_hits_20_000_apps_milestone

[2] International Telecommunications Union (a UN agency), "The World in 2009: ICT facts and figures," http://www.itu.int/newsroom/press_releases/2009/39.html, 2009.

sales of notebook computers in 2009 and that by 2012, smartphones will grow to 37% of mobile device sales.[3]

Looking at how people use their mobile phones today suggests patterns of behavior that will drive smartphone sales in the future. Increasingly, people are using their phones for more than phone calls: web browsing and the use of other mobile applications are growing. Market researcher comScore reports that global mobile Internet usage more than doubled between January 2008 and January 2009.[4] In Africa, a recent sharp increase in mobile phone adoption is attributed to the use of phones for banking and sending money to relatives via text messaging.

Even lower-end mobile phones typically bundle web browser, e-mail, and text messaging, but the power of the smartphones enables a wider array of applications. Smartphones are not just little computers that fit in your pocket. For many applications, they are actually more powerful devices than a laptop due to their built-in capabilities of camera, connectedness, and geolocation. Business people who can afford a laptop often prefer the longer-lasting battery power and portability of the smaller device. In an *Information Week* article, Alexander Wolfe collected real-world use cases of businesses adopting smartphones for applications that used to be only accessible with a desktop or laptop computer:

> At Dreyer's Grand Ice Cream, the Palm Treo 750 is being used by some 50 field sales representatives to access the company's back-end CRM database.
>
> The company's field-sales reps tried laptops and tablet PCs, but their battery life was too short and rebooting took too much time on sales calls, which number 20 to 25 a day, says Mike Corby, director of direct store delivery. Dreyer's reps also found the laptops to be too bulky to tote around, "not to mention the theft worries with notebooks visible on their car seats."
>
> At Astra Tech, a medical device maker, some 50 sales reps access Salesforce CRM apps on their smartphones. "Salespeople say they now check yesterday's sold or returned products plus the overall revenue trends, five minutes before meeting with a customer," says Fredrik Widarsson, Astra Tech's sales technology manager, who led the deployment on Windows Mobile smartphones (and is testing the app on iPhones). "Another interesting effect is that once a salesperson is back home for the day, the reporting part of their job is done. During waiting

---

[3] Christoph Hammerschmidt, "Smartphone market boom risky for PC vendors, market researchers warn," http://www.mobilehandsetdesignline.com/news/221300005; jsessionid=1JYPKFPGNOGE1QE1GHPCKH4ATMY32JVN, October 28, 2009.

[4] Dawn Kawamoto, "Mobile Internet usage more than doubles in January," http://news.cnet.com/8301-1035_3-10197136-94.html

periods throughout the day, they put notes into the CRM system, using their smartphone."[5]

In a recent article by Gary Kim, Forrester analyst Julie Ask identifies three things as the killer advantages of mobile devices: "immediacy, simplicity, and context."[6] When those are combined with usefulness, we're going to start to see a different flavor of software application emerge that will transform the way we use mobile phones. The use of software applications as "computing" will become archaic. The age of software as communications medium will have arrived.

What is a Smartphone?

Cell phones today are generally divided between the low-end "feature phones" and higher-end "smartphones." A smartphone has a QWERTY keyboard (either a physical keyboard or soft keyboard like the iPhone or BlackBerry Storm) and is more powerful than the feature phone with larger, high-resolution screens and more device capabilities.

Smartphone Landscape

Relative to desktop computers, smartphones have a diverse set of operating systems (see Table 1–1). Moreover, unlike desktop operating systems, the OS in mobile computing typically determines the programming language that developers must use.

When developing an application for the desktop, such as Microsoft Word or Adobe PhotoShop, application developers create their core application in a language such as C++ and share that core code across platforms, but then use platform-specific APIs to access the filesystem and develop the user interface. In the 1990s, a number of cross-platform desktop frameworks emerged, making it easier for companies to develop a single codebase that they could compile for each target platform (typically, just Mac and Windows). For mobile development, this is a bigger challenge.

---

[5] Wolfe, Alexander. "Is The Smartphone Your Next Computer?" October 4, 2008. http://www.informationweek.com/news/personal_tech/smartphones/showArticle.jhtml?articleID=210605369, March 16, 2009.

[6] Gary Kim, "Can Mobile Devices Replace PCs?" http://fixed-mobile-convergence.tmcnet.com/topics/mobile-communications/articles/66939-mobile-devices-replace-pcs.htm, October 19, 2009.

Table 1–1. *Smartphone Operating Systems and Languages*

OS	Symbian	RIM BlackBerry	Apple iPhone	Windows Mobile	Google Android	Palm webOS
Language	C++	Java	Objective-C	C#	Java	Javascript

Even focusing only on smartphones, there are four major operating systems that make up over 90% of the market: Symbian, RIM BlackBerry, Apple iPhone, and Windows Mobile, with the rest of the market shared by Linux and emerging mobile operating systems, Google Android and Palm's webOS. For most of these operating systems, there is a native development language, which is required to develop optimally for that platform, as illustrated in Table 1–1. While it is possible to develop using other languages, typically there are drawbacks or limitations in doing so. For example, you can develop a Java application for Symbian; however, several native APIs are unavailable for accessing device capabilities. Besides the differences in languages, the software development kits (SDKs) and paradigms for developing applications are different across each platform. While the device capabilities are almost identical, such as geolocation, camera, access to contacts, and offline storage, the specific APIs to access these capabilities are different on each platform.

Cross-Platform Frameworks

The fast-growing market for applications drives the need for faster time to market. Just as market opportunities led vendors to release cross-platform applications on desktop computers in the 1990s, mobile applications are more frequently available across devices. Operating systems vendors vie for the attention of developers and application vendors, but improve their tools incrementally. Where such dramatic challenges exist in developing across multiple platforms, it is natural for third party cross-platform frameworks to emerge.

The innovation in cross-platform frameworks for smartphone applications surpasses the patterns of abstraction seen in the cross-platform desktop frameworks of the 1990s. These new smartphone frameworks are influenced by the rapid application development techniques we are seeing in web development today. There are three specific techniques in web application development that are borrowed for these non-web frameworks: 1) layout with mark-up (HTML/CSS); 2) using URLs to identify screen layouts and visual state; and 3) incorporating dynamic languages, such as Javscript and Ruby.

A generation of designers and user interface developers are fluent in HTML and CSS for layout and construction of visual elements. Additionally, addressing each screen by a unique name in a sensible hierarchy (URL) with a systemized way of defining connections between them (links and form posts) has created a *lingua franca* understood by visual and interactions designers, information architects, and programmers alike. This common language and its standard implementation patterns led to the development of frameworks and libraries that significantly speed application development on the Web. These patterns are now being applied to the development of mobile applications as common techniques by individual developers as well as in cross-platform frameworks.

The new cross-platform frameworks (and the native Palm webOS) leverage these skills using an embedded web browser as the mechanism for displaying application UI. This is combined with a native application that transforms URL requests into the rendering of application screens simulating the web environment in the context of a disconnected mobile application.

The Branded Experience of Mobile Applications

New cross-platform smartphone frameworks support a trend where mobile applications, such as web applications, are a branded experience. The Web is a varied, diverse place, where the lines between application functionality, content, and branding blur. Web applications do not express the native operating systems of Mac, Windows, or whatever desktop happens to host the browser. Web applications are liberal with color and graphics, defying the UI conventions of the desktop as well as avoiding the blue underlined links of the early Web that Jacob Nielson erroneously identified as the key to the Web's usability.

As an example, the NBA released its NBA League Pass Mobile app for both iPhone and Android. "Multiplatform is a key tenet of our philosophy," said Bryan Perez, GM of NBA Digital. "We want our content available to as many fans as possible, and with more and more carriers adopting Android around the world, it's important to be there now."[7] Most businesses simply can't afford to focus on the niche of a single operating system or device. To reach customers, more companies are developing mobile applications, and the customers they want to reach are divided across the wide array of mobile platforms. Despite the challenges, businesses are driven to communicate with their customers through their mobile phones because of the enormous opportunity presented by such connectedness.

It may be effective shorthand to say that smartphones are the new personal computer; however, in reality they represent a new communications medium. This book covers frameworks and toolkits that make it easier than ever before to develop applications for multiple mobile platforms simultaneously. Leveraging these tools, you can take advantage of the widespread adoption of smartphone devices to broaden the reach of your business.

To provide some perspective on how application interfaces vary across platform, Figures 1–1 to 1–5 illustrate how two applications, WorldMate and Facebook, are realized across various platforms. These specific applications are not implemented using cross-platform frameworks, but are included to provide context on design decisions made in cross-platform implementation. As you will see, the two applications look quite

---

[7] Todd Wasserman, "So, Do You Need to Develop an Android App Too Now?," http://www.brandweek.com/bw/content_display/news-and-features/direct/e3iebae8a5c132016bcab88e37bc3948a44, October 31, 2009.

different from each other, even on the same platform. As is typical, these mobile applications choose a color scheme that is consistent with their brand, rather than adhering to defaults provided by the smartphone operating system.

Figure 1-1. *WorldMate iPhone*

Figure 1-2. *WorldMate 2009 Symbian*

Figure 1–3. *WorldMate BlackBerry*

Figure 1–4. *Facebook BlackBerry*

Figure 1-5. *Facebook iPhone*

Cross-Platform Development

Frequently, the industry produces multiple platforms that essentially provide the same solutions for different market segments. In the 1990s, Microsoft Windows and the Apple Macintosh provided GUI platforms with windows, mouse input, menus, and so forth. Software vendors needed to create applications for the both platforms and, inevitably software developers created libraries and frameworks that abstracted the differences, making it easier to develop one application that ran across platforms. In the 2000s, as more applications moved to the Web and browser syntax diverged, software developers created cross-platform libraries and frameworks, such as jQuery, Dojo, and OpenLaszlo. When there exists both a market for applications and enough processor speed and memory to support a layer of abstraction, developers naturally create cross-platform tools to speed time to market and reduce maintenance costs.

With the phenomenal growth of mobile, which has seen broad adoption across a diverse array of platforms, it is inevitable that software developers would create cross-platform mobile solutions. However, the challenge with mobile operating systems today is the diverse set of languages, in addition to platform-specific API syntax. Mobile cross-platform frameworks are addressing that challenge by leveraging the ubiquitous browser Javascript or scripting languages such as Lua or Ruby.

Web Techniques

We are seeing the influence of web development on emergent cross-platform techniques for mobile. Before any cross-platform frameworks existed, many developers found that embedding Web UI in a native application was a practical way to develop mobile applications quickly and make cross-platform applications easier to maintain. The user interface for mobile applications tends to be presented as a series of screens. From a high level, the mobile UI can be thought of as having the same flow-of-control as a traditional web site or web application.

It is common in a mobile application for every click to display a new screen, just as a click in a traditional web application displays a new page. By structuring the UI of the mobile application such as a web application, the coding can be simplified. By actually using Web UI controls, the implementation of the user interface can be created with a single source that renders and behaves appropriately across platforms. Also, it is much easier to hire designers and UI developers who are familiar with HTML and CSS than for any specific mobile platform, let alone finding developers who can develop a UI across multiple platforms using native toolkits.

What does it mean to have a web application architecture for an app that may not even access the network? Every smartphone platform has a web browser UI control that can be embedded into an application just like a button or a check box. By placing a web browser control in the application that is the full size of the screen, the entire UI of the application may be implemented in HTML. In reality, this has nothing to do with the Web, and everything to do with the sophisticated layout and visual design flexibility that even a bare-bones web browser is capable of rendering.

Cross-Platform Frameworks

In the past few years, many cross-platform frameworks have emerged. There has been an explosion of activity in this area as mobile devices become faster and more widely adopted, and particularly with a fast-growing market for applications. This book covers many of the popular frameworks that are focused on application development. The frameworks fall into two categories: those that let you create a native mobile application using cross-platform APIs, and HTML/CSS/Javascript frameworks that let you build cross-platform interfaces that run in a web browser. It is common practice to combine these to create cross-platform native applications. This book covers the native cross-platform frameworks of Rhodes, PhoneGap, and Titanium. These are listed below along with a number of frameworks that are not covered in this book.

- **Rhodes and RhoSync** from Rhomobile. Use Ruby for cross-platform business logic in this MVC framework and leverage HTML, CSS, and JavaScript for the UI. The optional RhoSync server supports synchronization of client-server data. With Rhodes, you can build applications for iPhone/iPad, Android, BlackBerry, and Windows Mobile. The client framework is MIT License; their RhoSync server framework is GPL with a commercial option. http://rhomobile.com/

- **PhoneGap** from Nitobi. Use HTML, CSS, and Javascript along with projects and libraries that support native application development to create applications that run on iPhone/iPad, Android, BlackBerry, Palm, and Symbian. Open-source MIT License. http://www.phonegap.com/

- **Titanium Mobile** from Appcelerator. Use JavaScript with custom APIs to build native applications for iPhone and Android. Titanium is an open-source framework, released under the Apache 2 license. http://www.appcelerator.com

- **QuickConnectFamily**. Use HTML, CSS, and JavaScript to build an application that runs on iPhone/iPad, Android, BlackBerry, and WebOS. The QuickConnectFamily templates give you access to behavior normally restricted to "native" apps. You can have full database access across all the supported platforms. http://www.quickconnectfamily.org/

- **Bedrock** from Metismo. A cross compiler converts your J2ME source code to native C++, simultaneously deploying your product to Android, iPhone, BREW, Windows Mobile, and more. Bedrock is a set of proprietary libraries and tools. http://www.metismo.com

- **Corona**. Develop using the Lua scripting language for native iPhone, iPad, and Android apps. Corona is a proprietary framework. http://anscamobile.com/corona/

- **MoSync SDK**. Use C or C++ to develop using MoSync libraries to build for Symbian, Windows Mobile, j2me, Moblin, and Android. MoSync is a proprietary framework. http://www.mosync.com/

- **Qt Mobility**. Use C++ and Qt APIs to target S60, Windows CE, and Maemo. Qt (pronounced "cute") is a cross-platform application development framework widely used for the development of GUI programs. The Qt mobility project moves it to mobile platforms. It is distributed as open source under the LGPL. http://labs.trolltech.com/page/Projects/QtMobility

- **Adobe Flash Lite**. Use ActionScript, a JavaScript-like proprietary scripting language, to build cross-platform application files (SWF) that will run as applications on a variety of devices that support Flash Lite. Adobe Flash Lite is a proprietary platform. http://www.adobe.com/products/flashlite/

- **Adobe AIR**. Adobe is working toward having the full features of Flash Player 10 work across a wide array of mobile devices; however, those efforts seem to be focused on web-based applications rather than native applications. Adobe AIR (as of this writing, in beta for Android) allows developers to run Flash applications outside of the mobile browser as stand-alone applications. http://www.adobe.com/products/air/

- **Unity**. A popular game development platform which allows you to deploy to Mac, Windows, or iPhone. Unity supports three scripting languages: JavaScript, C#, and a dialect of Python called Boo. They have announced support of Android, iPad, and PS3 to be released in Summer 2010. http://unity3d.com/

In addition to these frameworks for developing native applications, there are also many frameworks to create HTML, CSS, and JavaScript for mobile web applications. Many of these frameworks are little more than a collection of commonly used styles and graphical elements; however, when developing cross-platform applications using the techniques discussed in this book, these cross-platform HTML frameworks are essential time-savers. The last section of the book introduces Sencha, jqTouch, and iWebKit. These and others not covered in this book are listed as follows:

- **Sencha Touch**. A JavaScript framework that allows you to build native-looking mobile web applications in HTML5 and CSS3 for iOS and Android. Sencha Touch is an open-source framework available under the GNU GPL license v3, with a commercial license option available. http://sencha.com

- **JQTouch**. A JQuery plug-in for making iPhone-like applications that are optimized for Safari desktop and mobile browsers. Released under the MIT License. http://jQTouch.com

- **iWebKit**. An HTML5 and CSS3 framework targeting iOS native and web applications. iWebkit has been released under the GNU Lesser General Public License. http://iWebkit.net

- **iUI**. A JavaScript and CSS framework to build mobile web applications that run on iOS. iUI has been released under the New BSD License. http://code.google.com/p/iui/

- **xUI**. A lightweight JavaScript framework currently being used by PhoneGap. Currently targeting iOS applications with tentative future support for IE mobile and BlackBerry. Currently released under a GNU GPL license. http://xuijs.com

- **Magic Framework**. An HTML, CSS, and JavaScript framework. Used to make fast and smooth iPhone-feeling apps with native-feeling widgets, lists, and so forth. Also provides an easy HTML5 db storage interface. Currently released under the Creative Commons Attribution 3.0 United States License.
  `http://www.jeffmcfadden.com/projects/Magic%20Framework`

- **Dashcode**. A Framework developed by Apple to make simple, lightweight, dashboard widgets for OSX and mobile safari applications for iOS that utilize HTML, CSS, and JavaScript. Currently available under the Creative Commons Attribution-ShareAlike License.
  `http://developer.apple.com/leopard/overview/dashcode.html`

- **CiUI**. Developed by tech news site CNET.com to make an iPhone-friendly version of their web site. Released under the MIT License.
  `http://code.google.com/p/ciui-dev/`

- **Safire**. An open-source web application framework written in HTML, JavaScript- and CSS-targeting iOS. Released under the MIT License.
  `http://code.google.com/p/safire/`

- **iphone-universal (UiUIKit)**. An HTML and CSS framework for iPhone web development. Contains the iPhone-like Chat Balloons just like SMS on the iPhone. Released under GNU General Public License v3.
  `http://code.google.com/p/iphone-universal/`

- **WebApp.Net**. A lightweight, JavaScript framework to build applications that can take advantage of a WebKit browser control; namely, iOS, Android, and WebOS. Released under the Creative Commons Attribution-ShareAlike License. `http://WebApp.net`

- **The Dojo Toolkit**. A flexible and extensible JavaScript framework, primarily used to build web applications. `http://www.dojotoolkit.org`

- **Jo**. A lightweight JavaScript framework for HTML5 apps, built with PhoneGap in mind. Copyright 2010 Dave Balmer, Jr. this framework has a custom license ("as is" with attribution) `http://grrok.com/jo/`

There are more cross-platform mobile frameworks, libraries, and tools than are listed here. This list is provided to give you a sampling of what is out there.

About this Book

Part 1 of this book, the next four chapters (2-5), guide you through building native mobile applications. You will learn how to write code for simple applications and how to embed a browser control into a native application. These chapters are designed to give you a feel for what it is like to develop using native methodologies.

If you decide to develop using platform-specific techniques, then you will need to learn a lot that is outside the scope of this book; however, to save work in developing and maintaining your application across various mobile platforms, you can consider including some cross-platform UI by including a browser control and displaying part of your application UI using HTML. Each chapter in Part 1 reviews how to build for the device, both developer builds and distributable applications. This information is important even if you end up using one of the cross-platform frameworks, since at the end you are building a native application, which will be a native executable built with vendor tools. Lastly, each chapter reviews distribution options for applications on that platform.

In Part 2, chapters 6-9, you will learn about three popular cross-platform frameworks: Rhodes and RhoSync from Rhomobile, PhoneGap from Nitobi, and Titanium Mobile from Appcelerator. Finally, Part 3 will dive into techniques for creating a native look-and-feel using HTML techniques, as well as detail some of the limitations and capabilities of various platforms.

Platform Development and Distribution

Chapters 2–5 include tutorials of how to add a browser component to a native application for each of four platforms. This approach helps the developer by allowing them to write the structure of their application in HTML and have platform-specific CSS support for the visual layout and features of each platform.

Chapter 2

iPhone

To develop for the iPhone or iPod touch, you will need an Intel-based Macintosh computer running OS X v10.5.7 or later. You will also need to install the latest version of the iPhone SDK and verify that your device operating systems are up-to-date. Download the iPhone SDK from the Apple Developers site (http://developer.apple.com/iphone), which includes the Xcode IDE, iPhone simulator, and a suite of additional tools for developing applications for iPhone and iPod touch. These tools will help you develop your application and allow you to run it in the simulator. From this point on in the text, whenever we refer to building or creating applications for the iPhone, we also mean for the iPod Touch of iPad, interchangeably. The iPod Touch and iPad are compatible with the iPhone except that those devices lack a phone and camera.

This chapter includes a simple "Hello World" example, as well as an example of embedding a Web UI View, which you can use in conjunction with the techniques and toolkits in Part 3 to include cross-platform UI in a native application. However, the goal of these examples is to provide a taste of native iPhone development, so as to be able to contrast it with developing other native applications. The last part of the chapter, "Installing the App for the Device," details code signing and building for the device, which will be needed whether you are writing native code from scratch or using one of the cross-platform toolkits in Part 2.

Introducing Xcode

Xcode is Apple's integrated development environment for developing applications for Mac OS X and the iPhone. The preferred language in Xcode is Objective-C, which is required for iPhone applications, but Xcode also supports a myriad of other languages (C, C++, Fortran, Java, Objective-C++, AppleScript, Python, and Ruby). The Xcode IDE has a modified GNU compiler and debugger for its backend.

The Xcode suite includes Interface Builder and Instruments. Interface Builder helps you create user interfaces for your Mac and iPhone applications. Using the typical development process, Interface Builder is essential. Instruments provides a thorough analysis of your application's runtime performance and memory usage, allowing you to efficiently find memory leaks and bottlenecks to help improve the user experience.

iPhone Development Standard Practices

When building iPhone applications, you will need to be mindful of a few standard design patterns. First, the Model-View-Controller (MVC) pattern is a way to separate your code into three functionally independent areas. The model is usually defined by an Objective-C class that subclasses NSObject. The controller is referred to as a view controller and can either subclass UIViewController or UITableViewController. The view portion of your application is usually defined by an Interface Builder file called a nib. This is the preferred method of creating your views since Interface Builder handles the memory management of those views for you. The alternative is to define your view programmatically, which is considered a non-standard practice.

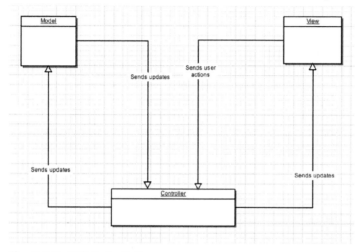

Figure 2–1. *MVC Design Pattern*

The delegation design patter is another important design pattern to be aware of. The delegation pattern allows a complex object to hand off some of its functionality to a helper object. On the outside, it would appear that you are calling the complex object to handle the task, but in reality it would use a helper object to outsource some of the complexity. We see this pattern a lot throughout iPhone development. Every time you find yourself declaring the delegate of an object (which happens a lot in an asynchronous environment), this pattern is being implemented.

Building a Simple iPhone app

As an introduction to building iPhone applications, you will build a simple "HelloiPhone" application, designed to introduce you to writing Objective-C code in Xcode and using Interface Builder to create the user interface of your application.

The goal of this application is to have the user enter his or her name into a text box, press a button, and have the iPhone greet them by name.

Create the Xcode Project

Start by opening Xcode and creating a new project (select **New Project** under the **File** menu or [Command+Shift+N] on the keyboard). Then select iPhone OS **Application** in the left-hand panel and **View-based Application** from the templates in the panel on the right side. Select **Choose** then name your new project "HelloiPhone" and save.

At this point, Xcode should present you with a project window (Figure 2–2), showing a list of files that were generated for you.

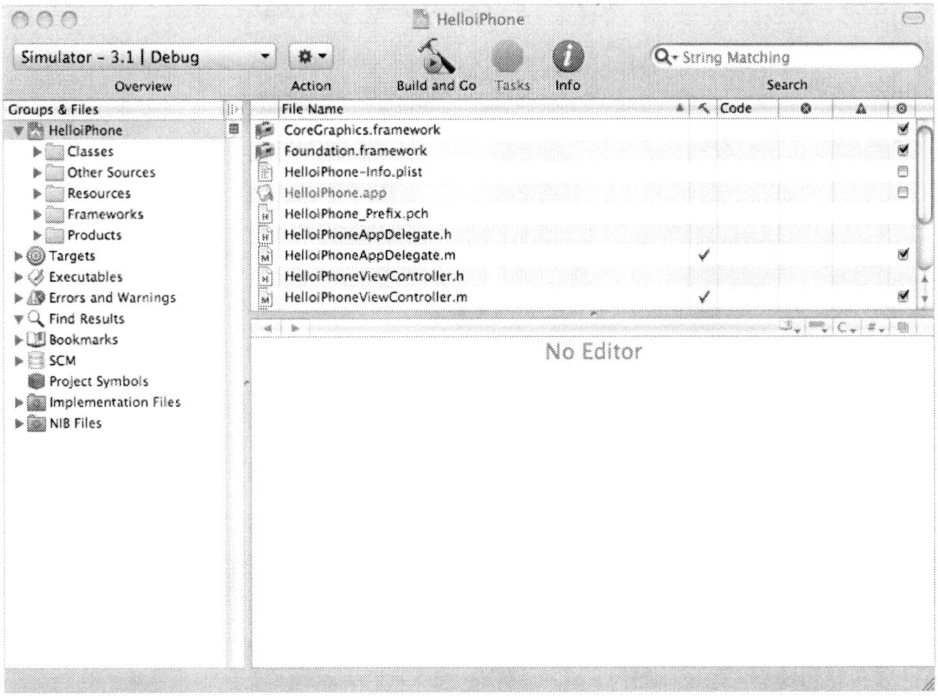

Figure 2–2. *XCode Project Window*

Table 2–1. *File types*

File Extension	Description
.m	Objective-C implementation files.
.h	Objective-C header files.
.plist	Property lists file that can contain configuration options or user settings for your application.
.app	The distributable application that you will be building.
.xib	Views from Interface Builder are saved as *.nib* files. A *.xib* file is the xml version of a *.nib* file. These files are still called "nibs" even though they have a different file extension.

Create the Interface

In this example, you will start with the interface of the application to set up the overall layout. The next step will be to create the corresponding code to interact with the views, and finally hook the code up to the views with Interface Builder.

Double-click on *HelloiPhoneViewController.xib* to open the view of your application in Interface Builder. Interface Builder will launch with four open windows (see Figure 2–3). One of the windows presented will be the view for the application. Initially this is just a gray box, which represents the application screen to which you can add UI components.

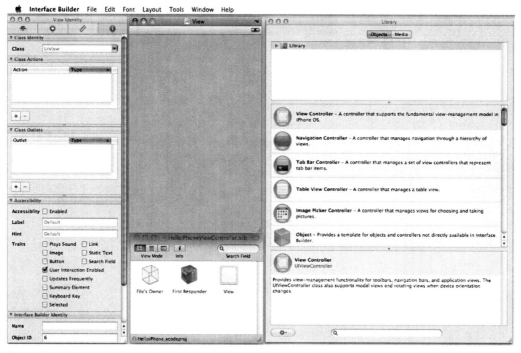

Figure 2–3. *Interface Builder showing four main windows*

If the Library window is not visible (on the right side of Figure 2–3), then choose Library from the Tools menu (or press Command-Shift-L) to bring up the Library window. In the bottom left corner of the window, there is a Settings drop-down menu that lets you decide how you would like to view the library. It is helpful at first to select the **View Icons and Descriptions** setting so that you can see what all the possible view objects do.

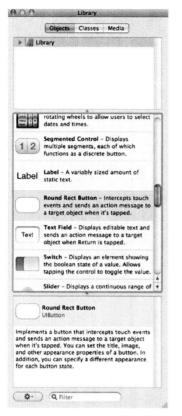

Figure 2–4. *Interface Builder Library Window*

Add UI Elements

Select **Round Rect Button** and drag and drop into our view window. (You can scroll to find it in the Library or type into the Search box at the bottom of the window to filter the list.) You also are going to need a *Label*, which will be used to display the text greeting, and a *Text Field* in which the user will enter his or her name. Search for those and also drag them to the view.

With all the UI components for the application placed in the view, you may align them properly on the screen.

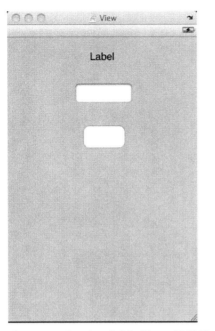

Figure 2–5. *Interface Builder View with UI Elements*

Align the Text Greeting

The Label element will display the greeting. In this example, it will display centered at the top of the screen. Start by taking the label and dragging it up to the top left corner of the view until it aligns with the blue guidelines provided by Interface Builder. Size the label horizontally, aligning once again with the provided guidelines.

To center the text, select the label and open the Attributes Inspector (under the **Tools** menu or Command+1 on the keyboard), then find the layout section. This section will look like a text-alignment section in a word processor, with a left-align, center-align, and right-align images. You will be selecting the center text alignment layout option or as an alternative you can go to the **Layout** menu, select "**alignment**, then choose **Center Alignment** from the drop-down.

Because you will be generating this text dynamically, the initial text should be the empty string. Double-click on the label, delete the text, and hit Enter to save.

Button and Text Field Layout

You will do something very similar with the button and text field layout. Select the text field and position it under the label on the left side, aligning with the blue guidelines. Then, drag the right edge horizontally until it lines up with the guidelines on the right side. Align the round rectangle button in a similar manner.

Next, add text to the button by double-clicking on it, then change the title to be "Hello iPhone!". You should also add text to the text field to give the user an idea of the kind of information you want them to insert. This user interface convention is supported directly in Interface Builder, which is referred to as a *Placeholder* attribute. This will display gray text in the field to provide in-context help text. Select the textbox and open the Attribute Inspector (Command-1), if not already open. Find the placeholder attribute and type "Name". This will give the text field gray initial text that will indicate to the user that a name should be placed there. When the user selects the text field, focusing it, the placeholder text will be cleared.

Now you should have something very similar to Figure 2–6.

Figure 2–6. *Interface Builder View with UI Layout and Text*

Make sure to save your file in Interface Builder and quit the program for now.

Writing the Controller Code

Now that you have created the application views, you will write the code to interact with it. Return to Xcode and open *HelloiPhoneViewController.h*. This file contains the outline for the view controller.

You will create code actions that correspond to the view. You do this with special keywords called IBAction and IBOutlet. These keywords establish a relationship between objects in the view and the code. You need to declare an IBOutlet for each UI component in your view that you will interact with programmatically. As you can see in Listing 2–1, you need to declare a UILabel and UITextField IBOutlets when you define their corresponding variables. IBActions are callback methods defined in your view controller; these are called by actions that happen in your view. You can assign these actions in Interface Builder or programmatically in your view controller.

The @property keyword will auto-generate accessors (that is, getters and setters). These correspond with an @synthesize statement that you will add in the implementation file. Declaring the UI components as properties allows you to easily modify and access them without writing additional code.

Lastly, the header file declares one IBAction *sayHelloToUser*, which performs the primary functionality of this simple application and later you will set to trigger when the user clicks the button.

Edit *HelloiPhoneViewController.h* to match Listing 2–1.

Listing 2–1. *HelloiPhoneViewController.h*

```
#import <UIKit/UIKit.h>
@interface HelloiPhoneViewController : UIViewController {
    IBOutlet UILabel *greetingLabel;
    IBOutlet UITextField *userNameField;
}

@property (nonatomic, retain) UILabel *greetingLabel;
@property (nonatomic, retain) UITextField *userNameField;

 -(IBAction) sayHelloToUser: (id) sender;

@end
```

Next, you will edit *HelloiPhoneViewController.m* to implement the functionality.

First, add an @synthesize statement directly underneath the HelloiPhoneViewController implementation declaration. This will auto-generate accessors for the greetingLabel and userNameField properties.

Listing 2–2. *HelloiPhoneViewController.m property accessors*

```
@implementation HelloiPhoneViewController
@synthesize greetingLabel, userNameField;
```

Next, you will add the implementation of the method *sayHelloToUser*. This method will create a formatted string concatenating "Hello" with the name that the user entered in the textbox and then displaying that string in the greetingLabel.

Below the @implementation declaration, you need to add the method in Listing 2–3.

Listing 2–3. *sayHelloToUser implmentation*

```
- (void) sayHelloToUser:(id)sender {
    greetingLabel.text = [NSString stringWithFormat:@"Hello %@", userNameField.text];;
    [userNameField resignFirstResponder];
}
```

The *sayHelloToUser* method gets the user's name from the text field and creates a helloMessage string. Because the greetingLabel is an IBOutlet, you can simply assign the string to the label to display it on the screen. Note that setting the userNameField text to null will clear it. Finally, calling *resignFirstResponder* will release the keyboard from the text field and hide the soft keyboard.

Lastly, you need to implement a *dealloc* method to release the memory for the label and text field elements. Changing the *dealloc* method of the implementation file to match listing 2–4.

Listing 2–4. *sayHelloToUser implementation*

```
- (void)dealloc {
     [greetingLabel release];
     [userNameField release];
   [super dealloc];
}
```

Connect the Code to the Views

In the final step of development for this application, you will connect the controller code to the views. Double-click *HelloiPhoneViewController.xib* to open in Interface Builder.

Interface Builder will display the IBOutlets and IBActions that you declared in the controller code, allowing you to connect them to the user interface elements with direct manipulation.

In the *HelloiPhoneViewController.xib* window, select the **File's Owner** cube and open the **Connections Inspector** under the **Tools** menu (Command-2). Under Outlets, you should see *greetingLabel* and *userNameField*. You need to drag their adjacent dots to the corresponding view objects to connect the UI elements to the code.

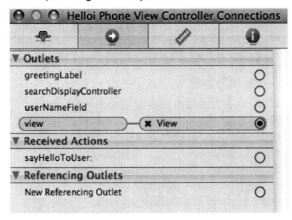

Figure 2–7. *Interface Builder Connections Inspector*

You should also see *Received Actions,* which lists the method *sayHelloToUser*. By dragging its dot to the **Hello iPhone!** button, you will set the user action to trigger the method. When you complete the drag action, a menu will appear over the button. Select **Touch Up Inside**. This will send an event when the button is released triggering the *sayHelloToUser* method.

Finally, drag the dot next to *New Referencing Outlet* and connect it to the text field. A menu option will appear; select **delegate** (which is the only option). This will allow the code to read from the text field.

That's it. All of your code is connected to your views. Now, you should click **Build and Go** (or press Command-R) in XCode to run your application in the simulator.

Skinning an iPhone Web View

This example will show you how to use a Web View to load a standard web page into a view inside a native iPhone application.

Start by opening Xcode and create a new project (select **New Project** from the **File** menu or [Command+Shift+N] on the keyboard). Then select **iPhone OS Application** in the left panel and **View-based Application** from the templates in the panel on the right side. Select **Choose** then name your new project "iWebDemo", and save. This will present you with the basic scaffold of an Xcode iPhone Project.

Your next step will be to add the UIWebView to your application through Interface Builder. Double-click on the file called *iWebDemoViewController.xib* in Xcode to launch Interface Builder. Verify the Library window is open (if not, select **Library** under the **Tools** menu [or Command+Shift+L] on the keyboard) and search for "Web View" either by scrolling the menu or by entering it as a search query in the Library filter text field.

When you find it, drag and drop the Web View onto your View window, allowing Interface Builder to help you guide it to the center. Currently, Interface Builder should resemble Figure 2–8.

Save Interface Builder and exit. You will come back later to activate the outlet to this view.

Back in Xcode, it's time to add the code side implementation that will allow us to manipulate the Web View. Open iWebkitDemoViewController.h to start adding in the declarations for your view object; this file will be very basic.

Start by adding *IBOutlet UIWebView *webView;* between the @interface braces; an IBOutlet will allow the code to interact with the view. The view will also need accessors to allow you to manipulate its web address. To auto-generate accessors for the view, declare *@property(nonatomic, retain) UIWebView *webView;* anywhere below the @interface declaration but before the @end declaration. There is another piece to this; the *@synthesize* keyword will complete the circuit for auto-generation in the implementation file. At this point, your code should like Listing 2–5.

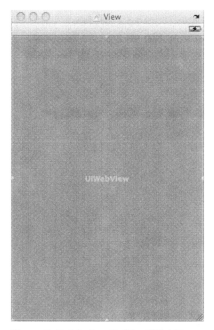

Figure 2–8. *Interface Builder UIWebView*

Listing 2–5. *iWebkitDemoViewController.h*

```
#import <UIKit/UIKit.h>
@interface iWebkitDemoViewController : UIViewController {
    IBOutlet UIWebView *webView;
}
@property (nonatomic, retain) UIWebView *webView;
@end
```

You just created the code representation of the Web View. This allows you to interact with the Web View and use getters and setters on it to manipulate it.

Save this file and turn to *iWebkitDemoViewController.m*. It's time to add the implementation that will turn your view into a semi-functional web browser.

The first thing you need to do in this file is finish the circuit that will auto-generate the accessors for your view. Directly under the @implementation iWebkitViewController add @synthesize webView; to finalize the auto-generation process, as in Listing 2–6. Now that we can alter the view, it's time to write the code to enable the view for web browsing.

Listing 2–6. *iWebkitDemoViewController.m*

```
@implementation iWebkitDemoViewController
@synthesize webView;
```

Toward the middle of the implementation file, uncomment the function -*(void)viewDidLoad*. This function gets called after the view loads successfully, so that makes it a perfect place to put the code to load a web page.

First, create a string containing the URL (such as http://www.google.com). Next, you will take that string and create an *NSURL* object, and embed that into an *NSURLRequest*. Finally, you will call the Web View to load the request object. This is shown in the code Listing 2–7.

Listing 2–7. *iWebkitDemoViewController.m*

```
// Implement viewDidLoad to do additional setup after loading the view, typically⏎
 from a nib.
- (void)viewDidLoad {
    [super viewDidLoad];
    // Create the URL string of the address
    NSString *urlAddress = @"http://www.google.com";
    // Bind that address to an NSURL object
    NSURL *url = [NSURL URLWithString:urlAddress];

    // Embed the NSURL into the request object
    NSURLRequest *requestObj = [NSURLRequest requestWithURL:url];

    // Tell the Web View to load the request
    [webView loadRequest:requestObj];
}
```

Next, finish hooking up the view in Interface Builder. (Double-click on *iWebkitDemoViewController.xib* in Xcode to launch it in Interface Builder.) You should, once again, have four windows in front of you. Start by looking for the window that represents your *nib* file, entitled *iWebkitDemoViewController.xib*. In the window, you should see three objects: File's Owner, First Responder, and View. Click on the **File's Owner** object and bring up the connection inspector by typing Command+1 on your keyboard. It should look like Figure 2–9.

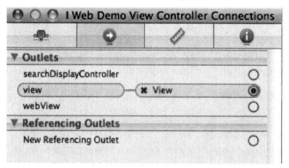

Figure 2–9. *Interface Builder Connection Inspector*

You should see your *webView* object listed under Outlets. You need to click and drag the objects circle to your view window. The Web View will illuminate when you hover over it, and that's when you will release your mouse button. The Attributes Inspector should now show your *webView* object connected to your Web View. That's it for your view in Interface Builder; you can save and exit.

It's time to run the iPhone simulator to check the status of your application. Verify you can load Google.com into the view; it should look like Figure 2–10.

Figure 2–10. *iPhone Web View Browser – Google.com*

Installing the App on the Device

Unlike running the application in the simulator, installing it on the phone requires signing credentials as is typical for mobile development. Before you can even think about building your application for the device, you need to go to developer.apple.com/ and enroll in the iPhone developer program. This will cost you $99 for the Standard program or $299 for Enterprise. The largest benefit to joining the program is the ability to distribute applications. With the Standard or Enterprise programs, you may provision an application for ad-hoc distribution, which is the way you will typically distribute your application for testing or early demonstration. In the Standard program, you are eligible to submit your app to the App Store. In the Enterprise program, you may provision your application for in-house distribution.

Once you have enrolled in the program, you will need to create a development provisioning profile and create a certificate. This can be as easy as using the Development Provisioning Assistant on the home page of the portal, or you can create the certificates and profiles manually.

Using the Development Provisioning Assistant

Use "development provisiong" in order to install an application on your device directly from Xcode. This will be useful for your own testing, but when you are ready to distribute to more devices for other people to test, you will need to use "ad-hoc provisioning," described shortly. The Apple iPhone Dev Center has an easy-to-use wizard that takes you through the many steps required to set up and install the provisiong profile. Choose **Launch Assistant** on the home screen of the iPhone Developer Program Portal. The assitant will ask you a few questions and guide you through the installation process. Its docuemntation is quite good, so we won't elaborate here.

Manually Setting Up iPhone Provisioning

There are many steps when creating your provisioning profile manually. The first thing to understand is the difference on the site between development and distribution. You will need a development provisioning profile to build applications directly to your device instead of the simulator. This does not give you the abilty to share that application with anyone else, for a Distribution provisioning profile is required. You will need certificates and profiles for each type of provisioning. You will also need to assosiate your profiles with device Unique Device Identifiers (UDIDs). Because the process is identical for development and distribution provisioning creation, we will walk you through development and assume you can explore distribution on your own.

The first step in creating your Provisioning profile is creating your certificates. In the iPhone Developers program portal, click on **Certificates** in the left-hand side bar. You should see an information bubble telling you that you currently do not have any valid certificates like in figure 2–12. Click on the **Request Certificate** button to get started. You will have to create the certificate using Keychain Access on the Mac; the instructions should be listed on the page.

After you upload the Signing Request, a certificate will be generated. Once it has been "approved," you need to download it to your computer. This To do this, click the Download button next to the certificate. When its finished downloading, click on the file to launch Keychain Access. This will launch the certificate and install it to the keychain.

The last step on the Certificates page is to get the Apple WWDR certificate. There is a link to download it directly under the certificate you just created. This is the Apple Worldwide Developers Relation (WWDR) certificate, you need to download it and add it to your keychain. All you need to do is click on the WWDR certificate after it has downloaded, to launch Keychain Access and install it to your keychain.

After you have succefully installed your certificates, you are ready to register devices to your provisioning profile. Select **Devices** on the left side of the program portal. Under the **Manage** tab, there will be an **Add Devices** button. Click this to add a new device to your profile.

Finding Your Device ID

Your device is identified by a Unique Device IdentifierUDID. To add a device to a profile, you will need the device id, which can be found in two places: iTunes and Xcode. Verify that the device is connected to the computer and go to iTunes. Select the device from the Devices section on the left. This should reveal the summary page with some device specific information at the top (name, capacity, and so forth). If you click on the serial number, the device identifier will be revealed (see Figure 2–11). The other way to find your device identifier is to open Xcode and go to the Organizer window. You can get there through the top menu bar [**Window ➤ Organizer**] or by using the keyboard (Shift+Command+O). Click on your device in the left-hand panel and it should reveal the summary page with the device ID. There is also a handy free application, AdHoc, that you can download from the App store that will automatically compose an e-mail with the UDID of the device.

iPhone

Name: Your Name

Capacity: 14.28 GB

Software Version: 3.1.2

Identifier (UDID): Device UDID

Phone Number:

Figure 2–11. *iTunes Device UDID*

Regardless of the way you choose to retrieve your device UDID, copy and paste it into the Device ID text field on the Developer Portals Device registration page, and give your device a name. This can be a common name, such as "Joe," or a device description, such as "Joe's work phone".

In the Program Portal, click on **App IDs** on the left side. App IDs are a unique combination of charactures used to differentiate applications. Click on the **New App ID** button to begin. It will then ask you for a general description or name for your App ID; this can be as simple as "MyiPhoneID" or "ProjectID." Try to keep the name specific to your application because this ID will be used throughout the portal to identify it. Next, you can choose to generate a new bundle seed ID or use an exisiting one if this application is part of a suite. Finally, you need to pick a Bundle Identifier for this application. To have this App ID cover *any* application that you are currently developing, simply put an astrisk (*) in this text field. This will allow any application to build, regardless of its name. To create a more specific App ID, the convention used is reversed domain-style strings, such as the example given in the portal "com.domainname.appname."

Create the Provisioning Profile

It's time to create your first provisioning profile. In the Program Portal, click on **Provisioning**. This area is where you will manage all of your development and distribution profiles. To start, click **New Profile**. Give your profile a name, such as "iPhoneAppDevPP" or "iPhoneAppDistPP." Check the certificate you created earlier, select the App ID you want to register with this profile, and finally select the devices you want to asociate with it. This will create your provisioning profile; all that's left is to download it and install it in Xcode.

Install the Provisioning Profile

Launch Xcode and go to the Organizer window located in the top menu bar at **Window ➤ Organizer** or launch with the keyboard (Shift+Command+O). Make sure the device is connected and select it in the devices drop-down, located on the left side. Find the provisioning profile you downloaded and drag and drop the file into the Provisioning section of the window. Your organizer window should look like Figure 2–12. It should also have a green-colored dot (apposed to an amber-colored dot) next to your device name on the left. The green dot signifies your device is set up correctly.

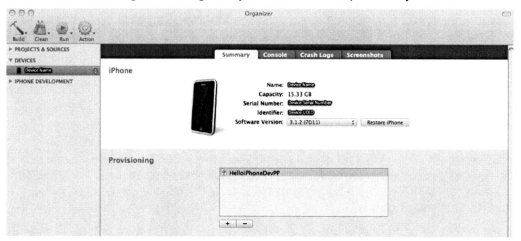

Figure 2–12. *Xcode Organizer Window*

Install and Run on the Device

Now that you have provisioning profiles set up on the device, you need to configure Xcode to use the proper profiles when you build your application. To do this, you need to modify the Project and Target Information windows.

Start by double-clicking the project file located under **Groups & Files** in Xcode. This file will be called *HelloiPhone*. This will launch the Project "HelloiPhone" Info window. Click on the Build tab and locate the section called Code Signing. Under Code Signing Identity, there should be an **Any iPhone OS Device** option. Clicking on the box to the right of this should provide you with a drop-down menu. Select the iPhone Developer that you created earlier in the iPhone Developers Portal. You need to do the exact same thing for the Target Info page now. Close the window and this time find the **Targets** drop-down under **Groups & Files** in Xcode. Double-clicking on the application "HelloiPhone" should reveal the Target "HelloiPhone" Info window. Once again, go to the Build tab and locate **Code Signing**. Drop-down **Code Signing Identity** and select the correct iPhone developer for the **Any iPhone OS Device** option. Close the window.

There is one final option you may have configured and that is the name of the application. If you decided to not use the asterisk (*) in the App ID section and gave your app a formal name, then you will need to edit the *info.plist* file. You can locate this file under resources in the HelloiPhone application drop-down in **Groups & Files**. Look for the Bundle identifier and name it exactly as you did in the portal. Save the *info.plist* file and you should be good to go.

In the top left-hand corner of Xcode, there is a drop-down that lets you decide whether you are building for the simulator or device. You want to have the active SDK set to the latest version of the device and the active configuration set to debug (unless you are building for distribution). Select **Build and Go** and the application will be compiled and installed to the device.

One last note: you can manage the applications that you are building from the Organizer window in Xcode. You may want to delete the application currently on the device before rebuilding it.

Chapter 3

Android

The Android operating system is released under the open source Apache License and is built on Linux kernel version 2.6. Android is a project of the Open Handset Alliance (OHA). Founded by Google, OHA is an association that includes 65 hardware/software companies and operators, such as KDDI, NTT DoCoMo, Sprint Nextel, Telefónica, Dell, HTC, Intel, Motorola, Qualcomm, Texas Instruments, Samsung, LG, T-Mobile, and Nvidia.

The first Android phone, T-Mobile G1 (also marketed as HTC Dream), was released in October 2008, followed by the release of 12 additional android phones in 2009. There are now dozens of Android mobile devices, including both phones and tablets. In addition to the natural fragmentation of screen size, capabilities, and OS version, developers saw incompatibilities between devices that require specific workarounds for both native applications and browser-based applications.

The Android mobile operating system has a rich set of features. 2D and 3D graphics are supported, based on OpenGL ES 2.0 specifications, and there is good media support for common audio, video, and image formats. Animated transitions and high-resolution, colorful graphics are integrated in the operating system and commonly seen in applications. The Android operating system supports multi-touch input (although it is not supported in every Android device). The web browser is based on the powerful WebKit engine and includes Chrome's V8 JavaScript runtime.

Multitasking of applications is supported. In Android, multitasking is managed by structuring applications as "activities." Activities have a distinct visual presentation and should be single-purpose, such as taking a photo, searching and presenting results, or editing a contact. Activities may be accessed by other applications as well. A simple application may implement a single activity, but more complex applications may be implemented as a number of activities cohesively presented as a single application.

Android lacks authoritative human interface guidelines, except for fairly narrow icon, widget, and menu design guidelines and broad advice about structuring activities.[1] This lack of standards can make it more challenging to design and develop for Android;

---

[1] http://developer.android.com/guide/practices/ui_guidelines/index.html

however, Android does include a set of common user interface components that are comparable to those available on the iPhone.

Android Development

To develop for the Android, you can use Windows, Linux, or Mac. Android applications are typically written in Java, but there is no Java Virtual Machine on the platform; instead, Java classes are recompiled in to Dalvik bytecode and run on a Dalvik virtual machine. Dalvik was specially designed for Android to reduce battery consumption and work well with the limited memory and CPU-power of a mobile phone. (Note that Android does not support J2ME.) Since the release of the Android NDK (Native Development Kit) in June 2009, developers may also create native libraries in C and C++ to reuse existing code or gain performance.

The most commonly used and recommended editor is Eclipse with the Android Development Tools plug-in. The plug-in provides a full-featured development environment that is integrated with the emulator. It provides debugging capabilities and lets you easily install multiple versions of the Android platform. As you will see in this chapter, the plug-in makes it easy to get a simple app up and running. If you don't want to use Eclipse, there are command-line tools to create a skeleton app, emulator, debugger, and bridge to an actual device.

In this chapter, you will learn how to set up your Eclipse development environment, create a simple "Hello World" application, launch the application in the emulator, and then build and install the application on an Android device. We also review Android distribution options are also reviewed at the end of this chapter.

Setting Up The Development Environment With Eclipse

You will need to install/set up the following components for your development environment to follow the tutorials in this chapter. Note that Android does not require that you use Eclipse, but it is an easy way to get started with native Android development.

- The Eclipse IDE. Any of the package downloads for the IDE should work fine. `http://www.eclipse.org/downloads/`

- Android Development Tools (ADT) Eclipse plug-in. `http://developer.android.com/sdk/eclipse-adt.html#installing`

- The Android SDK.

    Install the Android SDK by following the instructions in the Android developer site: `http://developer.android.com/sdk/installing.html`.

    The tutorial in this chapter assumes the tools are available on your system PATH:

- On Mac or Linux (in ~/.profile or ~/.bashrc): export PATH=${PATH}:<your_sdk_dir ➤ /tools

- On Windows, add the tools path to your environment variables.

- One or more versions of the Android platform (to simulate different devices). Unless you know that you'll be using new APIs introduced in the latest SDK, you should select a target with the lowest platform version possible. For compatibility with all devices, we recommend SDK 1.5, API 3.

1. On Mac and Linux, if you have set up your $PATH as described previously, you can just type on the command line: android (note: if you use the command-line tool, you will need to restart Eclipse to see the installed targets).

 On Windows, double-click *SDK Setup.exe* at the root of the SDK directory.

 Or in Eclipse, select **Window ➤ Android SDK and AVD Manager**.

2. Under Settings, select "Force https://..." (Figure 3–1).

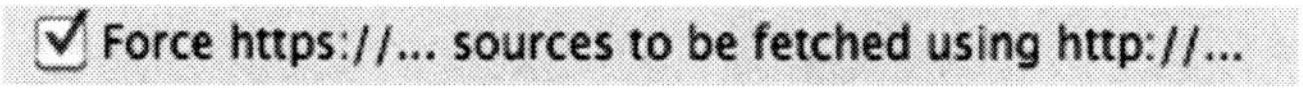

☑ Force https://... sources to be fetched using http://...

Figure 3–1. *Force https*

3. Then, under Available packages, select the SDK 1.5, API 3 and Google APIs for Android API 3 (Figure 3–2).

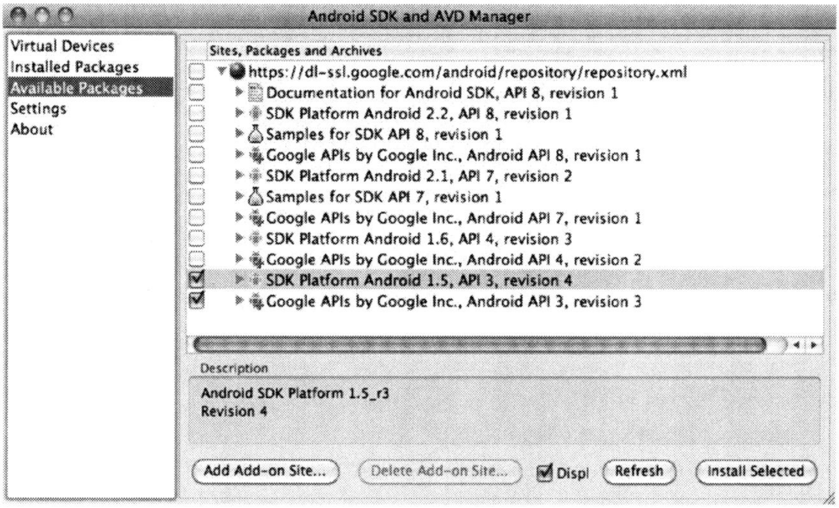

Figure 3–2. *Android SDK and AVD Manager: selecting packages to install*

4. Create an Android Virtual Device (AVD), as shown in Figure 3–3.

Figure 3–3. *Android SDK and AVD Manager: creating a virtual device*

5. Click **New** and fill in your desired values for virtual device properties (Figure 3–4).

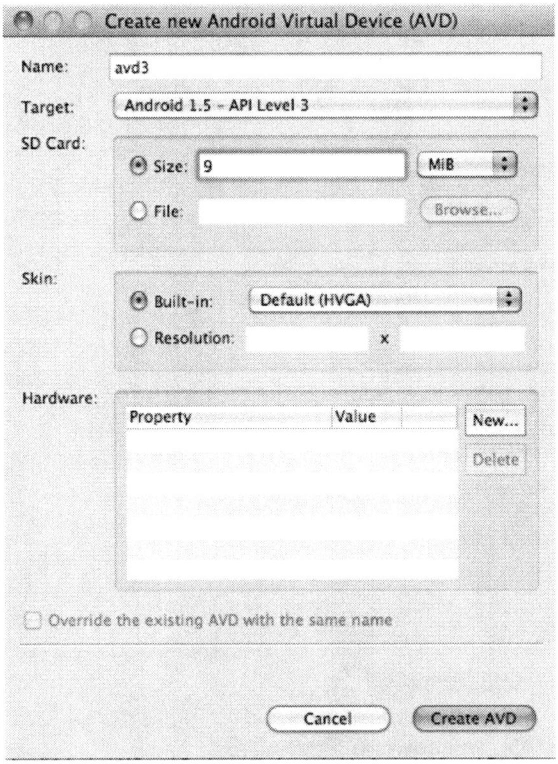

Figure 3–4. *Virtual device details*

Building a Simple Android Application

We will build a simple Hello World application and test it in the Android emulator. While there is a native development kit (NDK) that allows you to build code in C or C++, it is only for creating high-performance libraries. Android applications are always written in Java. This short tutorial will introduce you to building an Android application in Java using the Eclipse IDE.

The goal of this application is to have the user enter his or her name into a text box, press a button, and have the application greet them by name.

1. Select File ➤ New ➤ Project.

2. Select Android ➤ Android Project, and click **Next** (Figure 3–5).

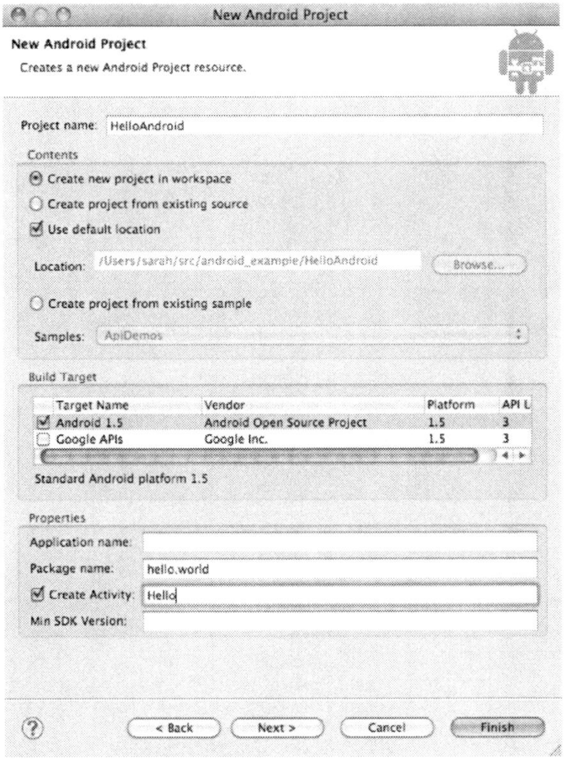

Figure 3–5. *New Android project*

You will need to provide a package name for your app. This can be something like *hello.world* or whatever you want it to be.

Make sure the box labeled **Create Activity** is checked and give your activity a name such as *Hello*. An activity is a UI class that allows you to display things on the screen and get user input. We will modify this class to create a simple UI.

If the box labeled **Min SDK Version** is empty, just click on the lowest SDK version you want to support in the list labeled **Build Target**. This will automatically fill in the correct number for you. This number will be important when you publish your app because it will enable devices to determine if they are able to run your application.

3. Click **Finish**.

Once you have completed the steps to create your application, take a look at the resulting structure in the Eclipse Package Explorer. It should look like Figure 3–6. Navigate into the *src* directory and find your activity class *Hello.java*. Double-click on it to open the file in the editor.

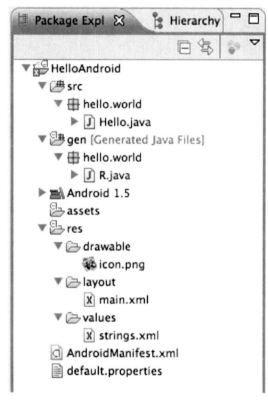

Figure 3–6. *Eclipse Package Explorer*

4. This class contains a method called "onCreate," which calls the method "setContentView" passing in "R.layout.main." This loads the layout that is defined in *res/layout/main.xml* (Figure 3–7).

```
package hello.world;

import android.app.Activity;

public class Hello extends Activity {
    /** Called when the activity is first created. */
    @Override
    public void onCreate(Bundle savedInstanceState) {
        super.onCreate(savedInstanceState);
        setContentView(R.layout.main);
    }
}
```

Figure 3–7. *Hello.java generated source code*

5. Double-click on *main.xml* to open it up in the Layout Editor. (You may need to click on the **Layout** tab in the lower left corner of the *main.xml* panel to see the Layout Editor, as illustrated in Figure 3–8.) The Layout Editor is a tool provided by the ADT plug-in for laying out UI widgets in your application. Notice that the main layout contains only a text widget that displays the text "Hello World, Hello!".

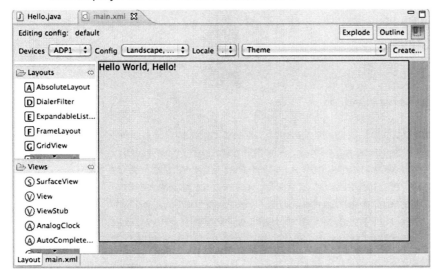

Figure 3–8. *ADT Layout Editor*

6. At this point, you can run your application. Go to the **Run** menu and click **Run**. Select **Android Application** from the list and click **OK**. This will launch the emulator and install your application.

> **NOTE:** If your project contains errors such as: "The project cannot be built until build path errors are resolved."
>
> Clean the project by choosing: **Project ➤ Clean**
>
> Then click **Run**.

7. The emulator takes a while to start up, and it may start up in a locked state and say "Screen locked, Press Menu to unlock." Just click the **Menu** button and your application will be launched. Your running application should look like the emulator shown in Figure 3–9.

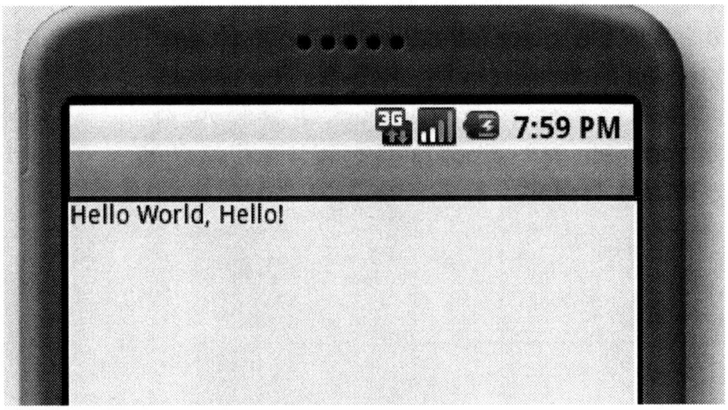

Figure 3–9. *Application running in Emulator*

8. Now that we have a simple application up and running, let's make it do something a little more interesting. We will add a text box in which the user enters his or her name, and a button that will prompt the Android device to say hello to the user. In the Eclipse editor, open up *res/layout/main.xml* in the Layout Editor. Remove the "Hello World" text from the screen by right-clicking on it and selecting **Remove** from the menu (and confirm when prompted by a pop-up message box).

9. Then add an input text field. Scroll through the **Views** menu (shown in Figure 3–10) to get to the **EditText** item. Click and drag **EditText** into the black layout window. You will now see an editable text item.

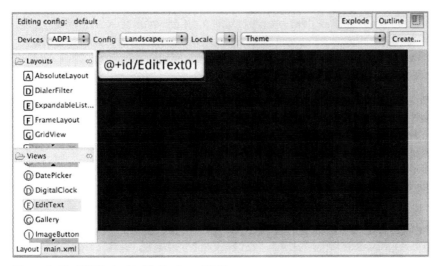

Figure 3–10. *Edit Text added in the Layout Editor*

10. The text that appears in the box is the default text. You can use this to
provide guidance to the user about what they should enter in the box. In
this application, we will ask the user to input his or her name into the
box so we will make the default text say "Name." To do this, click on the
Properties tab (shown in Figure 3–11). To make it appear, you may
need to double-click on the **EditText** item on the **Outline** tab.

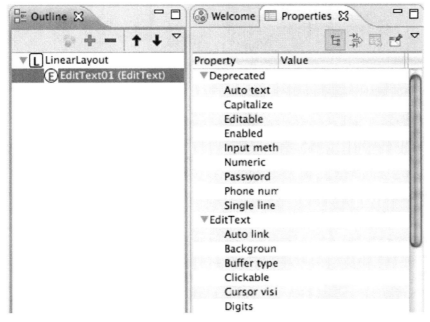

Figure 3–11. *Properties panel*

Scroll down until you see the **Text** property. Click on its value to edit it and change the value to "Name." We will also change the size of the text box to be more appropriate for a name. Scroll until you see the **width** property. Click on the row to set its value. Give it a value of "300px."

11. Next, find the **Button** control and add one to the layout. Edit the button's Text property to say "Hello Android!". When this button is clicked, we want to grab the contents of the name input box and display text that says hello to the user. We will need to add an empty text control to the layout to hold this text. Find the **TextView** control in the list and drag it under the button. Then delete the default text in the **TextView**.

12. Launch your app and see how the UI Widgets look in the layout. Your emulator should look like Figure 3–12. You should be able to type in the text field, but if you click the button at this point nothing will happen.

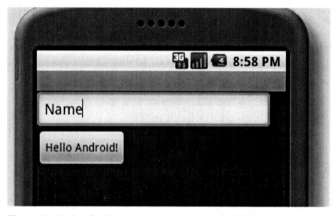

Figure 3–12. *Application running in emulator with UI Widgets.*

13. To make the button perform an action, you need to attach an event listener. Open up your activity class file *Hello.java* in the *src* directory. You can attach an event listener in the onCreate method. First, get a reference to the button using its ID, as shown in Listing 3–1.

Listing 3–1. *Button reference*

```
Button myButton = (Button) findViewById(R.id.Button01);
```

You can find the ID of your button by looking at its ID property in the properties list. When you first add this code, Eclipse will complain that it doesn't recognize the type Button. Eclipse will automatically add an import statement for you to import the Button class. Just click on the red **x** that appears to the left of that line of code and select **Import 'Button' (android.widget)** (Figure 3–13).

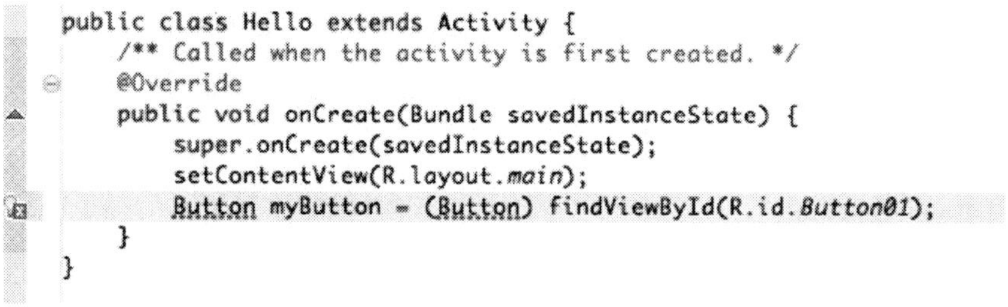

```
public class Hello extends Activity {
    /** Called when the activity is first created. */
    @Override
    public void onCreate(Bundle savedInstanceState) {
        super.onCreate(savedInstanceState);
        setContentView(R.layout.main);
        Button myButton = (Button) findViewById(R.id.Button01);
    }
}
```

Figure 3–13. *Find button reference*

Now that you have a reference to the button, you can add an event listener for the onclick event (see Listing 3–2).

Listing 3–2. *onClickListener*

```
myButton.setOnClickListener(new OnClickListener() {
    @Override
    public void onClick(View v) {
    }
});
```

Listing 3–2 shows the code to create an empty event listener. Any code you add inside the onClick method will be executed when the button is clicked. Get references to the EditText and TextView controls using the same method used to get the button object (shown in Listing 3–3).

Listing 3–3. *References to EditText and TextView from the Layout*

```
EditText et = (EditText) findViewById(R.id.EditText01);  TextView tv = (TextView)
findViewById(R.id.TextView01);
```

Then set the text in the TextView using the name that was entered into the EditText (with code shown in Listing 3–4).

Listing 3–4. *References to EditText and TextView from the Layout*

```
tv.setText("Hello " + et.getText());
```

The onCreate method should now look like Figure 3–14.

```
package hello.world;

import android.app.Activity;
import android.os.Bundle;
import android.view.View;
import android.view.View.OnClickListener;
import android.widget.Button;
import android.widget.EditText;
import android.widget.TextView;

public class Hello extends Activity {
    /** Called when the activity is first created. */
    @Override
    public void onCreate(Bundle savedInstanceState) {
        super.onCreate(savedInstanceState);
        setContentView(R.layout.main);
        Button myButton = (Button) findViewById(R.id.Button01);
        myButton.setOnClickListener(new OnClickListener() {
            public void onClick(View v) {
                EditText et = (EditText) findViewById(R.id.EditText01);
                TextView tv = (TextView) findViewById(R.id.TextView01);
                tv.setText("Hello " + et.getText());
            }
        });
    }
}
```

Figure 3–14. *Hello.java*

Now run your application and type your name into the box and click "Hello Android!". The device will display a customized hello message, including the name you typed.

Simple Application Using Android WebView

This section shows how to embed a WebView, which could allow you to add HTML UI to your native Android application. Create a project, as you did in the previous tutorial (Figure 3–15).

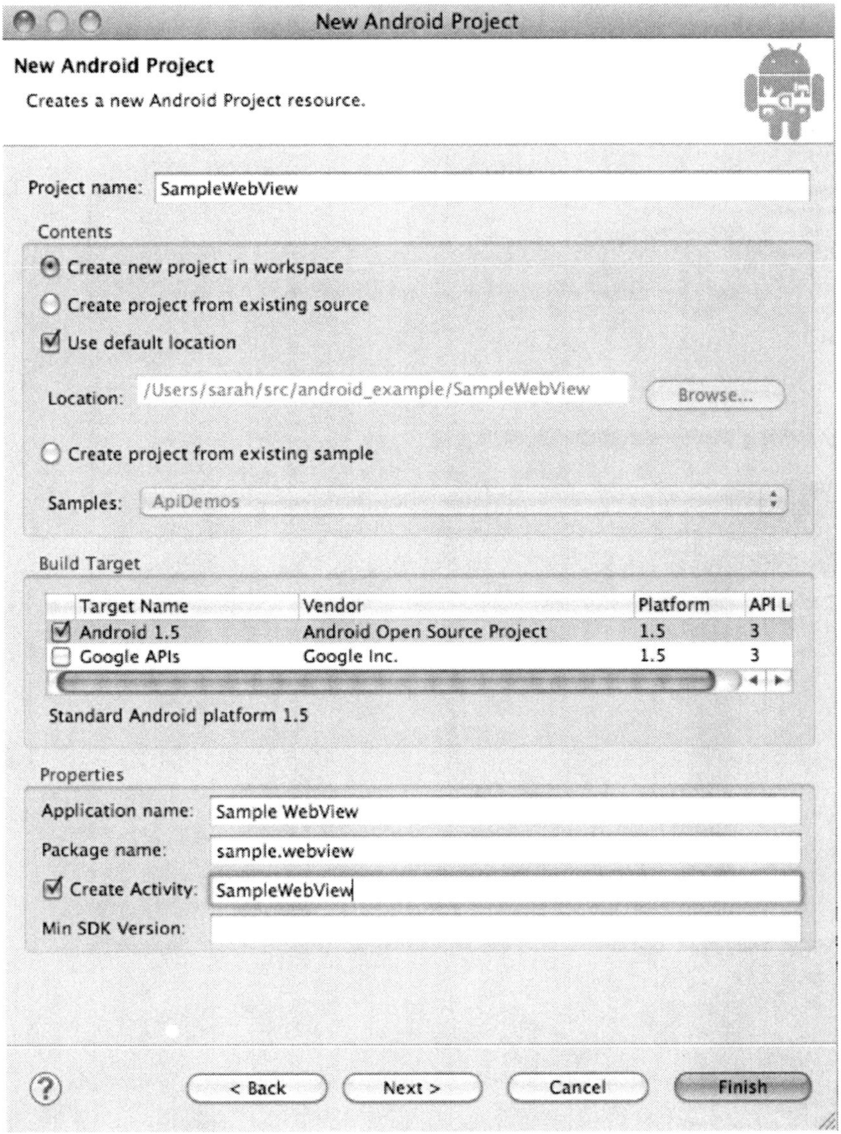

Figure 3–15. *Create Project.*

In this example, we don't use a layout (although you could). Instead, we simply create a new WebView and then set the ContentView to that instance of the WebView. Then we dynamically create some html and load it into the WebView (Figure 3–16). This is a very simply example of a powerful concept (Figure 3–17).

```
package sample.webview;

import android.app.Activity;
import android.os.Bundle;
import android.webkit.WebView;

public class SampleWebView extends Activity {
    /** Called when the activity is first created. */
    @Override
    public void onCreate(Bundle savedInstanceState) {
        super.onCreate(savedInstanceState);
        WebView webview = new WebView(this);
        setContentView(webview);

        String hello = "<html><body><p>This could be HTML UI</p></body></html>";
        webview.loadData(hello, "text/html", "utf-8");

    }
}
```

Figure 3–16. *Code for adding a WebView to SampleWebView.java*

Figure 3–17. *Application with WebView running in the Android simulator*

For more details on different ways to use WebView in Android, see
`http://developer.android.com/reference/android/webkit/WebView.html`.

Building for an Android Device

It is important to test your application on a range of target devices to understand its usability and responsiveness. For example, a G1 is significantly slower than a Nexus One. For some applications, that may make no difference, but for most it will be noticeable. Also, some device features (such as the accelerometer) cannot be tested in the emulator. Building for an Android Device is easier than other mobile platforms. You do not need to sign up for a developer program or sign your executable just to run it on a device. This section walks you through installing your application on an Android device with USB.

1. Set your application as "debuggable." In the *manifest.xml*, under the **Application** tab, set **Debuggable** to "true," as shown in Figure 3–18.

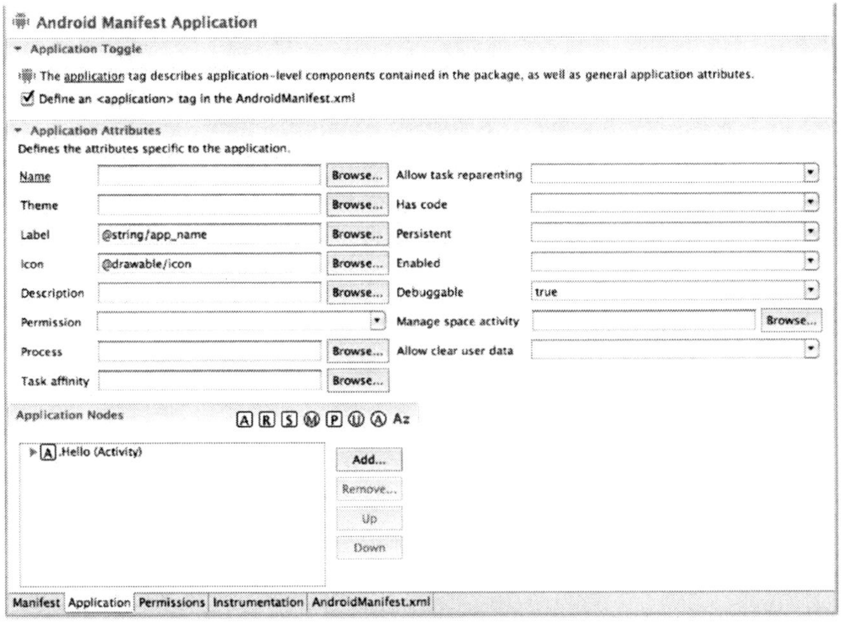

Figure 3–18. *Set application to debuggable in manifest.*

2. Set your device so it allows **USB Debugging**. In settings, select Application ➤ Development, and make sure **USB Debugging** is checked.

3. Set your system to detect your device. On Mac, this just works. On Windows, you need to install a driver. On Linux, you need to set up USB rules. You can verify that your device is connected by executing *adb devices* from your *SDK tools/* directory. If connected, you'll see the device name listed as a "device."

4. Then using Eclipse, run or debug as usual. You will be presented with a **Device Chooser** dialog that lists the available emulator(s) and connected device(s). Select the device upon which you want to install and run the application.

---

[2] Download driver: `http://developer.android.com/sdk/win-usb.html`.

[3] See detailed Linux instructions: `http://developer.android.com/guide/developing/device.html`.

Distribution on the Web

In order to publish your application, you will need to digitally sign it with a private key. This is a key that you can generate using standard tools, and that you, the developer, hold on to. Self-signed certificates are valid. You can easily generate your private key using Keytool and Jarsigner, both of which are standard Java tools. You can also use an existing key if you already have one.

The Eclipse ADT plug-in makes signing your application very easy, as it provides a wizard that will walk you through creating a private key if you don't already have one, and using it to sign your application. There is a wizard to sign and compile your application for release. For more information on signing your application, see the documentation in the Android developer site.

Once you have a signed .apk file, you can place it on a web site and if you browse to it from the web browser on an Android device, you will be prompted to install the application.

Android Market

The Android Market is the official Google directory for applications (Figure 3–19). With web distribution described previously, this marketplace is just one option for distributing your application. Some Android devices come preinstalled with an application called "Market," which allows people to access the Android Market. You may also access applications from the Android Market web site.

For developers who would like to submit their applications to the Market, there is a simple sign-up process with a $25 fee that must be paid with Google checkout.

Figure 3–19. *The Android Market*

---

[4] Signing your app: http://developer.android.com/guide/publishing/app-signing.html.

Chapter 4

BlackBerry

This chapter will discuss how to build native applications for BlackBerry smartphones. The BlackBerry is a product of Research in Motion (RIM), a public company based in Waterloo, Ontario. Founded in 1984, RIM released its first BlackBerry smartphone in 2002. Optimized for push email and with an easy-to-use QWERTY keyboard, the BlackBerry became the "gold standard" in smartphones for business professionals and executives in the US and Europe. The BlackBerry has the second largest market share of smartphones in the US. The platform has recently lost some buzz over the success of the iPhone and Android offerings. RIM has been criticized recently for being slow to introduce color screens and touch interfaces to its devices although this has been addressed with the release of its most current devices. The BlackBerry has a very large relative market share in the enterprise, particularly in the US, and must be taken into account when developing any enterprise application.

The web browser on the BlackBerry is proprietary and quite limited. RIM is expected to address this in the next OS release when it includes a WebKit-based browser.

BlackBerry Platform

The BlackBerry platform supports different ways of developing applications:

- *BlackBerry Web Development*: This is the newest offering from RIM using the Widget SDK. BlackBerry Widgets are small, discrete, standalone web applications that use HTML, CSS, and JavaScript.

- *Java Application Development*: This is the classic way in which BlackBerry apps are developed in Java using MIDP 2.0, CLDC 1.1 and RIM's proprietary APIs. We will cover this method shortly and it is assumed you have some experience programming in Java. Extensive documentation, training videos, and downloads are available at the BlackBerry Developers Web Site: `http://na.blackberry.com /eng/developers/`. The tools to develop for BlackBerry are free. Although the BlackBerry tools are based on Java, only the Windows 32-bit operating system is really supported for development. The learning curve to develop native BlackBerry applications in Java is relatively steep compared to other mobile platforms.

This chapter focuses on Java Application Development. See Chapter 14 for more detail on developing BlackBerry UI in HTML for use inside native applications with a Browser control or as web applications or Widgets.

The BlackBerry runs a proprietary multitasking operating system. 5.0 is the most current version, although you should be prepared to encounter much older versions since BlackBerry owners sometimes do not upgrade for a while, especially if the devices are being provided from their enterprise.

Central to understanding the BlackBerry platform is the BlackBerry Enterprise Server (BES). BES provides advanced functionality for IT administrators. A BES allows administrators to deploy and update applications, set policies for devices, and most importantly, synchronize email, calendar entries, contacts, and tasks wirelessly using push technology. BES is one of the reasons the BlackBerry is so dominant in the enterprise market.

Set Up for Classic Java Development

The system requirements are:

- Computer monitor with resolution 1024×768 or higher

- Intel Pentium 4 Processor (minimum 3 GHz)

- 1.5GB Hard drive

- 1GB RAM

- Microsoft Windows Vista, or Windows XP

In our experience, a fast Windows machine is recommended. It is possible to develop on a Mac by running these tools inside a Windows virtual machine, but for best performance you should run Windows natively.

You need to download and install the following tools if you do not have them already:

- Sun JDK (Java Development Kit) from http://java.sun.com/javase/downloads/index.jsp. The current version is JDK 6 Update 20, which includes the JRE (Java Runtime Environment).

- Eclipse IDE for Java Developers from www.eclipse.org/downloads/. Eclipse is a very popular, open source, multilanguage software development environment comprising an integrated development environment (IDE) and an extensible plug-in system. It is assumed that you are familiar with how to use Eclipse. If not, you can find documentation on the eclipse.org website. In this chapter, we will use Eclipse 3.4.1.

- BlackBerry Plug-in for Eclipse and BlackBerry JDEs from
  http://na.blackberry.com/eng/developers/resources/devtools.jsp.
  You will need the plug-in and at least one JDE. You should download
  the JDE for whichever version of the BlackBerry operating system you
  are targeting. Download all the available JDEs for the versions of
  BlackBerry operating systems that you need to support from 4.2 to
  5.0. In this chapter, we will use BlackBerry JDE Component Package
  4.70.

After you have downloaded and installed these tools, proceed to the next section.

Building a Simple BlackBerry Application

We will build a simple "Hello World" application and test it in the BlackBerry simulator.

Create the Eclipse Project

To create a new BlackBerry project from within Eclipse, choose New and then Project
from the File menu. A dialog box will appear (as seen in Figure 4–1) that prompts you to
pick what type of project you want to create. The BlackBerry project types are provided
by the BlackBerry plug-in referenced in the previous section.

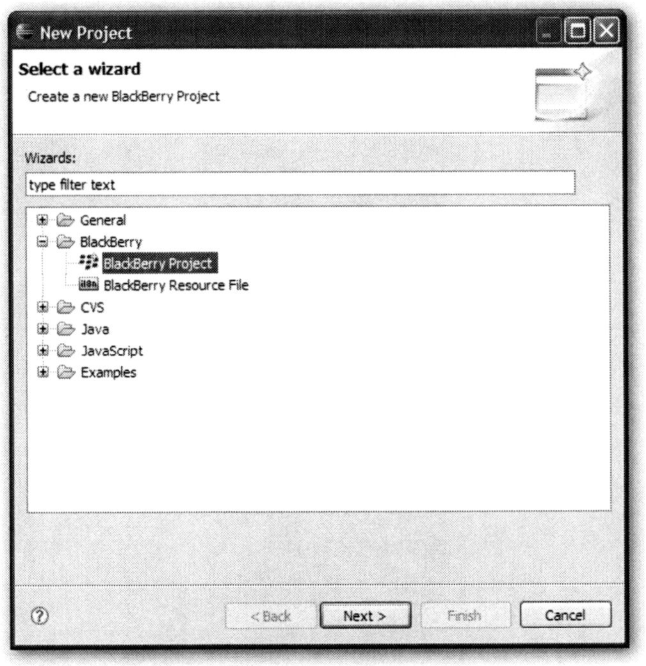

Figure 4–1. *"New Project" dialog in Eclipse*

Select **BlackBerry Project** and click the **Next** button. You will be prompted to enter the name of your project (as seen in Figure 4–2). Enter a name, such as "Hello World," and click **Finish**. "Hello World" will then be listed in the Projects pane, as shown in Figure 4–3.

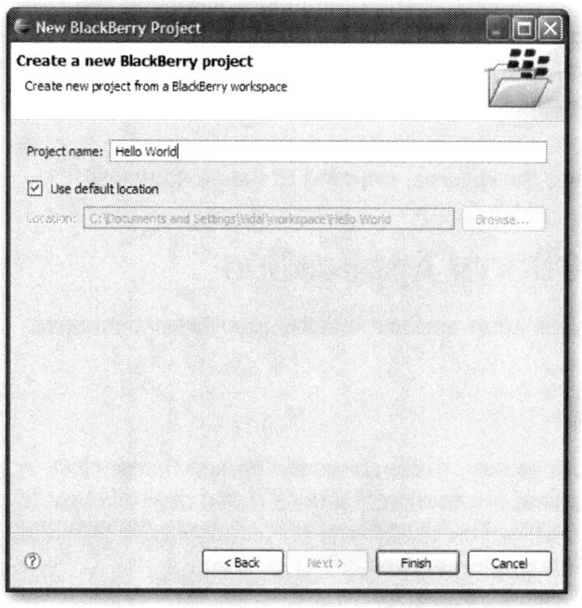

Figure 4–2. *BlackBerry Project creation dialog in Eclipse*

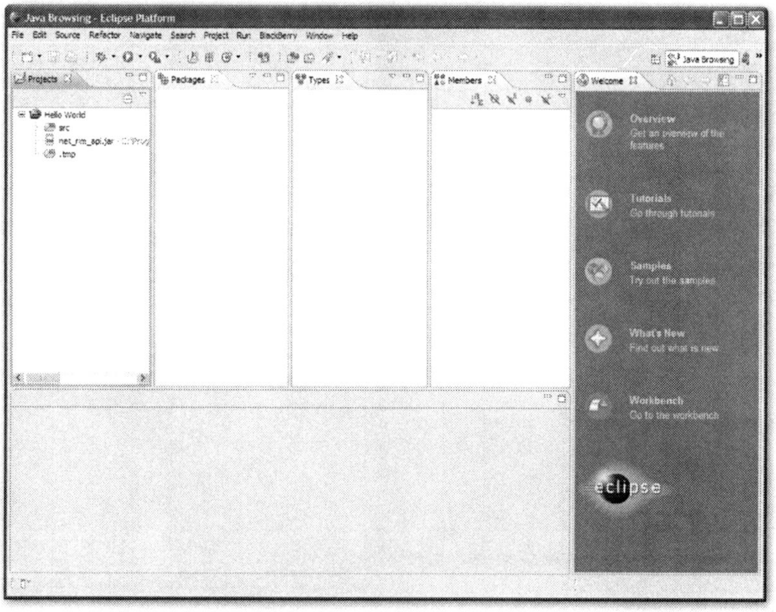

Figure 4–3. *BlackBerry Project in Eclipse*

From the **BlackBerry** menu, choose **Configure BlackBerry Workspace**. As seen in Figure 4–4, enter 1.0 for the Project Version and XPlatform for the Project Vendor.

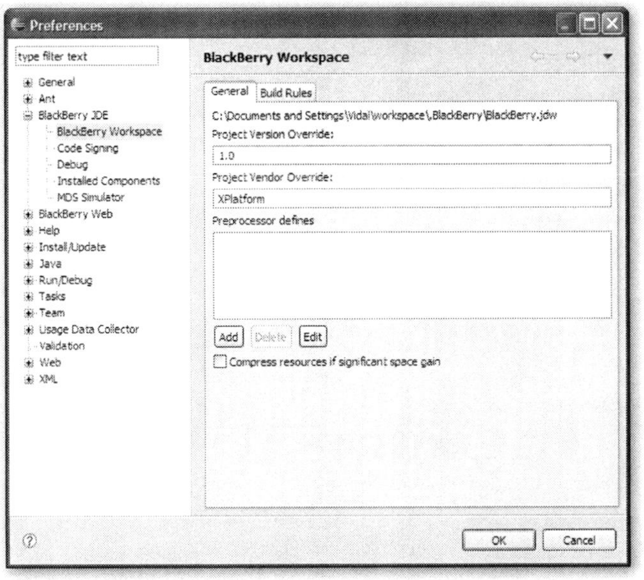

Figure 4–4. *Configuring the BlackBerry Workspace for Eclipse*

Next, click on **Installed Components** in the left panel. Choose the BlackBerry JDE that you want to build for. In this example, we choose 4.7.0. Click **OK** to close the BlackBerry Workspace Preferences

Create the Interface

When developing for BlackBerry, you will create the user interface programmatically by creating containers and UI elements as objects and then arranging and connecting them in a hierarchy. First, you need to create a Java class for your simple application.

1. From the **File** menu, click **New** and then **Package**.

2. Enter the name of the package as "com.xplatform.helloworld".

3. Click **Finish**.

4. From the **File** menu, click **New** and then **Class**.

5. Enter "HelloWorld" as the name of the new class. Leave all other fields with their default values (as shown in Figure 4–5) and click the **Finish** button.

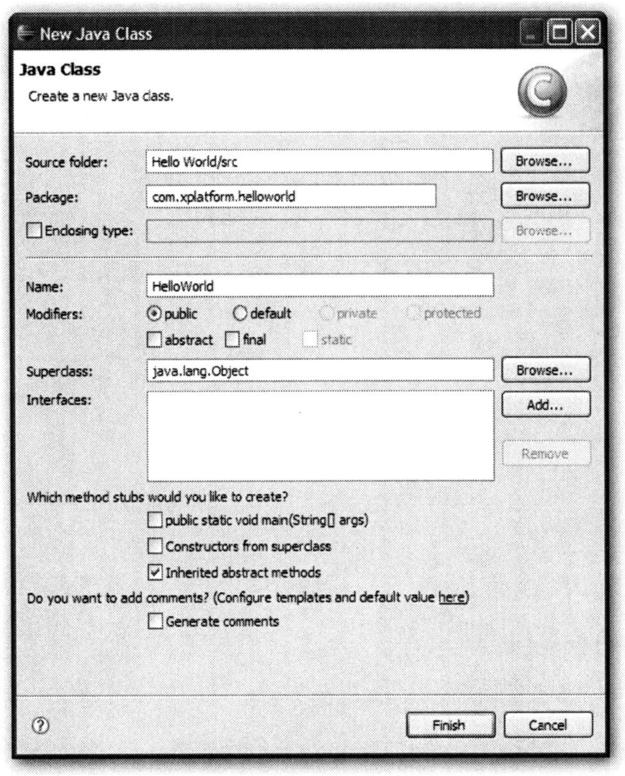

Figure 4–5. *Creating a Java class in Eclipse*

Replace the contents of the generated HelloWorld.java with the source code of the completed Hello World application that follows.

```java
package com.xplatform.helloworld;
import net.rim.device.api.ui.*;
import net.rim.device.api.ui.component.*;
import net.rim.device.api.ui.container.*;

public class HelloWorld extends UiApplication {

        public static void main(String []args)
        {
                HelloWorld theApp = new HelloWorld();
                theApp.enterEventDispatcher();
        }

        public HelloWorld ()
        {
                pushScreen (new HelloWorldScreen());
        }
}

class HelloWorldScreen extends MainScreen
{
```

```
public HelloWorldScreen()
{
        super();
        LabelField title = new LabelField("XPlatform Dev");
        setTitle(title);
        add(new RichTextField("Hello World!"));
}

public boolean onClose()
{
        System.exit(0);
        return true;
}
}
```

Code Explained

The following is a breakdown of the code sample just provided.

- Name the package. We do this on line number one with the package statement. This has to be the first line in the file.

- Import the packages we will be using from the BlackBerry SDK using import statements. Note, we can use the asterisk (*) at the end to import all the packages below a certain level in the hierarchy.

- Define our application class, called HelloWorld, by extending the UIApplication base class. UIApplication is the base class for all device applications that provide a user interface. Class HelloWorld must have one method main, which is the entry point into our application.

- Within main, create an instance of HelloWorld. Inside the constructor for HelloWorld, we instantiate a HelloWorldScreen custom screen object and call pushScreen() to display our custom screen for the application. We will define HelloWorldScreen below.

- Call enterEventDispatcher(). Our thread now becomes the event-dispatching thread that will execute all drawing and event-handling code. Note that under normal circumstances this method does not return.

- Define a custom screen for the application called HelloWorldScreen by extending MainScreen. MainScreen provides a full screen with features common to standard RIM device applications. Main screen objects contain a title section, a separator element, and a main scrollable section.

- In the HelloWorldScreen constructor, call super() to invoke our superclass constructor the MainScreen constructor. Then we create a LabelField and set it as the title of the MainScreen. And finally, we create a RichTextField and add it to main scrollable section of the screen. LabelField and RichTextField are UI elements provided by the BlackBerry SDK.

Build and Test the Application

Build and **Run As** then **BlackBerry Simulator**. This will compile your application, load it into the simulator, and launch the simulator. Once the simulator finishes starting, navigate it to its Downloads folder. Figure 4–6 shows the icon you will see for the HelloWorld application. Click it to launch.

Figure 4–6. *Finished Application Running in Simulator*

Simple User Interface Application Using a Label, Text Field, and Button

The goal of this application is to have the user enter his or her name into a text box, press a button, and have the BlackBerry greet them by name (Figure 4–7). You can compare this application and the process to the iPhone version from Chapter 2.

Figure 4–7. *Hello BlackBerry Application Running in the Simulator*

First, set up a new BlackBerry Project. We explained how to setup and configure a new BlackBerry project in the previous example. Next, we will create a new project called User Interface and a new class that extends UiApplication called UserInterface.

Replace the contents of the generated UserInterface with the source code of the completed User Interface application that follows.

```java
import net.rim.device.api.ui.*;
import net.rim.device.api.ui.component.*;
import net.rim.device.api.ui.container.*;

public class UserInterface extends UiApplication {

        public static void main(String []args)
        {
                UserInterface theApp = new UserInterface();
                theApp.enterEventDispatcher();
        }

        public UserInterface ()
        {
                pushScreen (new UserInterfaceScreen());
        }
}

class UserInterfaceScreen extends MainScreen implements FieldChangeListener
{
        LabelField greetingLabel;
        BasicEditField userNameField;
        ButtonField  helloBtn;
```

```
public UserInterfaceScreen()
{
        super();
        LabelField title = new LabelField("XPlatform Dev");
        setTitle(title);

        greetingLabel = new LabelField("");
        add(greetingLabel);

        userNameField = new BasicEditField("Name: ", "");
        add(userNameField);

        helloBtn = new ButtonField("Hello BlackBerry!",↵
ButtonField.CONSUME_CLICK);
        helloBtn.setChangeListener(this);

        add(helloBtn);
}
public void fieldChanged(Field field, int context) {
        greetingLabel.setText("Hello " + userNameField.getText());
}

public boolean onClose()
{
        System.exit(0);
        return true;
}
}
```

Code Explained

This code is similar to our previous example with the following differences:

- In our UserInterfaceScreen class, we declare that we implement FieldChangeListener interface. The method from this interface that we will define is "public void fieldChanged(Field field, int context)", described in the following section.

- We declare instance variables for our greetingLabel and our userNameField as LabelField and BasicEditField, respectively. BasicEditField allows us to set a label and initial value for the text field.

- We add these elements to the screen in our constructor.

- We also create a ButtonField with the label "Hello BlackBerry!". We call setChangeListener(this) on this button to tell it to refer to the UserInterfaceScreen object (this) when the button is clicked. The fieldChanged method will be called. This is why we implemented FieldChangeListener.

- In fieldChanged, we set the value of the greetingLabel to "Hello" plus the current value of the userNameField.

Simple Application Using BlackBerry Browser Field

You can also display HTML content in your application using the BlackBerry Browser Field. In this example we use BlackBerry OS 5.0 JDE, which supports the later Browser Field version 2. Read about the differences between Browser Field version 1 and version 2 in chapter 14. The code is very similar to the previous example. Instead of creating an instance of RichTextField, we create an instance of the BrowserField class.

```java
import net.rim.device.api.browser.field2.*;
import net.rim.device.api.ui.*;
import net.rim.device.api.ui.container.*;

public class HelloBrowser extends UiApplication {
    public static void main(String[] args)
    {
        HelloBrowser app = new HelloBrowser();
        app.enterEventDispatcher();
    }

    public HelloBrowser()
    {
        pushScreen(new HelloBrowserScreen());
    }
}
class HelloBrowserScreen extends MainScreen
{
    public HelloBrowserScreen()
    {
        BrowserField myBrowserField = new BrowserField();
        add(myBrowserField);
        myBrowserField.displayContent("<html><body><h1>Hello↵
 World!</h1></body></html>", "http://localhost");
    }
}
```

Figure 4–8 shows the Hello Browser App Running in the Simulator.

You change this application to display HTML content from a web page by switching:

```java
myBrowserField.displayContent("<html><body><h1>Hello↵
 World!</h1></body></html>", "http://localhost");
```

to

```java
myBrowserField.requestContent("http://www.blackberry.com");
```

Figure 4–8. *Hello Browser App Running in the Simulator*

Building for a BlackBerry Device

The BlackBerry simulator is quite good. There are versions for every BlackBerry model and it is effective for viewing your application with different screen dimensions and resolutions. However, there are always differences when you test on an actual device. For example, a UI element may seem usable when you are controlling it with mouse and key board shortcuts in the simulator, but on the physical device, you may find that a button is really too small to hit when you are using the Storm's touch screen. You should have a range of devices for testing and try it as early in the development process as possible.

Signing of applications is not required to run applications using the BlackBerry Smartphone simulator, but you must sign an application before you can install it on a BlackBerry smartphone device. Cryptographic keys can only be acquired from RIM.

You will need to fill out a web form [www.blackberry.com/SignedKeys/] to register for access to the BlackBerry runtime, application and cryptography APIs. Once registered, you will be sent a set of keys and installation instructions via e-mail that can be used to allow you to sign your applications using the BlackBerry Signature Tool. An administration fee of $20.00 will be charged to a valid credit card to complete the registration process. Allow a few days for RIM to process your application and send you your keys.

Code signing registration is solely for the purpose of monitoring usage of these particular APIs in third party application development and does not, in any way, indicate RIM's approval or endorsement of your application or your use of the APIs.

Over the Air (OTA) Distribution

You can distribute applications "over the air" by posting the files on the Web. BlackBerry Java OTA files consist of one .jad file and one or more .cod files.

Provide a link to the ".jad" file and when someone clicks that link in the Web browser on a BlackBerry device, the application will automatically download. If an application is too large to fit within the 128KB limit (64KB of application data and 64KB of resource data), it cannot be delivered as one large file, but must instead be broken up into a set of smaller files (as illustrated in Figure 4–9). This can be done automatically using the BlackBerry Java development tools.

```
RubyConf-1.cod                        100%    93KB   93.3KB/s    00:00
RubyConf-10.cod                       100%    83KB   83.2KB/s    00:00
RubyConf-11.cod                       100%    91KB   91.1KB/s    00:00
RubyConf-12.cod                       100%    85KB   85.4KB/s    00:00
RubyConf-13.cod                       100%    77KB   76.7KB/s    00:00
RubyConf-14.cod                       100%    57KB   56.6KB/s    00:00
RubyConf-15.cod                       100%    61KB   61.0KB/s    00:00
RubyConf-16.cod                       100%    49KB   49.4KB/s    00:00
RubyConf-17.cod                       100%    70KB   70.0KB/s    00:00
RubyConf-18.cod                       100%    81KB   80.6KB/s    00:00
RubyConf-19.cod                       100%    20KB   20.3KB/s    00:00
RubyConf-2.cod                        100%    65KB   65.0KB/s    00:00
RubyConf-3.cod                        100%    82KB   82.1KB/s    00:00
RubyConf-4.cod                        100%    83KB   83.4KB/s    00:00
RubyConf-5.cod                        100%    85KB   85.2KB/s    00:00
RubyConf-6.cod                        100%    79KB   78.6KB/s    00:00
RubyConf-7.cod                        100%    76KB   75.7KB/s    00:00
RubyConf-8.cod                        100%    81KB   81.4KB/s    00:00
RubyConf-9.cod                        100%    90KB   89.9KB/s    00:00
RubyConf.cod                          100%    90KB   90.1KB/s    00:00
RubyConf.jad                          100%  3140     3.1KB/s    00:00
```

Figure 4–9. *BlackBerry cod and jad files that compose the application for OTA distribution*

BlackBerry App World

Research in Motion offers a marketplace for applications called "BlackBerry App World." To make your application available in BlackBerry App World, you must apply for a "Vendor Portal" (Figure 4–10) – this is in addition to, and separate from, registration for signing certificates.

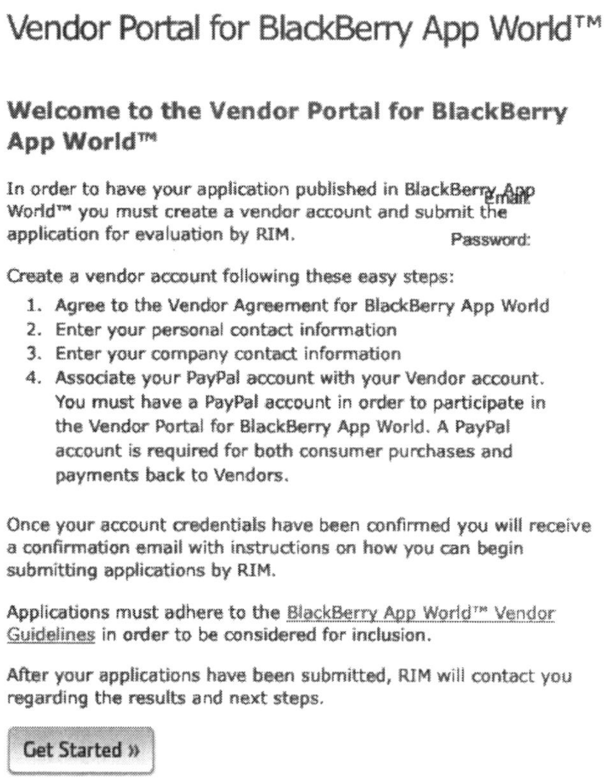

Vendor Portal for BlackBerry App World™

Welcome to the Vendor Portal for BlackBerry App World™

In order to have your application published in BlackBerry App World™ you must create a vendor account and submit the application for evaluation by RIM.

Email:

Password:

Create a vendor account following these easy steps:

1. Agree to the Vendor Agreement for BlackBerry App World
2. Enter your personal contact information
3. Enter your company contact information
4. Associate your PayPal account with your Vendor account. You must have a PayPal account in order to participate in the Vendor Portal for BlackBerry App World. A PayPal account is required for both consumer purchases and payments back to Vendors.

Once your account credentials have been confirmed you will receive a confirmation email with instructions on how you can begin submitting applications by RIM.

Applications must adhere to the BlackBerry App World™ Vendor Guidelines in order to be considered for inclusion.

After your applications have been submitted, RIM will contact you regarding the results and next steps.

Figure 4–10. Vendor portal

Research in Motion offers a marketplace for applications called "BlackBerry App World." After you create a vendor account, you will be contacted via email to provide official documentation verifying your identity (Figure 4–11). As a company, you must provide articles of incorporation or a business license. As an individual, you must fill out a form and have it notarized.

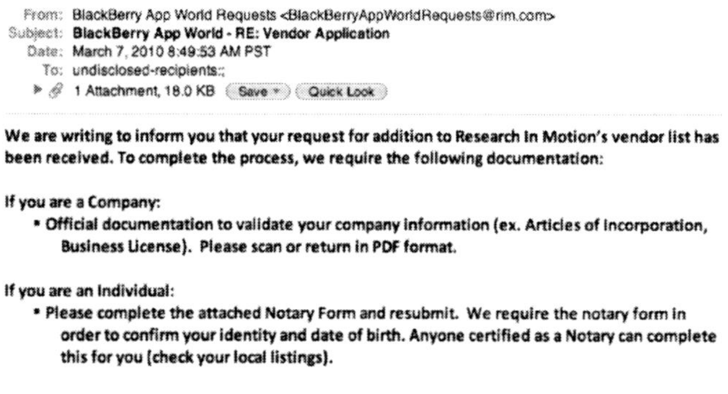

From: BlackBerry App World Requests <BlackBerryAppWorldRequests@rim.com>
Subject: **BlackBerry App World - RE: Vendor Application**
Date: March 7, 2010 8:49:53 AM PST
To: undisclosed-recipients:;
▶ 🖉 1 Attachment, 18.0 KB   (Save ▼) (Quick Look)

We are writing to inform you that your request for addition to Research In Motion's vendor list has been received. To complete the process, we require the following documentation:

If you are a Company:
  ▪ **Official documentation to validate your company information (ex. Articles of Incorporation, Business License). Please scan or return in PDF format.**

If you are an Individual:
  ▪ **Please complete the attached Notary Form and resubmit. We require the notary form in order to confirm your identity and date of birth. Anyone certified as a Notary can complete this for you (check your local listings).**

Figure 4–11. BlackBerry App World request for documentation

Chapter 5

Windows Mobile

The Windows Mobile operating system provides a more desktop-like user experience than other smartphones, adhering to the concepts of hierarchical organization with nested folders and menus. Approximately 15% of smartphones currently subscribe to a mobile plan run on the Windows Mobile platform, and Windows Mobile remains the third most popular platform for business users, commanding approximately 1/4 of the enterprise market. However, Windows Mobile market share has experienced a sharp decline over the past few years (30% between 2008 and 2009, 4% in the third quarter of 2009 alone) and it continues to drop. [1]

Additionally, usage patterns for devices on the Windows Mobile platform are vastly different from those found on more consumer-driven devices. A recent dataset released by AdMob, a mobile-centric advertising network, indicates that relative to market share, Windows Mobile users make approximately 1 request to every 15 requests made from the iPhone. Android users have usage patterns similar to BlackBerry devices. The diminished prevalence of web-based browsing on Windows Mobile devices undoubtedly has roots in user requirements and preferences, but is most likely impacted by ease-of-use and other usability issues.[2]

Although the Windows Marketplace for Mobile has only around 1000 applications, there are 18,000 applications available for the Windows Mobile platform distributed elsewhere, according to Microsoft.[3] In addition to distribution via an official channel, applications can also be distributed through several ad-hoc channels, including SMS, e-mail and physical media, as well as via direct web download.

---

[1] http://www.zdnet.co.uk/news/networking/2009/11/13/windows-mobile-loses-nearly-a-third-of-market-share-39877964/

[2] http://metrics.admob.com/wp-content/uploads/2010/03/AdMob-Mobile-Metrics-Feb-10.pdf

[3] http://www.informationweek.com/blog/main/archives/2008/07/windows_mobile_7.html;jsessionid=W2KHQFB3KLA2TQE1GHPSKH4ATMY32JVN

The forthcoming Windows Mobile platform has a new name: Windows Phone 7 and aims to provide a user experience better suited to mobile use patterns. Note that Windows Phone 7 will not be available as an upgrade for devices currently running Windows Mobile 6.5 and earlier operating systems. While the release of Windows Phone 7 may provide a boost to sales of Windows Mobile devices, the lack of continued support and development for legacy devices may provide the impetus for existing enterprise users to migrate to a different platform. Additionally, with the release of Windows Phone 7, ad-hoc distribution channels will no longer be available: devices running the Windows Phone 7 operating system will only run applications that have first been approved by Microsoft, and these applications will only be available via the Windows Phone Marketplace.

In addition to developing C++ and C#-based applications with the .NET Compact Framework, Windows Phone 7 will provide support for application development and game development using Silverlight and XNA, respectively. Microsoft Visual Studio 2010 and Expression Blend 4 for Windows Phone will be the primary tools used for Windows Phone 7 development. Unfortunately, Visual Studio 2010 does not support mobile application development for versions of Windows Phone prior to Windows Phone OS 7.0, so in order to develop for both devices, you will need to purchase licenses for both Visual Studio 2008 and 2010.

The focus of this chapter is Windows Mobile 6.5 Development, since that is the operating system prevalent on devices today.

Setting Up for Windows Mobile 6.5 Development

You should expect to spend a few hours downloading and installing what you need to build applications for Windows Mobile devices. The following tools are required to build the native application in this chapter, as well as to use the cross-platform frameworks covered later in this book.

- Microsoft Visual Studio 2008 Professional[4]
- Windows Mobile SDK.
- Windows Mobile 6 Professional and Standard Software Development Kits Refresh
- Windows Mobile 6.5 Developer Tool Kit
- ActiveSync

Visual Studio Express editions are not supported for mobile development, but you can download a free trial of Microsoft Visual Studio 2008 Professional from the MSDN web site.

Building a Simple Windows Mobile App

This section demonstrates how to build a simple Windows Mobile 6.5 application using MS Visual Studio 2008's drag-and-drop interface for assembling the UI and implementing functionality in C#, as well as building and deploying your application in the emulator and on a Windows Mobile device.

Creating a Smart Device Project

From the Visual Studio 2008 File menu, select **New ➤ Project**.

In the New Project window, find the Project Types pane on the left, expand Visual C# and select **Smart Device** (Figure 5–1). Select the **Smart Device Project template** from the Templates pane on the right, and click **OK**.

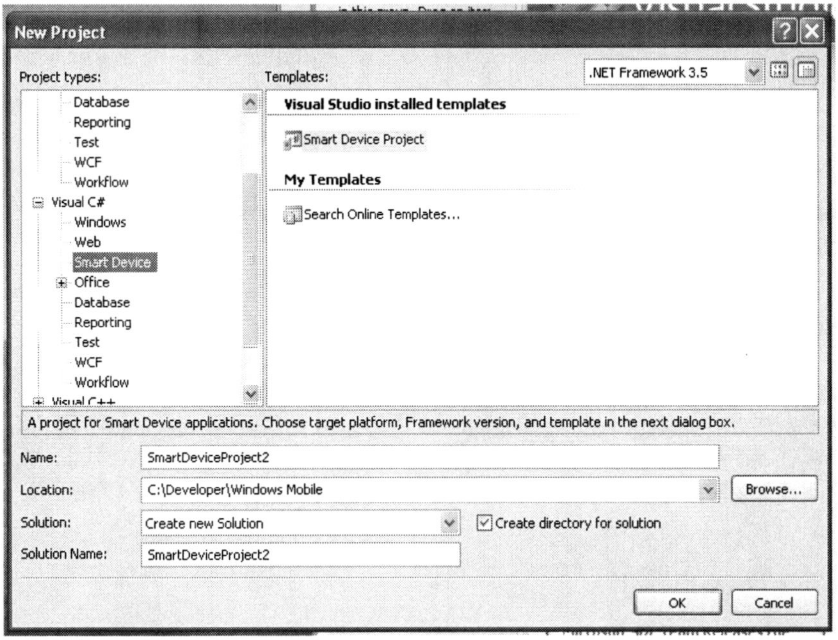

Figure 5–1. *Selecting the Smart Device Project template*

To create your application, in the Add New Smart Device Project wizard, select **Windows Mobile Professional 6 SDK** as the target platform (Figure 5–2). Select the **Device Application** template, and click **OK** to create the project.

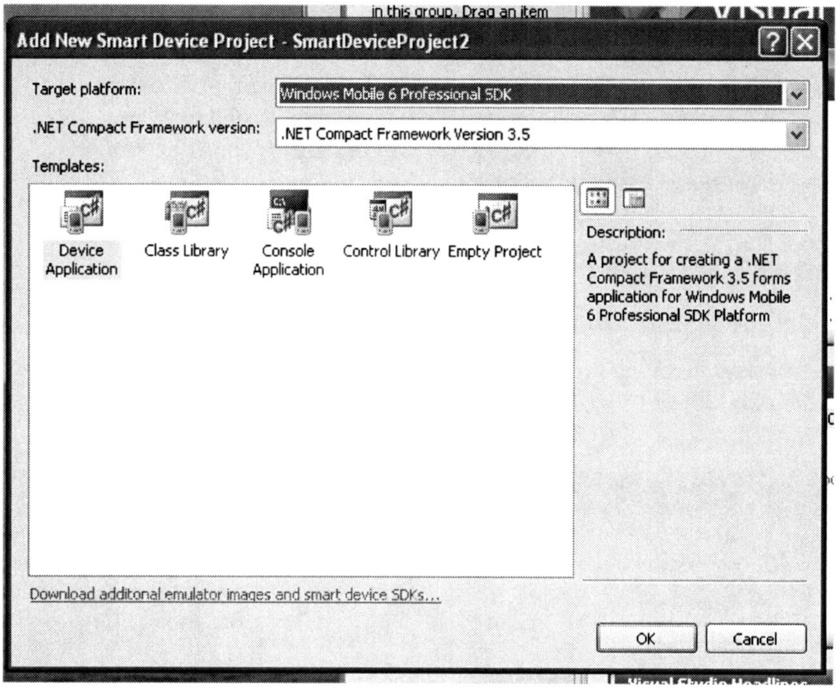

Figure 5–2. *The Add New Smart Device Project wizard*

Setting Up Base Functionality

Visual Studio allows you to build your application forms by selecting UI components in the Toolbox pane on the left and dragging them onto the form in the Design view. To make your application easier to work with, you should change the names of your UI components from the standard label1, label2...label37 to something more recognizable.

Add a Button to the View

From the Toolbox pane on the left, select a button and drag it onto the form (Figure 5–3).

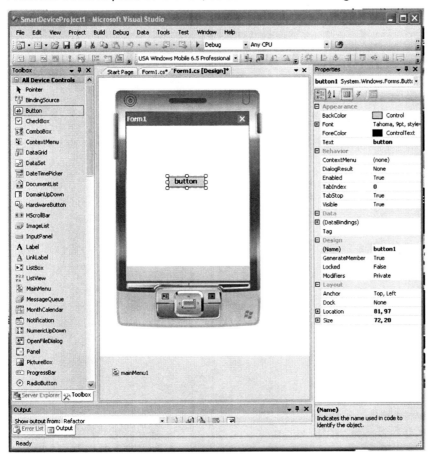

Figure 5–3. *Selecting a button from the toolbox pane*

Customize the Button

Click the button on your form once, and in the Properties pane under **Appearance**, change the label in the text field to "Submit," as shown in Figure 5–4. Then, under **Design**, set the name of the button to "submitButton," as shown in Figure 5–5.

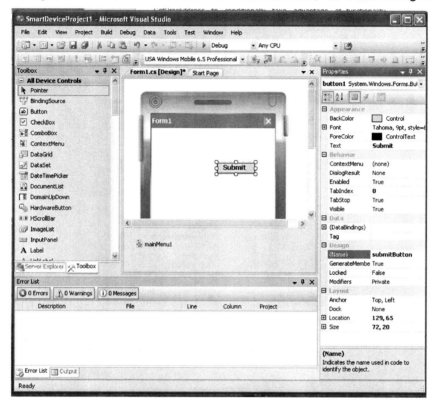

Figure 5–4. *Changing the label in the text field to "Submit"*

Figure 5–5. *Setting the name of the button to "submitButton"*

Create a Click Event Handler

Back in the design view, double-click the button you just created. This opens Form1.cs and generates an empty handler in the *Form1.cs* file (Figure 5–6).

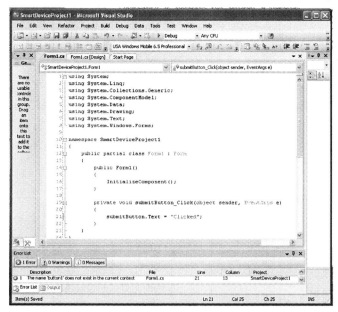

Figure 5–6. *The Form1.cs file*

In the handler, type the following line of code:

```
submitButton.Text = "Clicked";
```

Deploying and Test your Application

In order to start debugging your application in the emulator, press the F5 key. Select the **Windows Mobile 6.5 Professional Emulator** from the list of available emulators and devices, and click **Deploy** (Figure 5–7).

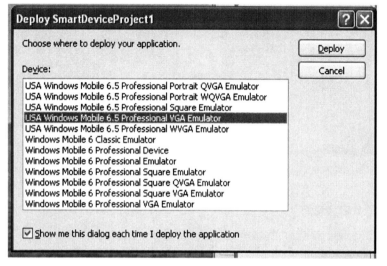

Figure 5–7. *Deploying SmartDeviceProject1*

It might take a few minutes for your application to load after the emulator launches–be patient.

When you click the button in your application, the button text should change from "Submit" to "Clicked" See Figure 5–8.

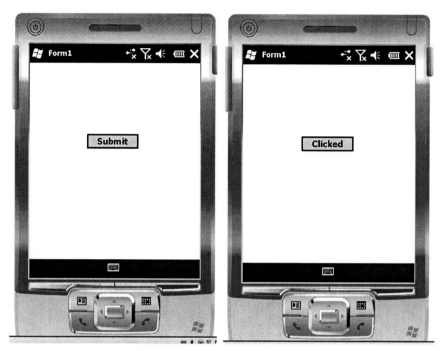

Figure 5–8. *The button text has changed to "Clicked"*

Fleshing Out the Application

Return to Visual Studio and select the **Form1.cs** Design view, where you will flesh out the rest of your application.

From the Toolbox pane on the left, select a label and drag it to the top of the form. Click the label a single time and in the Properties pane under Appearance, change the Text to "Name", and under Design, change the Name to "fieldLabel". Double-click the button to generate the handler.

Drag a TextBox from the toolbox and place it underneath the fieldLabel on the form. Click the label once and in the Properties pane under Appearance, leave the Text field empty. Under Design, change the Name to "textField" and double-click the button to generate the handler.

Position the submitButton below the textField.

Drag a Label from the toolbox to the bottom of the form. Click the label once and in the Properties pane under Appearance, remove all text from the Text field. Under Design, change the Name to "message" and double-click the button to generate the handler.

Your form should resemble Figure 5–9. Keep in mind that you will not be able to see the label field that will contain the result unless it is selected–simply press Ctrl+A to select all UI components in the design view if you wish to locate the hidden label field.

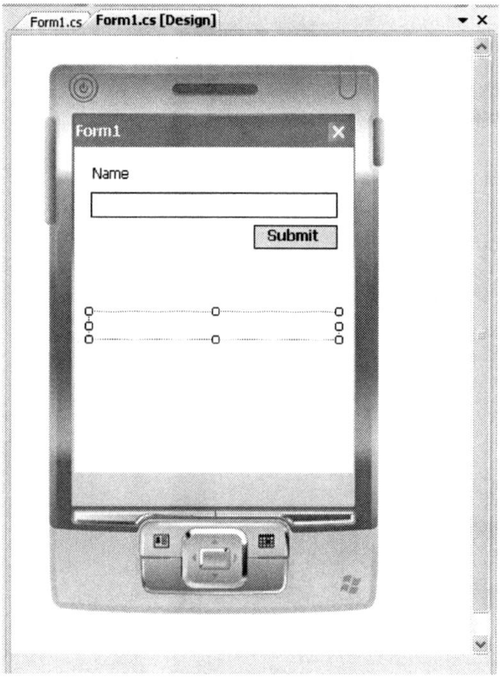

Figure 5–9. *The new form*

Update the submitButton handler to display a custom message when the button is clicked. Add:

```
message.Text = "Hi there, "+textField.Text+"!";
```

to the submitButton_Click handler. Your handler should look like the following:

```
private void submitButton1_Click(object sender, EventArgs e)
{
    button1.Text = "Click!";
    message.Text = "Hi there, "+textField.Text+"!";
}
```

Press the F5 key to deploy the application. Select **Windows Mobile 6.5 Professional Emulator** and click **OK**.

To test the application, enter your name into the text field then click the **Submit** button. "Hi there, [[your name]]!" will be displayed in the message box, as seen in Figure 5–10.

Figure 5–10. *The message box now contains the typed in name*

Embed a Web View in your Application

To embed a web view in your application, you can use the WebBrowser control.

Create an HTML page

First, you need to create a static HTML page that can be loaded from the browser. In the solution browser, right-click on your *project's* name, then click **Add ➤ New Item**. Select HTML Page, and name your file *test.htm* If you're not feeling creative, a simple text file containing the text "Hello World" will suffice.

To ensure that your HTML file is copied to the device, select the file name in the solution browser. In the Properties section, ensure that the **Copy to Output Directory** field is set to **Copy Always**.

Add a WebBrowser Control

Return to the Design view and from the toolbox drag a WebBrowser control onto your layout. Double-click the control to create the handler then return to the design view.

Load HTML in WebBrowser control

With the WebBrowser element selected, open the properties tab. Under Behavior, set the value of the absolute path to the HTML file using the format below:

```
file:///Program Files/MyProjectName/test.htm
```

Note that you can also set this value to access sites hosted on external web servers by entering the full URL with the http:// prefix. However, before you can access external sites from the emulator, you must ensure that you have cradled the emulated device. To connect to an emulator, select **Device Emulator Manager** from the **Tools** menu, select the emulator name from the list, and click **Actions ➤ Connect.** A green arrow will be displayed beside the emulator when it is running. To cradle the emulator, select its name once again, select **Actions ➤ Cradle,** and go through the motions with the ActionSync dialogues that are displayed.

You can redirect to a new page after your initial page loads by updating the webBrowser handler as follows:

```
        private void webBrowser1_DocumentCompleted(object sender, ↩
WebBrowserDocumentCompletedEventArgs e)
        {
            //string myUrl = "http://www.yahoo.com";
            //Uri myUri = new Uri(myUrl);
            //webBrowser1.Navigate(myUri);
            string myUrl = "file:///Program Files/SmartDeviceProject1/test.htm";
            Uri myUri = new Uri(myUrl);
            webBrowser1.Navigate(myUri);

        }
```

You can find code samples for building a full-featured browser at http://msdn.microsoft.com/en-us/library/3s8ys666.aspx

Packaging and Distributing Your App

Windows Mobile applications can be distributed on the Web or through the Windows Marketplace for Mobile. To compress and package application files for distribution, Windows Mobile uses Cabinet files, designated with the .cab extension. To distribute your application, you need to build your application as a signed CAB file. The following section provides an overview of the process required to release the "hello world" application built in the previous section. Additional advanced configuration options may be necessary for more complex applications outside the scope of this chapter.[5]

---

[5] Refer to http://msdn.microsoft.com/en-us/library/zcebx8f8.aspx for additional information on advanced cabfile properties.

Adding a CAB Project to the Solution

To create a CAB file, you first need to include a new CAB project to your application solution. From the File menu, point to Add, and then click New Project. The Add New Project dialog box will be displayed, as shown in Figure 5–11.

In the Project Types pane, expand Other Project Types, and select Setup and Deployment. From the Templates pane on the right, select the **Smart Device CAB Project** template.

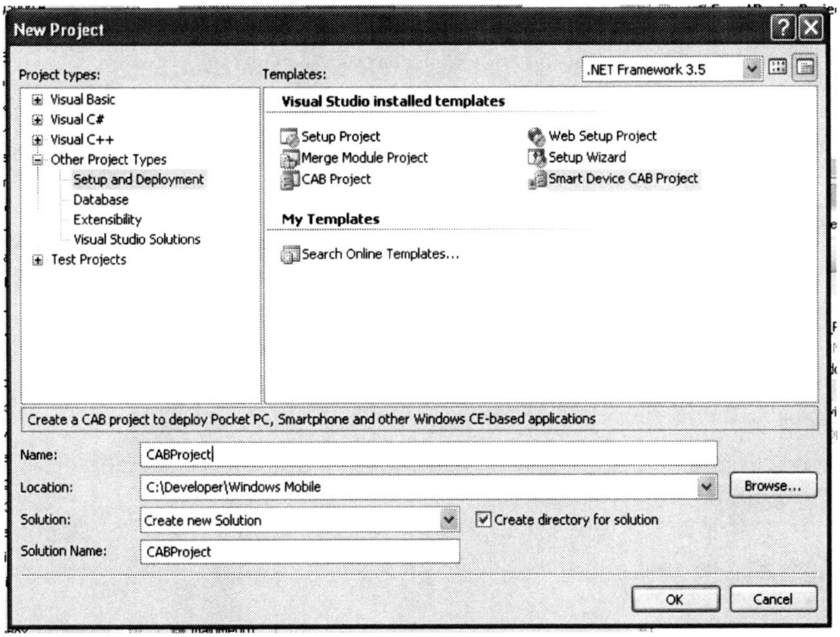

Figure 5–11. *The Add New Project dialog box*

In the Name field, type "CABProject". Click **OK** to add the CAB project to the solution. The CAB project will be displayed in the Solution Explorer.

Customizing Your Product Name

Open the Properties window by selecting select View ➤ Properties Window.

The value in the ProductName field defines the display name for the application in the application's folder names and the Add or Remove Programs screen. In the property grid, change the value of the ProductName field to "Hello World".
Customizing the CAB File name

In the Solution Explorer, right-click CABProject and select **Properties**.
In the CABProject Property Pages dialog, change the file name and path in the Output file name field to *Debug\HelloWorld.cab*. Click **OK** to update the file name.

Adding the Application to the CAB Project

In the File System Editor, you will find the File System on the Target Machine pane on the left. Note: if you cannot see the File System Editor, right-click the CAB project name in Solution Explorer, click **View**, and then click **File System**.

Your application should be installed into the Application Folder. Select **Application Folder** to specify that the files you select in the following steps will be installed in the appropriate location on the target device.
From the Action menu, select Add ➤ Project Output. In the **Add Project Output Group** dialog box, select **Hello World** from the Project drop-down list. From the list of outputs, select **Primary** output, ensure the Configuration is set to **Active**, and click **OK**.

Creating an Application Shortcut

To create a shortcut to allow users to easily access the application, from the right pane of the File System Editor, select **Primary output** from Hello World(active). Select **Action ➤ Create Shortcut to Primary output** from Hello World. Rename the shortcut to "Hello World" or another name of your choosing by right-clicking the Shortcut item ➤ Rename to.

Next, define where the shortcut should be accessed from on the target device. In the File System Editor's left pane, right-click File System on Target Machine then select either Add Special Folder ➤ Start Menu Folder or Add Special Folder ➤ Programs Folder.

Finally, drag the shortcut from the Application Folder into the Start Menu or Programs Folder in the left pane of the File System Editor.

Adding a Registry Entry

In the Solution Explorer, select the CAB project and open the Registry Editor by selecting View ➤ Editor ➤ Registry.

In the left pane of the Registry Editor, right-click **HKEY_CURRENT_USER**. Click **New Key**, and rename the New Key entry from "New Key #1" to "SOFTWARE".

Right-click **SOFTWARE**, and select New ➤ Key. Rename the New Key entry from "New Key #1" to "MyCompany".

Right-click **MyCompany**, and select Properties Window to verify the Name value has been changed to MyCompany.

Building and Deploying the CAB File

On the File menu, click Save All.

In Solution Explorer, right-click the **Smart Device Cab project**, and then click **Properties** on the shortcut menu.

On the Build page, select **Authenticode Signature**, and the **Click Select from Store** button.

In the Select Certificate dialog box, select the certificate you want to use and click **OK**.

If you don't have any visible certificates, click **Manage Certificates** to open the Manage Certificates dialog box. If you have a certificate on your system you wish to use, you can import it using the Import wizard. However, if you haven't created a certificate on this system before, you can do so from the command line. From the C:\Program Files\ Microsoft Visual Studio 9.0\SDK\v3.5\bin directory (or your local equivalent) issue the following command:

```
makecert -r -pe -n "CN=Your Name" -b 01/01/2000 -e 01/01/2099 -eku 1.3.6.1.5.5.7.3.3↵
 -ss My
```

Exit the Manage Certificates window and select the new certificate when it appears in the Select Certificate window, then click **OK**. The certificate will be displayed in the Certificate box of the Build page.

On the Build page, click **OK**.

On the Build menu, click **Build CABProject**.

-or-

Right-click **CABProject** in Solution Explorer, and click **Build**.

Installing the CAB File

In Windows Explorer, navigate to the folder where you stored this solution. You will find the CAB file in the CABProject\Debug folder of your solution.

To deploy your CAB file on a device, cradle your device normally using ActiveSync.

To connect to an emulator using ActiveSync, from Visual Studio menu bar, select Tools ➤ Device Emulator Manager. Expand Datastore ➤ Windows Mobile 6 Professional SDK and in the list of devices, double-click **USA Windows Mobile 6.5 Professional VGA Emulator**. When you see a green arrow, select Actions ➤ Cradle to launch ActiveSync, and complete the setup wizard.

In the ActiveSync window, click **Explore**, then copy the CAB file to a suitable location in the filesystem.

On the device, navigate to the CAB file in File Explorer and tap the CAB file name to automatically install the application and shortcuts into the appropriate locations on the device.

Distributing Your Application

There are several options for distributing your Windows Mobile 6 application:

- Include a link to download the .cab file in an e-mail message or SMS message. When the user clicks the link, the application will be downloaded and installed using Internet Explorer Mobile.

- E-mail the file as an attachment. When the user opens the attachment, the application will be installed automatically.

- Physically distribute the .cab file on removable media cards that can be inserted directly into the phone. You can include an autorun file to automatically start the installation script upon insertion.[6]

Distribute the application through the Windows Marketplace for Mobile.[7]

---

[6] You can find more information at http://msdn.microsoft.com/en-us/library/bb159776.aspx

[7] http://marketplace.windowsphone.com/

Cross-Platform Native Frameworks

In your hands is one of the most exciting devices to hit the market in quite some time: the iPhone 4. This Quick Start Guide will help get you and your new iPhone 4 up and running in a hurry. You'll learn all about the buttons, switches, and ports, and how to use the innovative and responsive touch screen and multitask with the new App Switcher bar. Our App Reference Tables introduce you to the apps on your iPhone 4—and serves as a quick way to find out how to accomplish a task.

Chapter 6

Rhodes

Rhodes is a cross-platform smartphone application framework developed by Rhomobile (www.rhomobile.com) a venture backed startup in Cupertino, CA. It was released in December of 2008. Rhodes is available for most major smartphones including the iPhone, Research in Motion (BlackBerry), Android, Windows Mobile, and Symbian. As of this writing, Symbian is not actively maintained and therefore not addressed in this chapter. A key value proposition for Rhodes is the ability for a company to build and maintain a single code-base across this wide variety of device operating systems.

Rhodes allows developers to create cross-platform smartphone applications using HTML, CSS, JavaScript and Ruby programming languages. It leverages developer experience in web development to make native mobile applications, and is aimed at developers who already have a background in web development and want to create mobile applications without having to learn platform SDKs and the native languages on each mobile device platform. The Rhomobile tools and framework can be used across Mac, Windows and Linux; however, to build for specific devices, the device SDK must be installed. BlackBerry and Windows Mobile devices require Windows; iPhone devices requires Mac; Android and Symbian devices run on Java and are cross-platform.

Rhodes is targeted primarily at enterprise applications. The framework makes it easy to create applications that present a series of screens that include standard UI widgets, including common phone UIs such as mapping. It is not suitable for fast-action games and other such consumer applications with demands for rich interactive graphic interfaces or platform-specific native UI controls. A strength of Rhodes is that it makes the traditional user interface patterns commonly found in most informational applications easy and portable.

Rhodes is a commercially-supported open source product licensed under the MIT License. Those companies requiring commercial grade support can purchase an Enterprise License from Rhomobile. Because Rhodes is open source, you can examine the code and see exactly what it is doing under the covers. You can extend it, contribute improvements and fixes, or customize your own version of Rhodes if you need to.

Rhodes takes much of its inspiration from web-oriented Model-View-Controller (MVC) style frameworks such as Ruby on Rails. However, it has several sfimplifications, extensions, and optimizations for the mobile scenario (see Differences Between Rhodes and Ruby on Rails later in the chapter). If you are a Ruby on Rails developer, you should find Rhodes familiar. Note that although certain patterns are borrowed from Rails, Rhodes is its own unique framework and not a port of Ruby on Rails. Even developers unfamiliar with Ruby on Rails can start developing quickly with Rhodes simply because there is much less code to write than for a native application.

Rhodes includes a local Object Relational Manager (ORM), called Rhom, and includes code to persist local data and sync remote data using RhoSync. Rhodes developers do not have to worry about writing data storage and sync logic into their applications and can focus instead on presentation and business logic.

The next sections provide details on creating device-only applications in Rhodes and you will see how to persist local data and use geolocation and other device features. However, the full power of the framework is seen when local data is synched to remote data sources, which can be easily achieved with Rhomobile's middleware server RhoSync (see chapter 7).

Complete details on Rhodes are available in the Rhomobile wiki (www.rhomobile.com/wiki) and the source to Rhodes is available at github (http://github.com/rhomobile). There are also open source example applications available. Finally, there is an active community of developers at http://groups.google.com/group/rhomobile.

Development Architecture

Rhodes applications are installed and run as native applications. However, you develop using the web development paradigm. You define the user interface of your application in HTML and CSS. Then, at runtime, the HTML and CSS is rendered in a native browser UI control that is embedded in your application by the Rhodes framework. JavaScript may be used for some interaction control the same way that you would use JavaScript in a web application.

You can also add application logic to your views using embedded Ruby (ERB), as you would in a Ruby on Rails application. ERB files are similar to PHP or JSP, where code can be mixed with markup to create dynamic HTML. Rhodes will generate the complete HTML, evaluating the Ruby code before the HTML is rendered by the browser UI Control, which will then dynamically execute any JavaScript that is on the page.

You also write Ruby code for the application logic that implements the flow of control for your application. Rhodes follows the Model-View-Controller (MVC) pattern that is similar to Ruby on Rails and other web frameworks. You implement methods in your controller to define actions that map to HTTP requests. Your controller action will typically fetch data from your model (implemented in the Rhodes ORM layer, Rhom) and render a view (implemented as HTML ERB).

In Figure 6–1 you can see the MVC pattern illustrated with the Rhodes object model and an example use case. In the example, there is a "New Product" page where the user can fill in the form field to provide values for the new product attributes. When the user clicks the **Create** button, a request is made to a lightweight embedded web server in Rhodes that only exists to respond to these UI request and RhoController actions. When a user clicks on a URL in the HTML view, a controller action is called. In this example, the ProductController create method is called. The controller action then calls the Product model, implemented with Rhom to save a new product in the local database. Then a view is rendered to display the result to the user. The entire web response cycle happens locally on the device.

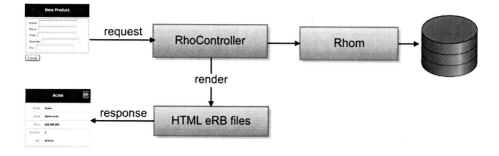

Figure 6–1. *The MVC Model*

Runtime Architecture

Rhodes development files are compiled into a native executable that is installed on the device or run in a desktop simulator using command line tools or the web interface on rhohub.com.

Since Rhodes apps are native binary applications, they can be submitted and distributed through the Apple iTunes App Store, BlackBerry World, Android Marketplace, and other distribution channels. To build for a device, you typically need to sign up for those developer programs and acquire cryptographic keys required to sign applications, even though you will not be writing in the platforms native SDKs. You also need to observe each platform's user interface guidelines so that your applications can be approved. (See Part 1 of the book on submitting apps for your target platform(s).)

On platforms where the primary development language is Java, such as BlackBerry, Rhodes applications are cross-compiled into Java bytecode that are then executed natively. On iPhone, Android, Windows Mobile and Symbian platforms, Rhodes applications are compiled into Ruby 1.9 bytecode. On these platforms, Rhodes includes a Ruby executor that runs the bytecode on the device. The Rhodes Ruby implementation is a subset of Ruby 1.9. It does not include all of the libraries that you would find on a desktop implementation of Ruby, although it is possible to extend it and add additional libraries into your application. (See http://wiki.rhomobile.com/ index.php/Rhodes#Adding_Libraries_to_Your_Rhodes_Application.)

To connect your Rhodes application with web services, you can use RhoSync or connect directly. You can connect directly via JavaScript, use the Ruby net/http library, or the optimized Rho:AsyncHttp. However, with remote data, you almost always want to cache it locally for offline use and using a RhoSync server is ideal for that use case. As detailed in chapter 7, you would write a source adapter that runs in the server environment where you have access to the full Ruby language and complete libraries.

Although Ruby is an interpreted language, using Rhodes, you cannot run arbitrary Ruby code at runtime by using, for example, string eval. That capability was intentionally removed in Rhodes Ruby interpreter to comply with iPhone App Store's Rule 3.3.2 that states:

> *An Application may not itself install or launch other executable code by any means, including without limitation through the use of a plug-in architecture, calling other frameworks, other APIs or otherwise. No interpreted code may be downloaded and used in an Application except for code that is interpreted and run by Apple's Published APIs and built-in interpreter(s).*
>
> (www.rhomobile.com/blog/2009/05/29/iphone-app-store-rules-and-guidelines-on-use-of-frameworks/)

Rhodes is a fully native application and embeds the device's built-in browser. This has implications for the markup, CSS, and JavaScript that can be supported on each platform. Some devices, such as the iPhone and Android, have full-featured browsers while others like the BlackBerry do not. This means that you cannot write HTML and CSS that take advantage of advanced or platform-specific browser features on one device and expect it to work on another device with a less capable web browser. While Rhodes apps are developed much like web apps, they run locally as native apps and not remotely like web apps. All processing and database access is local.

Device Capabilities and Native UI Elements

Rhodes provides access to device-specific capabilities such as GPS, PIM, camera, SMS, video player, accelerometer, proximity detector, and native UI controls. In some cases, the native controls are specific to the device, for example, every BlackBerry application has a menu that is invoked when you click the **Berries** button on the device; however, iPhone applications do not uniformly have a menu. So when you define a menu it appears on the BlackBerry, but is ignored if you were to build the same code for the iPhone. See the Rhodes Device Capabilities section for more details and examples.

Database (Rhom)

Rhom is a mini object-mapper implemented in Ruby. It provides database-abstraction functionality to the Rhodes micro-framework. It allows simple models to be used with a "property bag" database. Rhom is backed by a local device-side database such as SQLite or HSQLDB. The Rhodes framework abstracts the implementation details of the local database.

The main goal of Rhom is to provide a simple, intuitive model interface for a Rhodes application. Under the hood, Rhom operates on the RhoSync object values (http://wiki.rhomobile.com/index.php/Server_to_Backend_Sync_Process) table by collecting "property bags" or attributes for a given source into a model definition. This is the same table used by the Rhodes sync engine.

The methods on a Rhom object are inspired by but not exactly the same as those in the ActiveRecord ORM used by Ruby on Rails. Listing 6–1 shows sample client code to illustrate the Rhom syntax with an Account object. In this example, Account is the model object. Account.find in its simplest form takes the object's id as a parameter and returns the object (after fetching it from the local device storage). The second Account.find is shown with :all as the first parameter, which indicates that all records will be returned, the :select argument indicates the fields to lookup, optionally you could also pass :conditions if you wanted to retrieve a subset of the records.

Listing 6–1. *Rhom example code*

```
acct = Account.find "3560c0a0-ef58-2f40-68a5-48f39f63741b"
acct.name #=> "A.G. Parr PLC 37862"

 accts = Account.find(:all, :select => ['name','address'])
accts[0].name #=> "A.G. Parr PLC 37862"
accts[0].telephone #=> nil
```

Threading

Rhodes applications are multithreaded, however, applications cannot spawn their own threads; your code will run in a single thread. The three principal threads in a Rhodes application are:

- Main thread (controls the user interface)
- Ruby thread
- Sync thread (when RhoSync is used)

There are also auxiliary threads that come and go on demand. Examples include notifications, geolocation, client registration, and push.

One of the added benefits of Rhodes being multithreaded is that you can sync your data to RhoSync in the background while your user interface is not blocked. The impact is that many of the Rhodes API calls are non-blocking, asynchronous calls that you register callbacks to use, such as sync notification and login.

Differences Between Rhodes and Rails

- Rhodes is inspired by Ruby on Rails but is not a port of Ruby on Rails. It is significantly smaller and simpler.

- There are no separate directories for models, controllers and views. Each model is in its own directory. The controller file, model file, and view files for the model exist in the directory. Business logic is coded in the controller making Rhodes controllers somewhat fatter than Rails controllers.

- Many other directories available are not present in the Rhomobile app directory structure such as vendor, lib, log, and db. Their equivalents are generally in the root directory of the application.

- There are no validations on models. There is no schema.rb and no migrations.

- You cannot run Rhodes applications interactively using script/console. You need to compile your code and install it in the simulator to execute it.

- Many of the differences from Rails are to make it easier to run on mobile devices with limited memory. Rhodes is lighter weight because it is only providing the core necessary functions. Examples of features that either aren't necessary in Rhodes or not provided for space reasons are: web services, XML, pluralization, and YAML.

Creating a Rhodes App

This section details how you install and set up Rhodes and build a simple application that stores data locally on the device.

Installation and Setup

Before you install Rhodes, you will need to install Ruby and Ruby's library packaging system, RubyGems, as well as GNU make. Rhodes is distributed as a Ruby gem, which includes the Rhodes framework and all of the tools needed to work with each target smartphone platform.

- Ruby 1.8.6 or 1.8.7.

- RubyGems 1.3.5 or higher.

- GNU make 3.80 or higher (required by gem). You might already have it installed if you are running Mac OS X or Linux. On Windows, download it from http://gnuwin32.sourceforge.net/packages/make.htm and install somewhere. Ensure you have the location where it installed in your PATH environment variable.

To install the gem (sudo is recommended on Mac and Linux):

```
gem install rhodes
```

You will also need the device SDKs for your target platform. For details on installing the device SDKs, see chapters 2-5 or Rhomobile platform docs.[1]

Once you have the device SDK installed, run the Rhodes setup script (by typing "rhodes-setup" on the command line). Listing 6–2 shows sample output from this command run on a Mac with Android SDK installed. (Note: the iPhone SDK does not require configuration.)

Listing 6–2. *Rhodes setup commands*

```
$ rhodes-setup
We will ask you a few questions below about your dev environment.

JDK path (required) (/System/Library/Frameworks/JavaVM.framework↩
/Versions/CurrentJDK/Home/):
 Android 1.5 SDK path (blank to skip) (): ~/android/android-sdk-mac_x86-1.5_r2
Windows Mobile 6 SDK CabWiz (blank to skip) ():
 BlackBerry JDE 4.6 (blank to skip) ():
 BlackBerry JDE 4.6 MDS (blank to skip) ():
 BlackBerry JDE 4.2 (blank to skip) ():
 BlackBerry JDE 4.2 MDS (blank to skip) ():

 If you want to build with other BlackBerry SDK versions edit:
 <Home Directory>/src/rhomobile/rhodes/rhobuild.yml
```

Building a Rhodes Application

For your first application you are going to create an application that will let you enter product inventory on your phone. This is a basic application with one model that will allow you to create, edit, and delete inventory records on the device.

To create the initial skeleton of the application, you issue the "rhogen app" command. This will generate a starting directory with support files; Rhodes applications are organized in a fixed directory structure. The rhogen command is not required. You could create the files you need manually or simply copy and modify a previous application.

On the command line, type "rhogen app inventory" to generate the initial skeleton for the application (Listing 6–3).

Listing 6–3. *Rhodes app generation*

```
$ rhogen app inventory
Generating with app generator:
      [ADDED]   inventory/rhoconfig.txt
      [ADDED]   inventory/build.yml
      [ADDED]   inventory/app/application.rb
      [ADDED]   inventory/app/index.erb
```

---

[1] http://wiki.rhomobile.com//index.php?title=Building_Rhodes_on_Supported_Platforms

```
[ADDED]   inventory/app/index.bb.erb
[ADDED]   inventory/app/layout.erb
[ADDED]   inventory/app/loading.html
[ADDED]   inventory/Rakefile
[ADDED]   inventory/app/helpers
[ADDED]   inventory/icon
[ADDED]   inventory/app/Settings
[ADDED]   inventory/public
```

This creates the boilerplate files for the application including a "Settings" screen that is very useful in development, but will usually be replaced with one or more custom screens before the application is complete. Table 6–1 lists all of the top-level files and folders that are generated. Most of the development that you do will be to modify and create new files in the /app directory. These files and subdirectories are listed in Table 6–2.

Table 6–1. *Top-level files and folders generated by the "rhogen app" command*

File/Folder	Description
Rakefile	Used for building Rhodes applications from the command line.
rhoconfig.txt	Contains application specific options and configurations such as the start path definition, logging options, and the optional URL for your sync server. To change the default-landing page of your application, simply change start_path to point to a different page within the directory structure.
build.yml	Contains application-specific build information such as the name of the application, and the version of the SDK to use when building for specific platforms.
app/	This directory contains the models, device settings, default-landing page, and application layout page.
public/	This directory contains static files that are accessible by your application, such as CSS, images, and JavaScript libraries.
icon/	This directory contains the icons for your application.

Table 6–2. *Files and folders in the /app directory generated by the "rhogen app" command*

Application File/Folders	Description
/Settings	Responsible for login and device specific settings.
/helpers	Contains functions designed to help in the development process.
application.rb	Application specific setup and configuration.
index.erb	The default-landing page for the application. This page will typically have links to the controllers for at least some of the data models.
layout.erb	Contains the header file for the entire application.
loading.html	The initial loading page on startup

The file types that have been generated for you in the application include Ruby files (*.rb) that contain application business logic and configuration, and HTML with embedded Ruby files (*.erb) (www.ruby-doc.org/stdlib/libdoc/erb/rdoc/) for your user interface. These are the two main file types that you will be working with when writing Rhodes applications.

HTML, CSS, and Ruby are what Rhodes developers use to create the layout of the user interface; rather than writing code to build native UI controls with libraries such as UIKit on the iPhone.

Running the Application

To run the application in a simulator or on the device, you may simply run a rake task from your application directory. Rake is a simple Ruby build program with capabilities similar to make. See Table 6–3 for a list of commands. Note that running the application is not any harder on the device (and on some platforms it is faster than in the simulator), but you do need to set up cryptographic digital signatures (see platform chapters 2-5 for details).

Rhomobile also provides a desktop simulator for Rhodes that can be used on Windows platforms, which has a much faster startup time than the simulators and can be effective for quickly testing your application logic. To test your UI code, you need to run it on the simulator or device for the platforms you are targeting. The Windows simulator does not attempt to simulate the browser differences between the different smartphone platforms.

Table 6–3. *Rake commands for building and running Rhodes applications*

Command	Purpose
rake clean:android	Clean Android
rake clean:bb	Clean BlackBerry
rake clean:iphone	Clean iPhone
rake clean:win32	Clean Rhomobile Win32 Desktop Simulator
rake clean:wm	Clean Windows Mobile
rake device:android:debug	Build debug self-signed for Android device
rake device:android:production	Build production signed for Android device
rake device:bb:debug	Build debug for BlackBerry device
rake device:bb:production	Build production for BlackBerry device
rake device:iphone:production	Build production for iPhone device
rake device:wm:production	Build production for Windows Mobile device or emulator
rake run:android	Build and launch Android emulator
rake run:android:device	Build and install on Android device
rake uninstall:android	Uninstall application from Android emulator
rake uninstall:android:device	Uninstall application from Android device
rake run:bb	Builds app, loads, and starts BlackBerry Simulator and MDS
rake run:iphone	Builds app, launches iPhone simulator
rake run wm:emu	Build and run application on Windows Mobile 6 emulator
rake run wm:emucab	Build and install .cab on Windows Mobile 6 emulator
rake run wm:dev	Build and run application on Windows Mobile 6 device
rake run wm:devcab	Build and install .cab on Windows Mobile 6 device

Running on the iPhone

You will need the iPhone SDK that is only available for Macintosh computers installed for this section. For details on setting up the iPhone development environment, including building for a device, see Chapter 2. This section will walk you through how to build using the Rhodes platform, which depends on the Apple SDK and tools to build for the iPhone or iPad. In your application directory, on the command line, enter: "rake run:iphone". You will see a lot of text output and it may take a minute or so before the iPhone simulator launches. When the simulator appears, you won't see your application. You need to click on one of the dots on the bottom or drag the screen to show the screen to the right where your application is. (Note: the simulator may appear as an iPad or an iPhone Rhodes applications work on both. If you would like to see your application on a different device, select **Hardware ➤ Device** from the simulator menu and choose an alternate device.) See Figure 6–2 for an illustration of how the simulator looks after navigating to the screen with the application and then after the application is opened.

```
$ cd inventory/
$ rake run:iphone
```

If you get an error about it not finding the iphone sdk, please check your *build.yml* file and if necessary, edit it to match the iPhone SDK version that you have installed.

Figure 6–2. *Running on iPhone*

Running on Android

You can build for the Android on Mac, Windows or Linux. For details on setting up the Android development environment, including building for a device, see chapter 3. Note that you will need the Android Native development environment (NDK), as well as the SDK and related components, but you will not need Eclipse. After the initial setup, building for the Android and testing in the simulator is the same as building for the iPhone, except that the rake tasks have "android" instead of "iphone" in the name and the log files are found in different places.

In your application directory, on the command line, enter: "rake run:android". You will see a lot of text output and it will take several minutes before the Android emulator launches. When the emulator appears, you won't see your application. You need to select the menu tab on the bottom of the screen to reveal all applications and you will likely need to scroll to the bottom of that screen (Figure 6–3).

```
$ cd inventory/
$ rake run:android
```

Figure 6–3. *Running on Android*

Running on BlackBerry

BlackBerry requires Windows to run its tools and simulator. It also requires Java, but you won't typically use Eclipse. For details on setting up the BlackBerry development environment, including building for a device, see chapter 4. The business logic for a BlackBerry application can be identical to every other platform; however, the view implementation is often quite different due to limitations in the browser capabilities on the device. For more details on BlackBerry HTML UI, see chapter 14, but the basics will be covered in the rest of this section.

In your application directory, on the command line, enter: "rake run:bb". You will see a lot of text output and it will take several minutes before the BlackBerry simulator launches.

```
$ cd inventory/
$ rake run:bb
```

Running on Windows Mobile 6

Windows Mobile 6 requires Windows to run its tools and simulator. It also requires MS Visual Studio, even though you don't typically use it for development with Rhodes. For details on setting up the Windows Mobile development environment, including building for a device, see chapter 5. (As of this writing, Rhodes does not support Windows Mobile 7.) After the initial setup, building for Windows Mobile and running the application in the simulator will be very similar to the Android and iPhone – there are some browser differences, but the IE Browser is not as limited as the BlackBerry browser.

In your application directory, on the command line, enter: "rake run:wm:emu". You will see a lot of text output and it will take several minutes before the Windows Mobile simulator launches.

```
$ cd inventory/
$ rake run:wm:emu
```

Generating a Model

Rhodes also includes a script to generate code that implements the Model-View-Controller (MVC) pattern, similar to the Rails scaffold command. This will implement common actions to display a list of items, show an individual item's details, create, update, and delete. To create a model and the corresponding views and controller actions, use the "rhogen model" command. Note: more information about rhogen is available at http://wiki.rhomobile.com/index.php/Rhogen. Just as with the "rhogen app" command, you can also create the files by hand. Typically, your app will have one or more models.

The model for the application that is detailed in this tutorial will be called "Product" (see Listing 6–4). A product has attributes: brand, name, price, quantity, and sku. Issue "rhogen model Product name,description,done" to generate the Product model for your application.

Listing 6–4. *Generating a model with views and a controller*

```
$ rhogen model product brand,name,price,quantity,sku
Generating with model generator:
[ADDED]  app/Product/index.erb
    [ADDED]  app/Product/edit.erb
    [ADDED]  app/Product/new.erb
    [ADDED]  app/Product/show.erb
```

```
[ADDED]    app/Product/index.bb.erb
[ADDED]    app/Product/edit.bb.erb
[ADDED]    app/Product/new.bb.erb
[ADDED]    app/Product/show.bb.erb
[ADDED]    app/Product/product_controller.rb
[ADDED]    app/Product/product.rb
[ADDED]    app/test/product_spec.rb
```

As you can see, more files have been added to the file system. Each model is defined in its own subdirectory of the /app folder. The new files include the views for the default controller actions, the configuration file for the model, and the controller.

In the model's directory you will find *product_controller.rb*, which implements the controller for the model. You will also see *.erb* files for all of the views associated with the model. Finally, there is a *product.rb* file that sets properties on the model. Each Rhodes controller implements actions to perform basic CRUD (create, read, update, and delete) on the object generated by default by the scaffold. The template views generated are shown in Table 6–4.

Table 6–4. *Default views for Rhodes Model*

View	Purpose
index	lists all of the objects
new	displays the form to enter attributes for creating a new object
edit	displays a form for editing object attributes
show	displays the object attributes

The controller for the model (/app/Product/product_controller.rb) is very similar to a Ruby on Rails controller in the sense that it contains all the basic CRUD actions with consistent naming conventions. Most actions defined in the controller correspond to view files in the same directory that have the action name with an *.erb* file type.

Now that you have the scaffold of the application and a basic understanding of the structure, it's time to finish our application by connecting the model's view to our start screen.

To do this you need to edit your application index by opening *app/index.erb*. If you were to compile the application in its current state, you would still see the same start screen that you saw when you first ran the application that displays "Add links here...", with no way to view the UI for the model you just created. The code for the page should currently look like Listing 6–5. The Sync and Login buttons in the toolbar are connected to RhoSync by default (covered in the next chapter). You can delete them or modify the Settings controller to use a web service rather than RhoSync.

Listing 6–5. *Default start screen (app/index.erb)*

```
<div id="pageTitle">
    <h1>Inventory</h1>
</div>

<div id="toolbar">
    <div id="leftItem" class="blueButton">
        <%= link_to "Sync", :controller => :Settings, :action => :do_sync %>
    </div>
    <% if SyncEngine::logged_in > 0 %>
      <div id="rightItem" class="regularButton">
          <%= link_to "Logout", :controller => :Settings, :action => :logout %>
      </div>
    <% else %>
      <div id="rightItem" class="regularButton">
          <%= link_to "Login", :controller => :Settings, :action => :login %></div>
    <% end %>
</div>

<div id="content">
    <ul>
        <li>
            <a href="#">
                <span class="title">Add Links Here...</span>
                <span class="disclosure_indicator"></span>
            </a>
        </li>
    </ul>
</div>
```

To add a connection to your Product model, change the title "Add links here…" to "Products" and href to "Product" as shown in Listing 6–6. This will create a link to the Product model's index page: *app/Product/index.erb*–just with most web servers, the default page for a URL is index and the relative URL will look for a sibling page to *index.erb* that is also in the app folder. Note that most of the page is pure HTML and you could put other links here or add graphics with an <img> tag or add text. The part of the page that is embedded Ruby code is inside <% … %>.

Listing 6–6. *Modified start screen (app/index.erb)*

```
<div class="toolbar">
        <h1 id="pageTitle">
                Products
        </h1>
</div>

<ul id="home" selected="true" title="Products">
        <li><a href="Product">Product</a></li>
</ul>
```

Rhodes links work by assuming the /app directory is the root directory of your application. In the example you just wrote "Product" as the reference for the link. This is because "Product" is a subdirectory of /app and since you didn't specify a file in that directory, it uses the default: the index page. This linking convention can be used throughout your application.

Now that you have your model index page hooked up to your application index you are ready to build the application for one of the Rhodes supported platforms. Simply use the appropriate "rake:run" command for your platform of choice. See Figures 6–4 to 6–8 to see how all of the screens appear on the iPhone. The functionality is identical across platforms; however, the visual details conform to the target platform.

Figure 6–4. *Modified start screen (app/index.erb) as seen on iPhone*

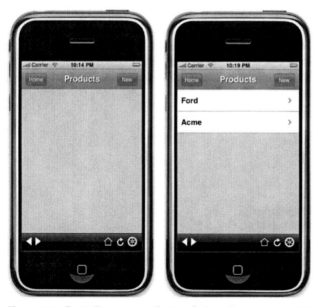

Figure 6–5. *Tasks list page (app/Product/index.erb), empty and with items in the list*

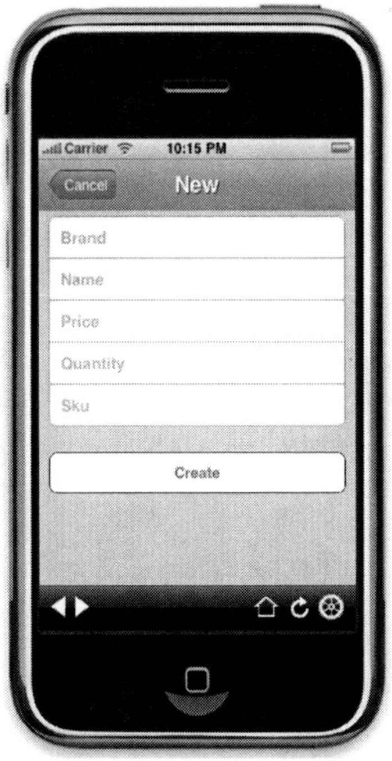

Figure 6–6. *Tasks new page (app/Product/new.erb)*

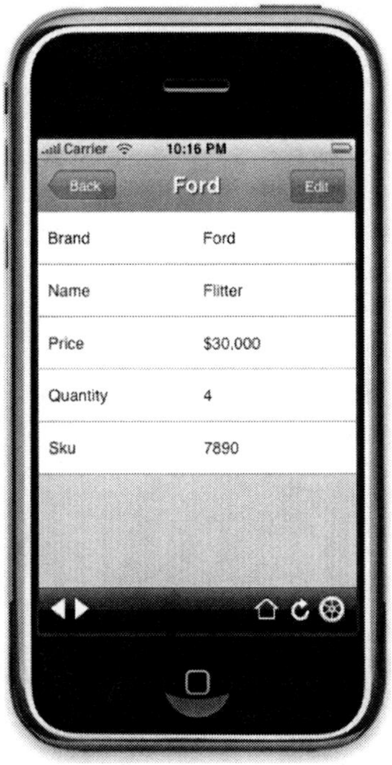

Figure 6–7. *Task details page (app/Product/show.erb)*

Figure 6–8. *Product edit page (app/Product/edit.erb)*

Debugging Tips

Finding the Rhodes log file and tips for effective debugging differs depending on the environment you are running for the application. Details are given below for some of the platforms that Rhodes supports. The latest version of Rhodes offers an interactive debugger, but you can also insert print statements (puts in Ruby) in your code and see the output the log file that Rhodes generates called *RhoLog.txt*. RhoLog includes the generated HTML that is being rendered, information about requests being sent to your controller, and even some logging about the sync process.

To enable debugging with the log file, you need to edit the *rhoconfig.txt* and make sure that "LogToOutput=1". Rhodes may run slower when debugging is on, so you should reset this to "0" when you build for production.

iPhone

You can find *RhoLog.txt* (and the sqlite DB) that rhodes uses in "~/Library/Application Support/iPhone Simulator/User/Applications". In this directory you may see several directories that are long hexadecimal strings. These correspond to the different applications you have installed in your simulator. Most likely you will just have one. Change into that directory (cd) and then cd to the Documents subdirectory. In there, you should file *RhoLog.txt*. You can watch this file with

```
tail -f RhoLog.txt
```

while the application is running.

You can also reset the simulator to a clean state using **Reset Content and Settings...** from the **iPhone Simulator** menu if things go wrong and you want to start over again.

The log provides a lot of useful information by default. You can also put statements, such as "p @product", in your controller to diagnose issues you may run into.

BlackBerry

Configure your BlackBerry simulator to use a directory as an SD card.

When running in the BlackBerry simulator, you can find the log here:

```
<your JDE directory>\simulator\sdcard\Rho\<your app name>\RhoLog.txt
```

Assuming you set <your JDE directory>\simulator\sdcard as the directory for the SD card. You can watch this file while the simulator is running using tail -f.

To manually remote everything from your simulator:

1. open this directory: <your JDE directory>\simulator

2. delete sdcard folder

3. run clean.bat

You should install the complete BlackBerry JDE, not the standalone simulator downloads. The standalone downloads do not contain clean.bat.

Android

Run the command:

```
adb logcat
```

Rhodes Device Capabilities

To create a compelling mobile application, you will want to take advantage of capabilities that are available on a phone, differentiating the experience from a web or desktop application. Most applications want to interface with native phone functionality such as the GPS, the camera, and the contacts. Access to these features is implemented quite differently on different smartphone platforms, but Rhodes lets you write simple, clean code that will work on all the supported platforms.

By writing your application in Rhodes your application gains access to the same native APIs that applications written directly in the native toolkits have access to. Moreover, by coding to the Rhodes API, you do not have to worry about rewriting your application on each platform where these APIs are implemented in completely different ways. Rhodes abstracts away and often simplifies accessing these capabilities so you can focus on your application and business logic instead. See Table 6–5 for the level of support for specific device capabilities across the platforms that are supportd by Rhodes.

Table 6–5. *Rhodes device capabilities matrix* [2]

Capability	iPhone	Windows Mobile	BlackBerry	Symbian	Android
GeoLocation	Yes	Yes	Yes	Yes	Yes
PIM Contacts	Yes	Yes	Yes	Yes	Yes
Camera	Yes	Yes	Yes	Yes	Yes
Date/Time Picker	Yes	2.0	Yes	2.1	Yes
Native Menu/Tab Bar	Yes	2.0	Yes	2.1	1.5
Audio / Video Capture	2.0	2.0	2.0	2.1	2.0
Bluetooth	2.0	2.0	2.0	2.1	2.0
Push / SMS	Yes	2.0	Yes	2.1	2.0
Landscape Orientation	2.0	2.0	2.0	2.1	2.0
Native Maps	Yes	2.0	Yes	2.1	1.5

In Rhodes, device capabilities are invoked from within the Ruby environment. Some device capabilities, such as geolocation, can also be invoked directly from JavaScript if the browser on the platform supports it. This is independent of Rhodes implementation of the same capability but gives you another option. Note, for example, if you code to the browsers JavaScript API for geolocation, that code may not be portable to other devices where the browser does not include this capability.

In this section we will explore three different device capabilities: contacts, camera, and geolocation. For the rest, the Rhodes system API samples project[3] has small examples that show how each API is used.

---

[2] http://wiki.rhomobile.com/index.php/Rhodes#Device_Capabilities_.2F_Native_UI_Elements

[3] http://github.com/rhomobile/rhodes-system-api-samples . API documentation is available on the Rhodes wiki: http://wiki.rhomobile.com/index.php/Rhodes

Contacts Example

Smartphones all have a built-in PIM (Personal Information Management) Contacts application that allows end users to store phone numbers and addresses. Smartphone platforms allow applications to access those contacts through APIs that differ per platform, but generally offer the same capabilities. In this section, we will step through writing a Rhodes application that will allow you to show and edit native PIM contacts using Rhodes APIs on both the iPhone and Android. This example is written using Rhodes 2.0.2.

The complete source code to the completed application is available online at: http://github.com/VGraupera/Rho-Contacts-Sample.

Generate a skeleton application using the rhogen command as shown in Listing 6–7.

Listing 6–7. *Creating the Contacts application using the rhogen command*

```
> rhogen app Contacts
```

Generating with app generator:

```
[ADDED]  Contacts/rhoconfig.txt
    [ADDED]  Contacts/build.yml
    [ADDED]  Contacts/app/application.rb
    [ADDED]  Contacts/app/index.erb
    [ADDED]  Contacts/app/index.bb.erb
    [ADDED]  Contacts/app/layout.erb
    [ADDED]  Contacts/app/loading.html
    [ADDED]  Contacts/Rakefile
    [ADDED]  Contacts/app/helpers
    [ADDED]  Contacts/icon
    [ADDED]  Contacts/app/Settings
    [ADDED]  Contacts/public

 > cd Contacts/

> rhogen model Contact first_name,last_name,email_address,business_number
```

Generating with model generator:

```
[ADDED]  app/Contact/index.erb
    [ADDED]  app/Contact/edit.erb
    [ADDED]  app/Contact/new.erb
    [ADDED]  app/Contact/show.erb
    [ADDED]  app/Contact/index.bb.erb
    [ADDED]  app/Contact/edit.bb.erb
    [ADDED]  app/Contact/new.bb.erb
    [ADDED]  app/Contact/show.bb.erb
    [ADDED]  app/Contact/contact_controller.rb
    [ADDED]  app/Contact/contact.rb
    [ADDED]  app/test/contact_spec.rb
```

Edit your rhoconfig.txt file and change

```
start_path = '/app'
```

to

```
start_path = '/app/Contact'
```

Edit your *contact_controller.rb* file to look like Listing 6–8.

Listing 6–8. *Contacts/app/Contacts/contact_controller. rb*

```ruby
require 'rho/rhocontroller'
require 'rho/rhocontact'

require 'helpers/browser_helper'

class ContactController < Rho::RhoController
  include BrowserHelper

  #GET /Contact
  def index
    @contacts = Rho::RhoContact.find(:all)
    @contacts.to_a.sort! {|x,y| x[1]['first_name'] <=> y[1]['first_name'] } if @contacts
  end

  # GET /Contact/{1}
  def show
    @contact = Rho::RhoContact.find(@params['id'])
  end

  # GET /Contact/new
  def new
  end

  # GET /Contact/{1}/edit
  def edit
    @contact = Rho::RhoContact.find(@params['id'])
  end

  # POST /Contact/create
  def create
    @contact = Rho::RhoContact.create!(@params['contact'])
    redirect :action => :index
  end

  # POST /Contact/{1}/update
  def update
    Rho::RhoContact.update_attributes(@params['contact'])
    redirect :action => :index
  end

  # POST /Contact/{1}/delete
  def delete
    Rho::RhoContact.destroy(@params['id'])
    redirect :action => :index
  end
end
```

You require 'rho/rhocontact' to load the Rhodes PIM contact API.

In the index action, you create an array of all the contacts on the device using Rho::RhoContact.find(:all) and assign to an instance variable

```ruby
@contacts = Rho::RhoContact.find(:all)
```

Rho::RhoContact.find(:all) will return all the contacts on the device. Unfortunately, there is no way to limit it to a certain number of contacts or to specify a sort order, so in the next line you sort the contacts array manually in Ruby by first_name provided, of course, there are any contacts at all.

Next, edit the *Contact/index.erb* to look like Listing 6–9.

Listing 6–9. *Contacts/app/Contact/index.erb*

```
<div id="pageTitle">
        <h1>Contacts</h1>
</div>

<div id="toolbar">
    <div id="leftItem" class="regularButton"><%= link_to "Home",
Rho::RhoConfig.start_path %></div>
    <div id="rightItem" class="regularButton"><%= link_to "New", :controller =>
:Contact, :action => :new %></div>
</div>

<div id="content">
    <ul>
        <% @contacts.each do |obj| %>
            <li>
                <a href="<%= url_for :action => :show, :id => obj[1]['id'] %>">
                    <span class="title"><%= "#{obj[1]['first_name']}
#{obj[1]['last_name']}" %></span>
                    <span class="disclosure_indicator"></span>
                </a>
            </li>
        <% end %>
    </ul>
</div>
```

In this ERB template, you iterate through the array of contacts and output each one in a list. Because of the special HTML CSS classes you use, the list will look like a native iPhone table.

Now, build and run the application for the iPhone simulator:

```
> rake run:iphone
```

Before launching our Rhodes Contacts application in the simulator, open the native Contacts application in the simulator and add some contacts. By default the iPhone simulator address book is empty. I added two contacts: John Doe and Abraham Lincoln.

Now launch our Rhodes Contacts application, and you will see the same contacts (Figure 6–9).

Figure 6–9. *Rhodes Contacts application*

Similarly, rebuild the application for the Android using

> `rake run:android`

Again, add some contacts to the native Contacts application in the Android emulator and then launch our Rhodes Contacts application.

The Rhodes Contacts API also allows you to create, update and delete native contacts. The controller methods for these actions can be seen back in Table 6–4. These will work with the standard views that were generated using the rhogen model command.

Camera Example

In this section, we will step through writing an application that will allow you to take pictures using the camera and also pick images that are already on the smartphone using Rhodes APIs on both the iPhone and Android. This example requires Rhodes 1.5.

The full source code to the completed application is available online at: http://github.com/VGraupera/Rho-Photos-Sample

Generate a skeleton application using rhogen by typing the following into the command line:

> `rhogen app Photos`

Then create a model for the Photos using

```
> cd Photos
> rhogen model Photo image_uri
```

In *rhoconfig.txt* at the root of your application directory, change the start_path to change the startup page for your application:

```
start_path = '/app/Photo'
```

In your Photo directory, you can delete all the ERB files except for *index.erb*. Edit your *index.erb* to look like the Listing 6–10.

Listing 6–10. *Contacts/app/Photo/index.erb*

```
<div class="toolbar">
        <h1 id="pageTitle">Photos</h1>
</div>

<div id="photos" title="Photos" selected="true">
        <%= link_to '[Choose Picture]', { :action => :choose }%>
        <%= link_to '[Take Picture]', { :action => :new }%><br/>

        <% @images.reverse_each do |x|%>
                <img src="<%=x.image_uri%>" width='300px'></img><a
href="<%=url_for(:action => :delete, :id =>x.object)%>">Delete</a><br/>
        <% end %>
</div>
```

Edit the *photo_controller.rb* file to look like the Listing 6–11.

Listing 6–11. *Contacts/app/Photo/photo_controller.rb*

```
require 'rho/rhocontroller'

class PhotoController < Rho::RhoController

    def index
      puts "Camera index controller"
      @images = Photo.find(:all)
    end

    def new
      Camera::take_picture(url_for :action => :camera_callback)
      redirect :action => :index
    end

    def choose
      Camera::choose_picture(url_for :action => :camera_callback)
      redirect :action => :index
    end

    def delete
      @image = Photo.find(@params['id'])
      @image.destroy
      redirect :action => :index
    end

    def camera_callback
      if @params['status'] == 'ok'
        #create image record in the DB
```

```
        image = Photo.new({'image_uri'=>@params['image_uri']})
        image.save
        puts "new Image object: " + image.inspect
        WebView.navigate "/app/Photo"
      end
    end
end
```

You will save your photos using the Photo model. You can create new photos either by
using the camera with

```
    Camera::choose_picture(url_for :action => :camera_callback)
```

or selecting a pre-existing image on the phone using

```
    Camera::choose_picture(url_for :action => :camera_callback)
```

Both of these APIs are asynchronous and require you to provide a callback method (see
the camera_callback method in Listing 6–11 that is called after the picture is taken or
chosen by the user. In your callback, you navigate back to the home page that will load
all the photos including any new ones. You have to call WebView.navigate rather than
redirect because this callback is called in a different thread than the main Rhodes UI
thread.

Geolocation and Mapping Example

Geolocation is supported on all of the devices that are compatible with Rhodes. Native
mapping is only supported on the iPhone, BlackBerry, and Android. You can still do
mapping on any platform using the web browser and you can use geolocation features
without mapping, although they are often used together. The example in this section
follows such a typical use case that integrates the results of geolocation into a map.

The example application illustrated in this section allows the user to fill in a web form
and check a box to use the current location or optionally fill in a zip code, and then
displays all of the locations on a map. The complete application was built to show where
conference attendees originated from and can be found at
http://github.com/blazingcloud/rhodes_rubyconf—it is a connected application that
saves data to a server via RhoSync, but that isn't required for using geolocation. The
example code in this section could be used offline or with other means of connecting to
a server.

When testing on the device simulators, you need to be aware of how to simulate your
location. On the iPhone simulator, your current location is always 1 Infinite Loop,
Cupertino, CA (Apple's headquarters). On the BlackBerry, you can set the location
through the menu on the simulator. On the Android, you connect to the emulator using
netcat (see Listing 6–12) and send a "geo fix" command. Note that the two numbers
following geo fix are longitude then latitude.

Listing 6–12. *Using netcat to set the current location in the Android emulator.*

```
nc localhost 5554
Android Console: type 'help' for a list of commands
OK
geo fix -122.1 37.2
OK
```

For the native mapping to work on the Android, you need to install the "Google APIs by Google Inc., Android API 3"package and then you can use the Google Map capabilities. To do that, run android/android-sdk-r04-mac_86/tools/android (you'll see a window appear), click **Settings**, check **Force https://... sources to be fetched using http://...** and press **Save&Apply**. Then select the **Available** item in left list, expand **https://dl-ssl.google.com/....**, check package **Google APIs by Google Inc., Android API 3, revision x** and press **Install selected**.

Then you'll need to obtain your own Google API key for Android as described here: `http://code.google.com/intl/en/android/add-ons/google-apis/mapkey.html` and add it to application's *build.yml* (see Listing 6–13).

Listing 6–13. *Section of build.yml file with Android configuration*

```
android:
  mapping: yes
  # http://code.google.com/intl/en/android/add-ons/google-apis/mapkey.html
  apikey: "XXXYYYcZzZzvAaBbCcdddDDDXXX999"
```

Creating the application

Generate the application and a "person" model to which you will add geolocation and mapping, using commands illustrated in Listing 6–14.

Listing 6–14. *Generating the application and model using rhogen commands*

```
rhogen app map_example
cd map_example
rhogen model person name,latitude,longitude,zip,twitter
```

Then modify the "new person" form, adding a checkbox for "Use Current Location." This will not be saved in the model, but is a flag that will be sent to the controller (see create action in Listing 6–15).

Listing 6–15. *In map_example/app/Person/new.erb*

```
<form title="New Person"
        class="panel"
        id="person_new_form"
        method="POST"
        action="<%=url_for(:action => :create)%>" selected="true">
    <fieldset>
            <input type="hidden" name="id" value="<%=@person.object%>"/>

                <div class="row">
                    <label>Name: </label>
                    <input type="text" name="person[name]"/>
                </div>
```

```
            <div class="row">
                <label>Use Current Location: </label>
                        <input type="checkbox"
name="person[use_current_location]" />
                </div>

            <div class="row">
                    <label>City, State or Zip: </label>
                    <input type="text" name="person[zip]"/>
                </div>

            <div class="row">
                    <label>Twitter: </label>
                    <input type="text" name="person[twitter]"/>
                </div>


        </fieldset>
        <input type="submit" value="Create"/>
</form>
```

When the user submits the "new person" form (defined in *new.erb*), the create action will be called (defined in the create action of the PersonController class). Modify this code to detect the current location if the user has checked the **use current location** checkbox. In Listing 6–16, you see how to access GPS data programmatically: using the GeoLocation class built into Rhodes. These are synchronous calls that return immediately, and return floating-point numbers.

If either latitude or longitude are 0, it means the GPS is not ready to use. Note that calling GeoLocation.latitude or GeoLocation.longitude for the first time will trigger a call to the underlying geolocation capability; however, the devices will typically take several calls to return a result since the user must allow the app to access their location and the hardware can take several seconds to become responsive. Also note that Rhodes requires that data be saved in String format, so the Ruby to_s (to string) method must be called on each value after retrieving the location.

Listing 6–16. *In map_example/app/Person/person_controller.rb, create action*

```
def create
    person_attrs = @params['person']
    if person_attrs['use_current_location'] == "on"
      person_attrs.delete('use_current_location')
      sleep(5) until GeoLocation.latitude != 0
      person_attrs['latitude'] = GeoLocation.latitude.to_s
      person_attrs['longitude'] = GeoLocation.longitude.to_s
    end
    @person = Person.new(person_attrs)
    @person.save
    redirect :action => :index
  end
```

This application also includes an example of mapping, showing the location of each person on a map. Listing 6–17 shows the code; the MapView class in Rhodes produces a map overlay. There are small differences in the map user interface that are appropriate to each platform: on the iPhone it has close button, on the BlackBerry a close menu item, and on Android the user can simply use the back button. When the close/back action is triggered, the previously displayed view is revealed.

Native map UI is available on the iPhone, BlackBerry, and Android.

Listing 6–17. *Controller method to instantiate a map overlay of a view*

```ruby
def map
  @people = Person.find(:all)

    platform = System::get_property('platform')
  if platform == 'APPLE' or platform == 'Blackberry' or platform == 'ANDROID'
    annotations = @people.map do |person|
      result = {}
      unless person.latitude.nil? or person.latitude.empty?
        result[:latitude] = person.latitude
        result[:longitude] = person.longitude
      end
      result[:title] = person.name
      result[:subtitle] = person.twitter
      result[:street_address] = person.zip
      result[:url] = "/app/Person/#{person.object}/show"
      result
    end
    p "annotations=#{annotations}"
    MapView.create(
      :settings => {:map_type => "hybrid", :region => [33.4,-150,60,60],
                    :zoom_enabled => true, :scroll_enabled => true,↵
 :shows_user_location => false},
      :annotations => annotations
    )
    redirect :action => :index
  end
end
```

Chapter **7**

RhoSync

Synchronization servers provide the ability for mobile users to access information even when the device is offline or disconnected. They can also dramatically simplify the programming model. Developers can assume the data that they need is available locally in a database instead of writing code to access the network and take apart the data from some wire format.

In the past, synchronization servers assumed access to an underlying database for the application they wanted to mobilize. This was true of sync servers such as IntelliSync (now discontinued by Nokia) and Motorola Starfish. With the advent of Software As A Service (SaaS), such as SalesForce, Siebel On Demand, SugarCRM On Demand, and others, direct access to a database can no longer be assumed. This invalidated the approaches of the whole first generation of mobile sync servers. And it's now known to be a worst practice to integrate via databases.

The good news is that all SaaS vendors now expose some form of web services interface, typically a SOAP or REST web service. This creates an opportunity for a new kind of sync server for mobile devices targeted to enterprise apps exposing web services. A new sync server can also focus on today's much more powerful smartphones.

RhoSync is a new sync server framework concentrating on mobilizing applications exposing web services to smartphones. Like Rhodes, the RhoSync server is open source (but distributed under GPL), providing freedom and flexibility if needed. RhoSync is written in Ruby, but more importantly, connections to back-end services (which are pluggable extensions to RhoSync) are written in Ruby. RhoSync facilitates mobile development by providing a simple way to integrate data from external web services into Rhodes-based smartphone applications. The complexity and lines of code required to connect users to your back-end services are orders of magnitude smaller than the size and effort that has typically been associated with sync projects: for example, a basic RhoSync source adapter requires only 20 lines of easily understandable code.

In this chapter, you'll get the background you need to develop an understanding of the RhoSync server, then it will guide you in using RhoHub, a hosted RhoSync server, or setting up your own RhoSync server with a very simple application. The chapter concludes with a complete sample application to demonstrate end-to-end integration and to introduce a real-world use case for using RhoSync with Rhodes.

How the Sync Server Works

The RhoSync server acts as a middle tier between a mobile application and the web service that it accesses for remote data. The RhoSync server stores information from back-end systems in its data store as object-attribute-value (OAV) "triples" capable of representing any type of arbitrary data. OAV triples allow small changes between the device and the back end to be communicated back and forth very efficiently. Because RhoSync operates on individual attribute values rather than entire objects, RhoSync handles conflicts elegantly.

Using the RhoSync server framework, you will create an **application**. An application consists of one or more **sources**, subclasses of the SourceAdapter class, each of which contains instructions for how the RhoSync server should perform sync operations. The **source adapter** contains the instructions used to populate the data store on the RhoSync server with information from a web service. When a client device syncs, the source adapter manages the process used to take data from the device's data store, update its own data store, then populate your back-end system.

The RhoSync server framework also manages user authentication for your application. All client applications connecting to a RhoSync server require authentication. However, if your application does not require users to authenticate individually, you can simply accept all client connections, and automatically authenticate anyone using the application.

Data Storage: Why Triples?

RhoSync stores copies of data asOAV triples (see Table 7–1). This common data representation technique is often referred to as either an Entity-Attribute-Value (EAV) schema or a "property bag." Wire formats for synchronization almost always use such a format, as it allows more efficient handling of incremental changes, particularly in conflicts where two users have changed the same record. The OAV triple format is also good for handling arbitrary data types from the back end, in the event the data may not be a simple relational database record. Additionally, the triple format handles changes to database structure in a flexible way, without the need to migrate your database in yet another environment.

Table 7–1. *Object-attribute-value triples*

Column	Purpose
object	ID of the object instance on the back-end system
attrib	Attribute name
value	Attribute value for the specified object

RhoSync Source Adapters

A RhoSync source adapter is a Ruby class that contains a set of methods that are called as needed by the RhoSync server. Source adapters are subclasses of the SourceAdapter class. If you are running your own RhoSync server, you can run a command-line script to generate your source adapter (see Listing 7–1). If you are using RhoHub, a source adapter will automatically be generated for each object in your application. The following two sections provide a detailed walkthrough of setting up an application using RhoHub or a locally installed RhoSync server.

Listing 7–1. *Commands for generating server app and source adapter*

```
rhosync app storemanager-server
cd storemanager-server/
rhosync source product
```

The default source adapter class will resemble Listing 7–2.

Listing 7–2. *Source Adapter Class Skeleton*

```
class Products < SourceAdapter
    def initialize(source, credential)
        super(source, credential)
    end

    def login
    end

    def query(params=nil)
    end

    def sync
      super
    end

    def create(create_hash, blob=nil)
    end

    def update(update_hash)
    end

    def delete(object_id)
    end

    def logoff
    end
  end
```

Source adapters most commonly include seven core methods: login, query, sync, create, update, delete, and logoff. To implement the functionality desired for your app, simply implement the methods included in the source adapter. The following sections provide an overview of these methods.

Initialize

The initialize method is the ideal location for any setup you may need to include in your source adapter. In the Ruby language, the initialize method is the class constructor.

The arguments passed to initialize are source and credential. Source is a reference to the source settings in *app/Settings/setting.yml*. Credential is provided for backwards compatibility, and is always nil in RhoSync 2.0.

Authenticating with Web Services: Login and Logoff

If your back-end application requires authentication in order to perform web service queries, you will need to add a login method to your source adapter.

The login method shown in Listing 7–3 is taken from the source adapter for the SugarCRM source adapter—you can find the full implementation in *RhoSync/vendor/sync/SugarCRM*.

Listing 7–3. *Login method with back-end authentication*

```
def login
    u=@source.login
    pwd=Digest::MD5.hexdigest(@source.password)
    ua={'user_name' => u,'password' => pwd}
    ss=client.login(ua,nil)  # this is a WSDL
    if ss.error.number.to_i != 0
        puts 'failed to login - #{ss.error.description}'
    else
        @session_id = ss['id']
        uid = client.get_user_id(session_id)
    end
end
```

This login method accesses parameters that have been set for the source as attributes of the @source variable. The @source variable has several attributes that are stored on the RhoSync server for each user for each app.

When accessing the session, it is recommended that you use the same instance variable across all source adapters. In this example, you should use the @session_id variable to access the state of the current session in subsequent source adapter methods.

Note that writing such a login method in your source adapter class does not manage authentication of the user with the RhoSync server. The source adapter login method merely performs the oft-required first step when interacting with a web service. RhoSync requires that every client authenticate to allow them to use the RhoSync server.

There is also a current_user method you can use: *current_user.login* returns the current username that was passed to authenticate.

Should you need to terminate the session with the back end, create a custom logoff method. Often this is not required, since many web services simply timeout. This method would most typically be used in the event that the application allowed an end user to log out for security reasons or to manage multiple identities.

Retrieving Data: Query and Sync

To populate data to your device, you'll need to implement a query method in your source adapter. The sync code then dissects the query results.

Query

Whether your web service uses SOAP, JSON, XML, or any other protocol or data format (including direct access to a database), Ruby offers a wide assortment of standard and third-party libraries that you can use to easily integrate with any kind of web service or data source.

Imagine a simple back-end application where the web services are published as REST interfaces and return JSON. A sample query method to interact with this simple product catalog web service will retrieve all products in a JSON request. A sample result is given in Listing 7–4.

Listing 7–4. *JSON response returned from back end*

```
[
    {
      "product":
        {
            "name": "inner tube", "brand": "Michelin", "price": "535",
            "quantity": "142", "id": 27, "sku": "it-931",
            "updated_at": "2010-03-25T08:41:03Z"
        }
    },
    {
      "product":
        {
            "name": "tire", "brand": "Michelin", "price": "4525",
            "quantity": "14", "id": 29, "sku": "t-014",
            "updated_at": "2010-03-25T08:41:03Z"
        }
    },
    {
      "product":
        {
            "name": "wheel", "brand": "Campagnolo", "price": "4525",
            "quantity": "8", "id": 31, "sku": "w-422",
            "updated_at": "2010-03-25T08:41:03Z"
        }
    }
]
```

In the Ruby language, a simple way to make web requests using the REST pattern is to use the "rest-client" standard library and, likewise, JSON can be parsed with the 'json' library (see Listing 7–5). These dependencies must be explicitly specified with the Ruby "require" command at the top of the file. (This would be true of any Ruby application.)

Listing 7–5. *Source adapter class with query implementation*

```ruby
require 'json'
require 'rest-client'

class Product < SourceAdapter
  def initialize(source,credential)
    @base = 'http://rhostore.heroku.com/products'
    super(source,credential)
  end

  def login
  end

  def query
    parsed=JSON.parse(RestClient.get("#{@base}.json").body)

    @result={}
    if parsed
       parsed.each do |item|
          key = item["product"]["id"].to_s
          @result[key]=item["product"]
       end
    end
  end

  def sync
     super
     # this creates object value triples from an @result variable
     # containing a hash of hashes
  end
end
```

The first part of the query method fetches the data from the web service and parses the result into an interim format (stored in the variable "parsed"). The code then loops through the items returned from the query, and creates name-value pair objects in the format expected by the RhoSync server.

The RhoSync server expects the query method to return data by populating the @result instance variable. In this example, as is typical, @result is returned as a hash of hashes, indexed using each product's id obtained from the JSON returned from the web service.

Each hash key in the inner hash represents an attribute of an individual object. All data types must be strings; therefore, the hash values, including the product id numbers in this example, need to be strings rather than integers. (This is accomplished by calling to_s, which converts any Ruby object to a string.) The response to the client is formatted as shown in Listing 7–6.

Listing 7–6. *Result format returned to client device*

```
{
"27"=> {"name"=>"inner tube","brand"=>"Michelin"} ,
"29"=> {"name"=>"tire","brand"=>"Michelin"},
"31"=> {"name"=>"wheel","brand"=>"Campagnolo"}
}
```

Sync

The sync code dissects the query results and puts them into the RhoSync data store. If you populate @result with a multidimensional hash as was illustrated in the previous example, you can avoid this task and use the default sync method (see Listing 7–7).

Listing 7–7. *Default sync method*

```
def sync
      super
    end
```

However, if you have a very large volume of data (hundreds of thousands of records), populating @result as a hash of hashes would add too much time and memory consumption. In those cases, using the "stash_result" function in your query method will take the current @result and incrementally stash it in RhoSync's data store. Then when sync is called, all of the stashed data will be stored in RhoSync's data store master document.

Submitting Data: Create, Update, and Delete

To send information from your device to the back-end system, you'll need to write code for create, update, and delete methods in your source adapter (though you don't have to implement all of them if your app doesn't require it).

Create

In the create method, you can assume that you will receive an object in the form of a hash of name-value pairs. The default name assigned to this argument is "create_hash," although since this is just the name of the argument to the method, you can feel free to assign any name to the argument in your implementation.

In an inventory-tracking application, the hash returned from the client for a new record might resemble Listing 7–8.

Listing 7–8. *Create parameter format*

```
{"sku"=>"999","name"=>"tire", "brand"=>"Michelin", "price"=>"$49"}
```

The create method needs to make use of the data in this parameter to do its work. Listing 7–9 shows an example of a create method that posts to http://rhostore.heroku.com/rhostore/products (defined as the instance variable @base in the beginning of the previous example). The rhostore web service is a Rails application, where the create takes parameters like: product[brand] = Michelin. Note that this example continues to use the RestClient Ruby library, assuming that the dependency was declared with a "require" statement with the previous example. You need to return the ID of the newly created object from your create call.

Listing 7–9. *Source adapter create method*

```
def create(create_hash, blob=nil)
    result = RestClient.post(@base,:product => create_hash)

    # after create we are redirected to the new record.
    # The URL of the new record is given in the location header
    location = "#{result.headers[:location]}.json"

    # We need to get the id of that record and return it as part of create
    # so rhosync can establish a link from its temporary object on the
    # client to this newly created object on the server

    new_record = RestClient.get(location).body
    JSON.parse(new_record)["product"]["id"].to_s
end
```

Update

To allow editing an object from the client, include an update method in your source adapter (Listing 7–10). This method will receive a similar hash of attribute values discussed previously in the Create section. For updated records, the "update_hash" parameter contains the updated values for the specified object, which can be identified by retrieving the value of the attribute named "id." Use this method to invoke the backend system to perform the update. The rhostore web service expects an http put action with a hash passed that has a single item with the name "product" and the value of a hash containing attribute values to modify.

Listing 7–10. *Update method*

```
def update(update_hash)
    obj_id = update_hash ['id']
    update_hash.delete('id')
    RestClient.put("#{@base}/#{obj_id}",:product => update_hash)
end
```

Delete

To allow users to delete objects from the back end, include a delete method in your source adapter. This method receives the id of the object to delete. The delete method can then instruct the back-end system to delete the object. In this example, the rhostore API deletes the object when an http delete action is sent to a specific URL that includes the object id.

Listing 7–11. *Update and Delete Method*

```
def delete(object_id)
    RestClient.delete("#{@base}/#{object_id}")
end
```

User Authentication

The RhoSync server requires every device to authenticate with the server, but that doesn't require authentication with your back end. If your back-end services require authentication, you write your authentication code in a file called *application.rb*, which is at the root of your server app directory.

The authenticate method receives the login and password strings from the device, and a reference to the client server session object. Note that the session isn't encrypted, and is sent between the client/server, so it shouldn't include sensitive information. Instead, the Store interface can store sensitive info server-side.

Listing 7–12. *Authentication example*

```
class Application < Rhosync::Base
  class << self
    def authenticate(username,password,session)
      true # do some interesting authentication here...
    end

    # Add hooks for application startup here
    # Don't forget to call super at the end!
    def initializer(path)
      super
    end

    # Calling super here returns rack tempfile path:
    # i.e. /var/folders/J4/J4wGJ-r6H7S313GEZ-Xx5E+++TI
    # Note: This tempfile is removed when server stops or crashes...
    # See http://rack.rubyforge.org/doc/Multipart.html for more info
    #
    # Override this by creating a copy of the file somewhere
    # and returning the path to that file (then don't call super!):
    # i.e. /mnt/myimages/soccer.png
    def store_blob(blob)
      super #=> returns blob[:tempfile]
    end
  end
end
```

```
Application.initializer(ROOT_PATH)
```

When the authenticate method is called, it should return true or false (nil evaluates to false in Ruby, so that is also acceptable) to indicate if this user should be allowed to log in to RhoSync. If a user does not exist on the RhoSync server, but authenticate returns true, a new RhoSync user with that login is created. However, although user authentication is delegated to the back end, authorization to access restricted data will require some user data to be stored on the RhoSync server. In order to associate data with an account, the username (but not the password) will be saved in the RhoSync data store.

If you want to store additional data about the user, you can put and get data in the RhoSync data store using the user's login as a key. See Listing 7–13 for an example.

Listing 7–13. *Storing and retrieving user data*

```
Store.put_value("#{current_user.login}:preferences","something")

my_pref = Store.get_value("#{current_user.login}:preferences")
```

Product Inventory Example

In this chapter, you will create an application that connects to a remote web service for tracking inventory. People using the app will be able to view product inventory from the device, as well as create and edit records.

You can build the example in this chapter for either RhoHub or a local RhoSync server. First, we will guide you through building on RhoHub, then the identical application will be illustrated using local installations of RhoSync and Rhodes.

Creating Your Application on RhoHub

RhoHub is a service hosted by Rhomobile at http://rhohub.com. It is free for open source applications and has tiered pricing for private applications. It is great for getting started quickly. RhoHub significantly simplifies the development and deployment experience by providing hosting for your source adapter, which is automatically conveniently re-deployed when you edit and save the source in the web-based IDE. It also has a GUI wizard to generate an application and allows you to build the platforms that Rhodes supports (Figure 7–1).

As of this writing, RhoHub is not yet running Rhodes and RhoSync 2, so the code examples in this section do not match those detailed previously. However, it is likely that the workflow will be similar and version 2 code changes are minor.

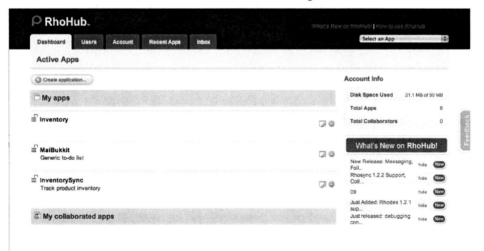

Figure 7–1. *Rhomobile GUI wizard*

To set up an application with RhoHub, simply log in and click **Create Application**. For this example, we'll use the name "Inventory," as shown in Figure 7–2.

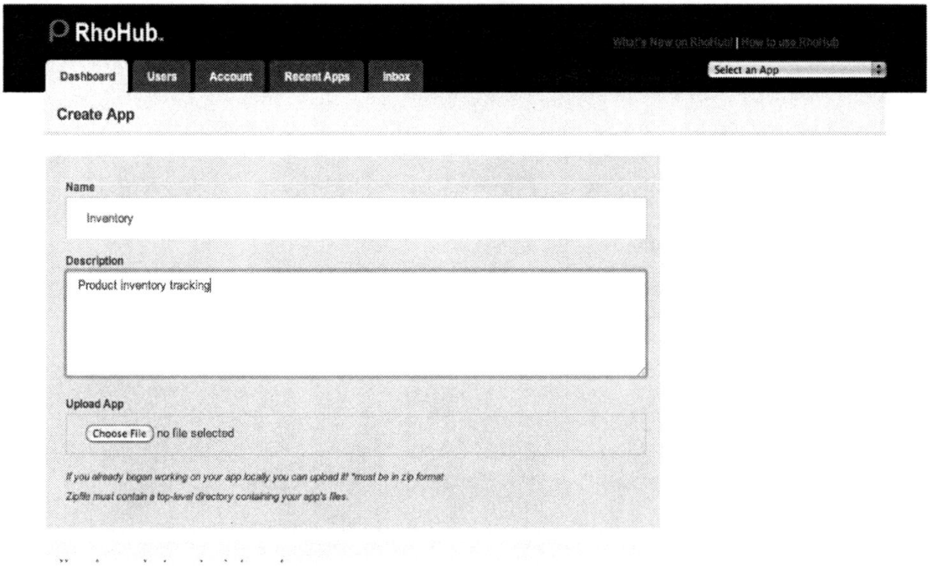

Figure 7–2. *Naming the application*

It is important to note that your application source code will be public by default, so if you want to keep it private, you will need to sign up for a premium account.

Fill in the fields on the **Create New Object** page as shown in Figure 7–3, then click **Create Object**.

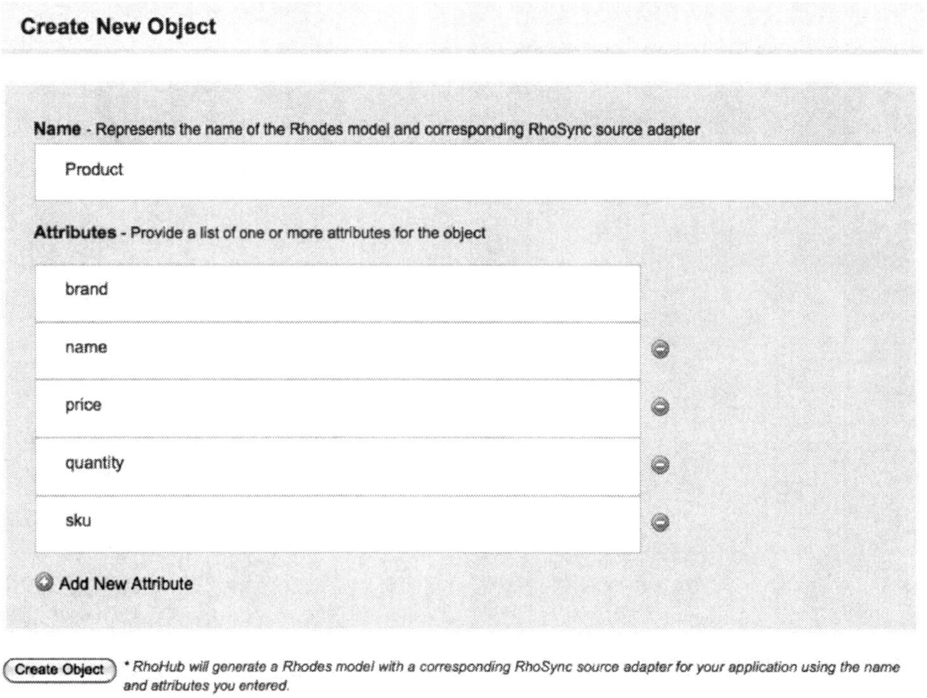

Create New Object

Name - Represents the name of the Rhodes model and corresponding RhoSync source adapter

Product

Attributes - Provide a list of one or more attributes for the object

brand

name

price

quantity

sku

⊕ Add New Attribute

(Create Object) * RhoHub will generate a Rhodes model with a corresponding RhoSync source adapter for your application using the name and attributes you entered.

Figure 7–3. *Filling in the fields of the Inventory application*

This generates both the code for your client application as well as the skeleton for your source adapter (Figure 7–4).

Figure 7–4. *The generated client and server code for your application*

At least one user must be subscribed to the application. This example will connect with a user called "tester" (Figure 7–5, top screen). To create the "tester" user, from your account **Dashboard**, select the **Users** tab (Figure 7–5, bottom screen), and add a user with the login and password both set to "tester."

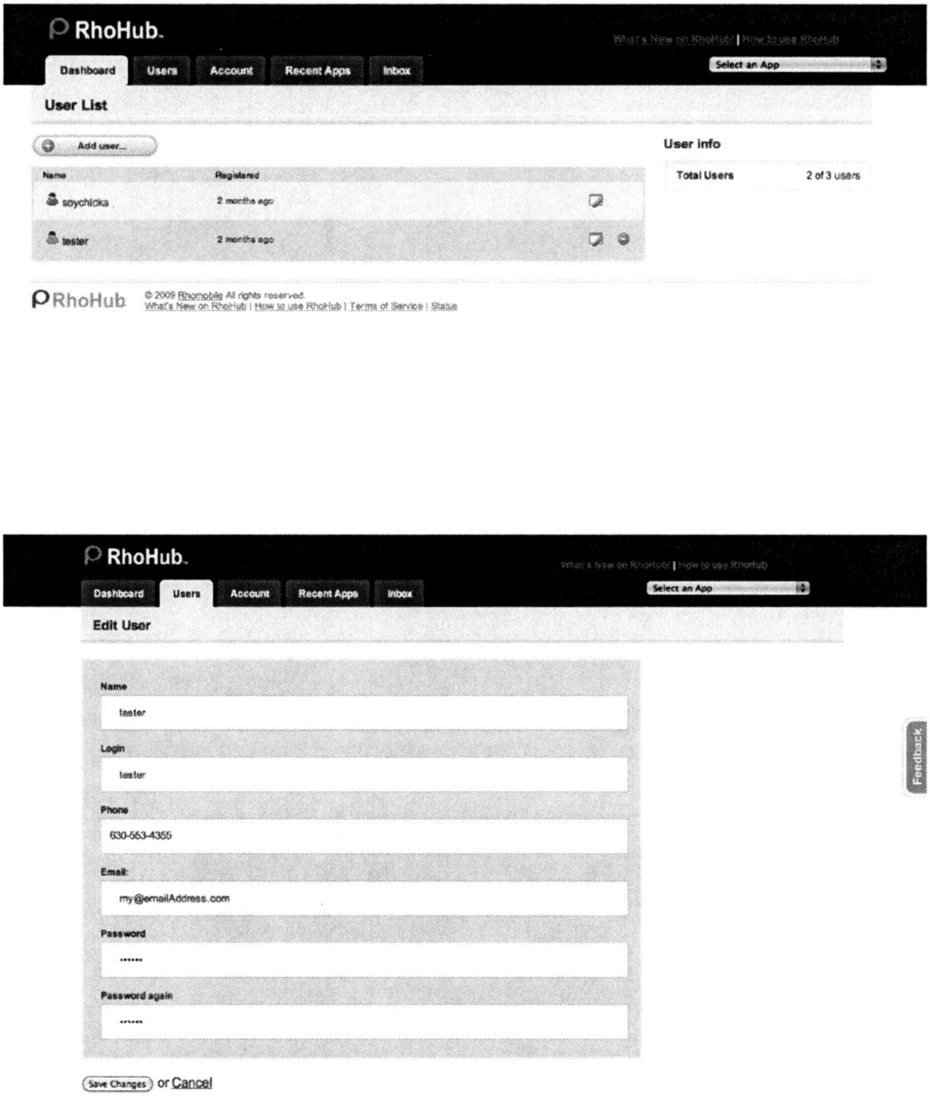

Figure 7–5 *Connecting a user*

After the user is created, you need to subscribe the user to your application. From the **Dashboard** tab, select your application. Select the **Settings** and scroll to the bottom where you can subscribe users. Select the check box next to the user you just created, and click **Save**. Figure 7–6 shows that the user "tester" is subscribed. The fields under

Associated Attributes for Backend Credentials only need to be filled in if they will be used by the source adapter's login method (as detailed in the previous Login section). They do not need to be filled in for this application.

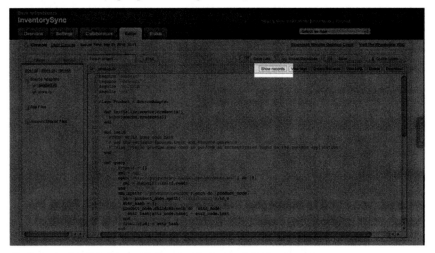

Figure 7–6. *Subscribe user with RhoHub*

Implementing Your Source Adapter

Next, you would complete the implementation of the source adapter using the online editor, which you can see by clicking on the **Editor** tab and then selecting the **Server** tab. The source adapter will be named the same name as the object you just created. In the preceding example, it would be named *product.rb* and by selecting the file name on the left, the code will be displayed on the right.

To follow this example, simply comment out the raise in login and add the query method detailed earlier in the chapter.

Testing Your Source Adapter

When using RhoHub, the source adapter is automatically loaded when it is generated, and reloaded whenever you save a change to your code.

The generated source adapter class is already easily testable. In your **Editor** screen, select the **Server** tab, select your *product.rb* source adapter in the left panel, then click **Show Records** (highlighted in Figure 7–7).

Figure 7–7. *RhoHub Editor with Source Adapter product.rb selected.*

This will display a list of records retrieved from the web service, as illustrated in Figure 7–8.

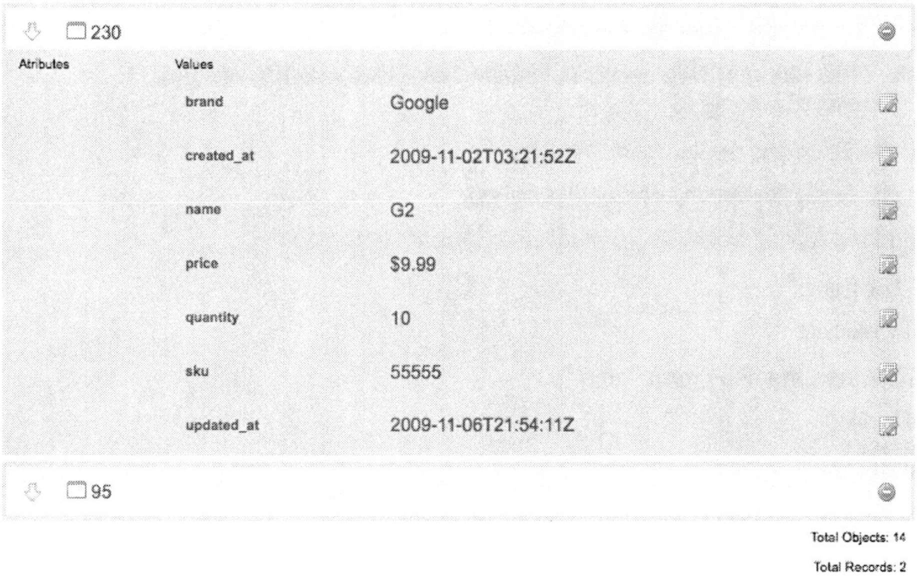

Atributes	Values	
⬇ ☐ 230		◉
brand	Google	▨
created_at	2009-11-02T03:21:52Z	▨
name	G2	▨
price	$9.99	▨
quantity	10	▨
sku	55555	▨
updated_at	2009-11-06T21:54:11Z	▨
⬇ ☐ 95		◉

Total Objects: 14

Total Records: 2

Figure 7–8. *RhoHub Show Records (with first record opened)*

Creating Your Application on a Local RhoSync Server

An alternate approach to using the hosted sync on RhoHub is to deploy your own RhoSync server application. During development, you will typically run RhoSync on your development machine, which is effective for connecting via a simulator. However, in production and for testing on devices, you will typically need to deploy on a server with a host name or fixed IP that is generally available on the network.

RhoSync is typically installed as a Ruby gem. If you want to use the very latest RhoSync, it is straightforward to run from source.[1] To prepare your environment, install the following dependencies:

- Ruby 1.8.7
- RubyGems 1.3.7 or higher
- Redis 1.2.6
- Ruby Web Server

---

[1] You can find additional instructions at: http://wiki.rhomobile.com/index.php/RhoSync_2.0 #Installing_RhoSync.

- RhoSync is tested with mongrel. WEBrick, the default web server that ships with Ruby, is known to cause problems with HTTP headers/cookies and is not recommended.

- The Mongrel web server is installed as a Ruby gem: `sudo gem install mongrel`

Download the RhoSync server from GitHub:

`git clone git://github.com/rhomobile/rhosync.git`

or download the tarball from `www.github.com/rhomobile/rhosync`

OR install the gem.[2]

`gem install rhosync`

You will also need the rRby gem "rake."

```
gem install rake
rake db:create
rake db:bootstrap
```

Generate the RhoSync Application

To use the RhoSync server, we need to generate an application. To generate the skeleton of a source adapter on your local RhoSync server, type the command "rhogen source product," which will create a file called *product.rb* in the RhoSync application's *sources* subdirectory along with a spec file *product_spec.rb* in the *spec/sources/* subdirectory. Source adapters are loaded from the *rhosync/lib* directory or *rhosync/vendor/sync* (or a first-level subdirectory). Listing 7–14 shows the creation of the source adapter from the command line.

Listing 7–14. *Generating a RhoSync application*

```
$ rhosync app storemanager-server
Generating with app generator:
      [ADDED]   storemanager-server/config.ru
      [ADDED]   storemanager-server/settings/settings.yml
      [ADDED]   storemanager-server/settings/license.key
      [ADDED]   storemanager-server/application.rb
      [ADDED]   storemanager-server/Rakefile
      [ADDED]   storemanager-server/spec/spec_helper.rb
$ cd storemanager-server/
$rhosync source product
Generating with source generator:
      [ADDED]   sources/product.rb
      [ADDED]   spec/sources/product_spec.rb
```

---

[2] As of this writing, Rhodes 2.0 is in beta. To install the beta version: `[sudo] gem install rhosync --pre`

Setting up RhoSync Server

The first time you run the server, you will need to run the following steps (within the application directory that you generated previously).

On Mac and Linux:

```
[sudo] rake dtach:install
```

On all platforms:

```
[sudo] rake redis:install
```

Start Redis:

```
rake redis:start
```

Start your RhoSync server:

```
rake rhosync:start
```

If everything went well, you should see something like the following output on your console:

```
[07:01:15 PM 2010-05-04] Rhosync Server v2.0.0.beta7 started... [07:01:15 PM 2010-05-04]
**************************************************** [07:01:15 PM 2010-05-04]
WARNING: Change the session secret in config.ru from <changeme> to something secure.
[07:01:15 PM 2010-05-04]   i.e. running `rake secret` in a rails app will generate a
secret you could use.  [07:01:15 PM 2010-05-04]
****************************************************
```

The RhoSync server has a web console that you can access at http://localhost:9292, or use the command-line shortcut:

```
rake rhosync:web
```

Testing Your Source Adapter

If you are running your own RhoSync server, then you will need to restart the server when you update a source adapter or authentication code in *application.rb*. Once you have done this, you can generate the application shown in Listing 7–15.

First, create an application that has a product model with the following attributes: brand,name,price,quantity,sku

Listing 7–15. *Client application code*

```
$ rhogen app inventory_app
Generating with app generator:
     [ADDED]  inventory_app/rhoconfig.txt
     [ADDED]  inventory_app/build.yml
     [ADDED]  inventory_app/app/application.rb
     [ADDED]  inventory_app/app/index.erb
     [ADDED]  inventory_app/app/layout.erb
     [ADDED]  inventory_app/app/loading.html
     [ADDED]  inventory_app/Rakefile
     [ADDED]  inventory_app/app/helpers
     [ADDED]  inventory_app/icon
```

```
      [ADDED]   inventory_app/app/Settings
      [ADDED]   inventory_app/public

$ cd inventory_app/

$ rhogen model product brand,name,price,quantity,sku
Generating with model generator:
      [ADDED]   app/Product/config.rb
      [ADDED]   app/Product/index.erb
      [ADDED]   app/Product/edit.erb
      [ADDED]   app/Product/new.erb
      [ADDED]   app/Product/show.erb
      [ADDED]   app/Product/controller.rb
```

Debugging RhoSync Source Adapters

The statement "puts @result.inspect" is an example of a debugging technique commonly used when building Rhodes applications. Here, puts is used to inspect the structure of the hash before returning from the method. If you are running your application using your own RhoSync server, the output goes to regular standard output. There is no built-in support for file logging, but you can create any logging you like in Ruby.

If you are new to Ruby, there is one catch with the use of puts as a debugging technique: never use puts on the last line of your method. The puts method outputs your data to the screen, but will return nil from the method, so when debugging your application, always make sure to have the value you wish to return as the last line executed within your method.

In RhoHub, you can view this output in the console.

Testing Your Application

Once your source adapter has been set up on the RhoSync server, you can try out the application in the device simulator of your choice.

In the default scaffold-generated app, the user login is performed from the Options menu, **Login** screen. Sync will be triggered automatically after login.

Chapter 8

PhoneGap

PhoneGap (`http://phonegap.com/`) is an open source framework for building native mobile applications using HTML, CSS, and Javascript for iPhone, Android, BlackBerry, Palm webOS, and Symbian WRT (Nokia). PhoneGap is a perfect for transforming a mobile web application to a native application. It is easy to use for web developers. In order to use PhoneGap, a web developer will need to learn how to build using one or more device SDKs and tools, but all the application code can be HTML, CSS, and JavaScript. In fact, a developer must be fairly expert in JavaScript to take advantage of this platform. Depending on the perspective of the developer, it is a benefit or a drawback that it provides little in the way of design patterns for mobile applications. It will not help you with an application that works off-line, which means it is possible on Android and iPhone with Webkit's Web Storage support,[1] but not on BlackBerry (as of this writing).

PhoneGap provides a rich collection of client-side JavaScript APIs with a method for hosting your web application within a native mobile application. PhoneGap is a sponsored project of Nitobi (`http://nitobi.com`), a software consultancy headquartered in Vancouver BC. The framework started in 2008, and is free to use under an MIT license.

The key advantage of creating a native mobile application with PhoneGap is that you can drop in a mobile web application and build it into a native application that an end user may install (or purchase). As a native application, it can access certain capabilities not available from a web application, such as access to contacts data, geolocation, camera, and accelerometer using PhoneGap's JavaScript APIs.

To create a native application with PhoneGap, you start by writing a mobile web application using HTML, CSS, and Javascript using whatever tools you are most comfortable with. PhoneGap does not require your application to conform to any

---

[1] The Web Storage spec is still in working draft (and now considered separate from HTML 5 by the World Wide Web Consortium (W3C). It has been implemented already by many browsers including Android and iPhone mobile WebKit browsers. For more information, see: `http://dev.w3.org/html5/webstorage/`.

particular structure, nor does it provide any specific guidance about how to create your app. If you already have an existing mobile web application, you may be able to easily convert it to use in PhoneGap. PhoneGap works particularly well on such platforms as iPhone and Android that include the WebKit browser with the advanced JavaScript and CSS of HTML 5.

In fact, PhoneGap tracks advanced features of HTML 5 and the work of standards bodies such as the W3C Device API Group (http://www.w3.org/2009/dap/) that defines standards for Javascript APIs for mobile phone features. PhoneGap attempts to implement emerging APIs to interact with device services such as contacts, camera, and so forth today and make them available as part of its framework ahead of these APIs being available in mobile browsers. The goal of PhoneGap is to cease to exist once mobile browsers expose these APIs. A selling point of PhoneGap is that you are not coding to a proprietary API but instead to what may in the future turn out to be W3C standards.

> *An express goal of the PhoneGap project is for the project to not exist. We believe in the web and devices should too. The web is moving off the desktop and into the pockets of people all over the world. Phones are the new window to the internet and, currently, they are second class. PhoneGap aims to move your device to a nice first class window. With a foot rest. Maybe a pillow.*
>
> —phonegap.com

Note that while PhoneGap attempts to be a non-proprietary API and tracks standards from W3C, those standards are not fully developed. PhoneGap exists to bridge the gap between the standard and what is required to build a real application, so it contains APIs that diverge from the standard. This is also perhaps a reason why the PhoneGap APIs change frequently.

PhoneGap is well-suited for anything you could do with a mobile web application. Like all of the cross-platform frameworks that leverage the browser for UI, it is not well-suited for applications that require intense math calculations or 3-D animations. Neither is it well-suited for developers needing to write data-driven applications, like most enterprise applications, that must work offline using sync'd local data. PhoneGap does not provide specific database support and relies on HTML5 database APIs for persistence, which are not widely available.

The key benefit of being able to package and distribute your mobile web application is that you have a marketplace for your application, such as the Apple App Store, Nokia's OV Store, or Blackberry App World. Your application will then have screen real-estate wherever the phone installs applications and users can typically configure their phone to display the application for quick access.

When running inside PhoneGap, your application can access certain devices capabilities from JavaScript that are not otherwise available to web apps. The PhoneGap API provides access to the following device capabilities:

- Geolocation

- Contacts

- Vibration

- Accelerometer

- Camera

- Sound playback

- Device information

- Click to call

For a complete list of device capabilities (which differ across platform), see `http://wiki.phonegap.com/Roadmap`. Some capabilities, such as orientation, recording audio, and maps are available on only one or two platforms.

Nitobi also provides a JavaScript library optimized for mobilize devices similar to jQuery called XUI (`http://xuijs.com`). XUI is much faster and lighter-weight than jQuery but has only a subset of the functionality.

There are a large number of PhoneGap applications at the Apple App Store: `http://phonegap.com/projects`.

Getting Started with PhoneGap

In this chapter, we will build a sample application for iPhone, Android, and BlackBerry. PhoneGap also supports Symbian and Palm webOS, but we will not cover those in this chapter. You need to download and install the SDKs for whichever platforms you want to develop for. If you are going to follow along for iPhone, you need to download and install the iPhone SDK and sign up for the Apple iPhone developer program. The free version will allow you to test your application in the simulator. (For details on how to build for the iPhone device, see Chapter 2.) If you are developing for BlackBerry, you need to install BlackBerry SDK, as well as Eclipse and several plug-ins—Phonegap documents these in detail at `http://phonegap.pbworks.com/Getting-Started-with-PhoneGap-%28BlackBerry%29`, or see Chapter 4. As with iPhone, BlackBerry development is free with preview in the simulator, but you need to sign up and purchase keys to build on the device. If you want to develop for Android, you will need to download the latest Android SDK at `http://www.android.com/` (see Chapter 3).

The PhoneGap project is separated into native projects for each device that you will compile using the native toolkits for each device. Download the PhoneGap source from `http://phonegap.com/download` or `http://github.com/phonegap`. If you want to easily stay up-to-date with the latest releases, you can download the source using git. The PhoneGap source code is not large and fairly transparent to read over. PhoneGap maintains a wiki at `http://phonegap.pbworks.com/`.

Because PhoneGap is still in pre-release (at version 0.9.1 as of this writing), the authors have found it most effective to keep the code up-to-date using git. Note that the git repository uses submodules, so there are extra steps to get all of the source. As noted in the *readme*, use the commands from Listing 8–1 in your terminal or at a command line (with git installed) to access the PhoneGap source.

Listing 8–1. *Downloading PhoneGap Source Using git*

```
git clone git://github.com/phonegap/phonegap.git
  cd phonegap/
  git submodule init
  git submodule update
```

Sample Application

PhoneGap includes a system sample application that shows some of the basic device capabilities of the framework. We will use this to also verify that we have everything installed to build correctly.

PhoneGap iPhone

To develop for iPhone, you will need a Mac OS X computer. PhoneGapLib is a static library that enables users to include PhoneGap in their iPhone application projects, and also create new PhoneGap-based iPhone application projects through an Xcode project template. Xcode is Apple's development environment for Mac OS X and iPhone that comes included with the iPhone SDK.

First you need to build and install the Installer Package:

1. Download *phonegap-iphone* source.

2. Launch *Terminal.app*.

3. Navigate to the folder where the Makefile is (in git repository, this is *phonegap/iphone*).

4. Type "make", then press Enter. If you see: "Warning: "Require Admin Authorization" is recommended but not enabled. Installation may fail.", you can safely ignore this warning.

5. The make command should build *PhoneGapLibInstaller.pkg* into this folder. Make sure XCode is not running. Launch *PhoneGapLibInstaller.pkg* to run the PhoneGap installer, which installs PhoneGapLib and the PhoneGap Xcode Template.

Then create a PhoneGap project:

1. Launch Xcode, then under the File menu, select New Project.

2. Navigate to the **User Templates** section, select **PhoneGap**, then in the right pane, select **PhoneGap-based Application.**

3.   Select the **Choose** button, name your project, and choose the location where you want the new project to be.

4.   To build your own application instead of the system sample, simply replace the contents of the *www* folder with your web application HTML and assets. We will cover this in the next section.

5.   Select **Simulator** as the target, and then **Build and Run**. See Figures 8–1 and 8–2.

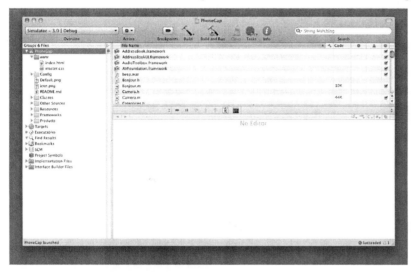

Figure 8–1. *PhoneGap project loaded in XCode*

Figure 8–2. *PhoneGap system sample application running in iPhone Simulator*

Android

For Android, you need to install the Android SDK and Eclipse plus the Android Development Tools (ADT) development plug-in for the Eclipse. ADT extends the capabilities of Eclipse to let you build Android projects and export signed (or unsigned) APKs in order to distribute your application.

PhoneGap includes an Eclipse project in the *Android* directory. From your Eclipse workspace choose File ➤ Import.... Select **General, Existing Project into Workspace** and select your *phonegap/android* directory.

Next, right-click over the project and select **Android Tools** ➤ **Fix Project Properties**.

Next, select **Build and Run as Android Application**. You will need to create an android virtual machine, aka AVD, the first time you run. See Figures 8–3 and 8–4.

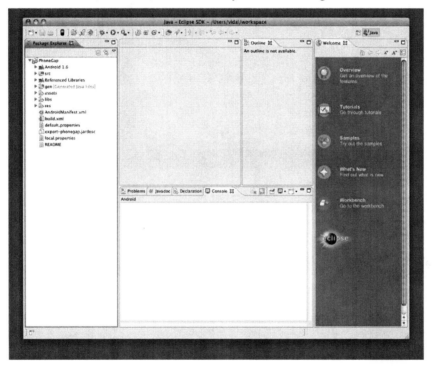

Figure 8–3. *PhoneGap Project loaded into Eclipse*

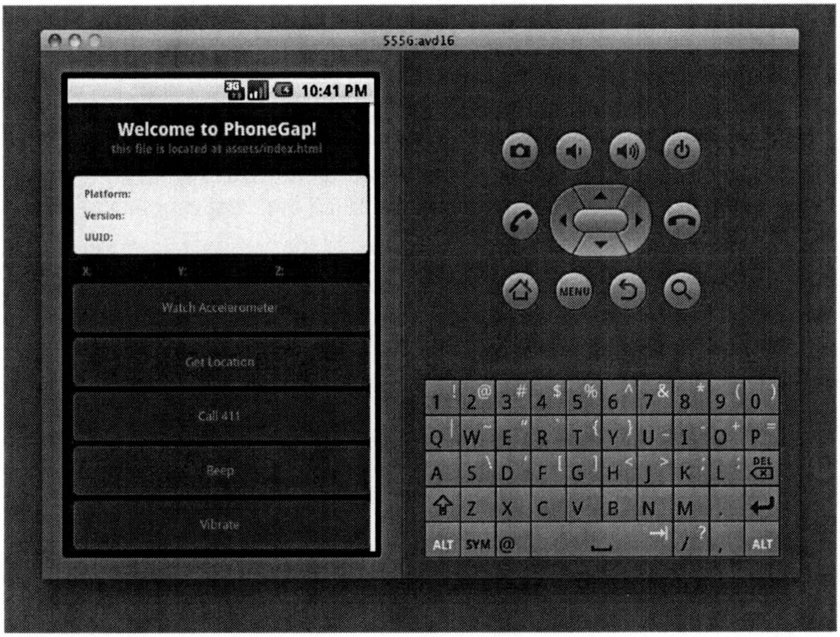

Figure 8–4. *PhoneGap running in Android 1.6 Simulator*

BlackBerry

To develop for BlackBerry, you will need a Windows PC. Refer to the PhoneGap wiki for detailed installation and setup instructions: `http://phonegap.pbworks.com/Getting+Started+with+PhoneGap+(BlackBerry)`.

Download and install Eclipse 3.4 or 3.4.1. You will need to install the BlackBerry JDE Plug-in for Eclipse, and the Eclipse Software Update for the BlackBerry JDE v4.6.1 Component Pack to allow you to develop BlackBerry apps in Eclipse. You can download these from the BlackBerry Developers site.

Create a PhoneGap project with Eclipse as follows:

1. Launch Eclipse, go to File ➤ Import ➤ Existing BlackBerry project.

2. Navigate over to where you downloaded the phonegap-blackberry source code, and point it to the *phonegap.jdp* file located in *blackberry/framework/*.

3. Before running, right-click on project root and make sure **Activate for BlackBerry** is checked.

4. Run or debug from Eclipse as desired.

PhoneGap Simulator

You can also test your application in a cross-platform (Windows, Mac, and so forth) PhoneGap simulator written in Adobe Air. You can find the simulator at http://phonegap.com/download.The simulator uses the WebKit browser that is built into Adobe Air to run your application. Start the simulator and choose your starting *index.html* file or equivalent. This is very helpful since the build and test process can be very time-consuming using the native device SDKs.

You must always test using the device simulator and the real device for full compatibility verification; however, using the PhoneGap simulator for parts of your development cycle will speed up the process. See Figures 8–5 and 8–6.

Figure 8–5. *PhoneGap Simulator Control Panel*

Figure 8–6. *PhoneGap running in PhoneGap Simulator with BlackBerry Skin*

Writing Hello World in PhoneGap

Now that you have built the sample application to verify that you have installed PhoneGap correctly, you can build your own application. You start by deleting (or setting aside) the default *index.html* in the /*www* folder, as we will be replacing it in this example. The *index.html* file is the entry point for your application. Any code, HTML layout, or images used by your application must be loaded or linked to by this file.

As of this writing (PhoneGap 0.9), the *www* folder is in a different location for each platform supported by PhoneGap. See Table 8–1 for platform-specific locations (or, on the command line, type: "find . | grep www").

Table 8–1. *Where to Put Your Application Files by Platform*

Platform	Where to Put Your Application Files
iPhone	/iphone/PhoneGap-based Application/www
Android	/android/framework/assets/www
BlackBerry	/blackberry/framework/src/www
Windows Mobile	/winmo/www
Symbian	/symbian.wrt/framework/www
Palm	/palm/framework/www

Edit the *www/index.html* so that it contains only the lines in Listing 8–2, then build and run it in the simulator. See Figure 8–7 to see how it looks in the iPhone simulator. You can see that it is a simple rendering of the *index.html* web page.

Listing 8–2. *Hello World code*

```
<html>
  <h1>Hello World</h1>
</html>
```

Figure 8–7. *Hello World running in an iPhone Simulator*

Writing a PhoneGap Application

PhoneGap is completely unstructured. It does not require you to organize your application in any particular way. To start writing your mobile app, it is easiest to begin by writing a web application using whatever tools you are familiar with. In this example, we will write a simple tip calculator and restaurant bill-splitting application. This is a single-page application that uses JavaScript to change the contents of the page based on user interaction.

The code for our sample application is shown in Listing 8–3. This was first written and tested on the desktop using Firefox and Safari. Another advantage of writing this first for a desktop browser is that you can use JavaScript debugging tools such as Firebug or the Safari developer tools to get your programming logic correct. The Safari desktop browser is very close in functionality to the WebKit mobile browsers on iPhone and Android. This version of the application uses jQuery, which is compatible with iOS and Android, but does not work on BlackBerry (more detail on BlackBerry to come). The key take-away here is that this could be any mobile web application. The example in this chapter is provided to help illustrate that fact, and to demonstrate how to build a custom application across platforms–the actual code is not particularly important.

Listing 8–3. *Code for the Simple Tip Calculator Application for WebKit*

```html
<html>
<head>
        <script src="jquery-1.3.2.min.js" type="text/javascript" charset=↵
"utf-8"></script>
        <script>

            $(document).ready(function() {
                        $("#amount").focus();
                        $("#click").click(function(){$('form')[0].reset();});
                        $("#split_form").submit(function(){
                                console.log($("#amount").val(), $("#gratuity").val(), ↵
 $("#num_diners").val());

                                var result = $("#amount").val() * $("#gratuity").val()↵
 / $("#num_diners").val();

                                $("#result").text("$"+result.toFixed(2));
                                return false;
                                });
                });
        </script>
</head>
<body>
        <div id="index">
        <h1>Tip Calculator and Bill Splitter</h1>
        <form action="#" id="split_form">
                <p><label>Amount</label><input type="text" name="amount"↵
 id="amount"></p>
                <p><label># Diners</label><input type="text" name="num_diners"↵
 id="num_diners" value="1"></p>
                <p>
                        <label>Gratuity</label>
                        <select id="gratuity" name="gratuity">
```

```
                        <option value="1.0">None</option>
                <option value="1.10">10%</option>
                <option value="1.15" selected="1.15">15%</option>
                <option value="1.18">18%</option>
                <option value="1.20">20%</option>
              </select>
          </p>
          <p><span id="result"></span></p>
          <p><input type="submit" value="Calc"></p>
          <p><a href="#" id="click">Clear</a></p>
        </form>
        </div>
  </body>
  </html>
```

To mobilize this application, simply delete the existing contents of the PhoneGap *iphone/www* directory and copy the *index.html* and *jquery.js* files to that directory. Choose **Build and Run**. Note: we chose to use jQuery here only because it made the JavaScript simpler. It is absolutely not required, and in fact, does not work on some mobile browsers (like BlackBerry). See Figures 8–8 and 8–9.

Figure 8–8. *Tip calculator code in PhoneGap XCode project*

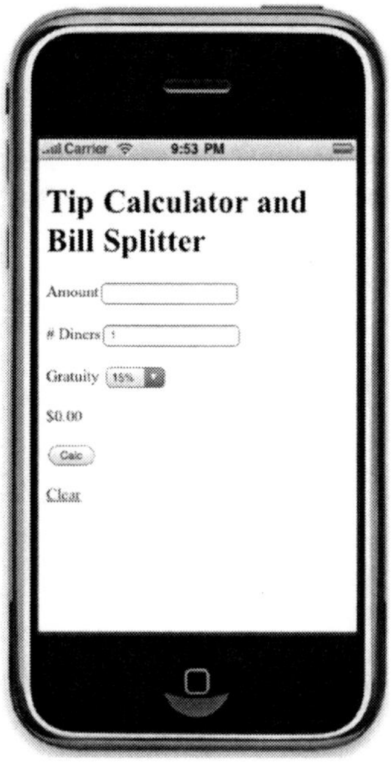

Figure 8–9. *Tip calculator running inside iPhone Simulator*

To build this application for Android, copy the same *index.html* and *jquery.js* into the
PhoneGap android/assets/www directory. Then run as Android Application. See Figure 8–10.

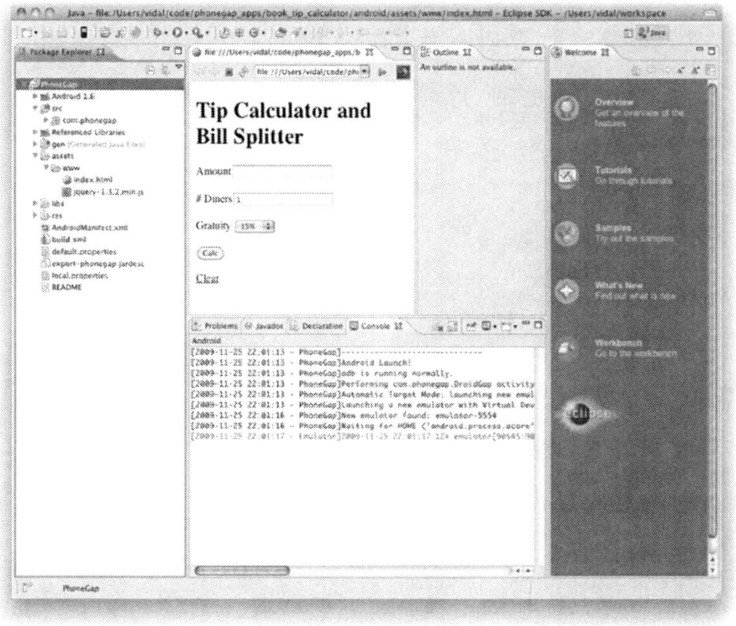

Figure 8–10. *Tip calculator code in PhoneGap Eclipse project for Android*

You can see that the application looks and functions identically off a single code base on both platforms.

For BlackBerry, the application needs to be modified not to use jQTouch. As detailed in Chapter 14, the BlackBerry browser supports limited JavaScript capabilities. Listing 8–4 shows a modified application that runs on BlackBerry (as shown in Figures 8–11 and 8–12). To create this application, copy the code into *phonegap/blackberry/framework/src/www/* and then build the project in Eclipse as detailed previously.

Listing 8–4. *Code for the Simple Tip Calculator Application for BlackBerry*

```
<html>
<head>
        <script>

                window.onload = function() {
                        document.getElementById("amount").focus();
                        document.getElementById("clear").addEventListener('click',↵
 function(event){document.forms[0].reset();}, false);

                        document.getElementById("split_form").addEventListener↵
('submit', function(event){

                                try {
                                var result = document.getElementById("amount").value *
                                        document.getElementById("gratuity").value /↵
 document.getElementById("num_diners").value;
                                        document.getElementById('result').value=↵
"$"+result.toFixed(2);
                                } catch(err)
                                {
                                        txt="There was an error on this page.\n\n";
  txt+="Error description:\n\n" + err.message + "\n\n";
  txt+="Click OK to continue.\n\n";
  alert(txt);
                                }

                                return false;
                        }, false);
                };
        </script>

</head>
<body>
        <div id="index">
        <h1>Tip Calculator and Bill Splitter</h1>
        <form action="#" id="split_form">
                <p><label>Amount</label><input type="text" name="amount"↵
 id="amount"></p>
                <p><label># Diners</label><input type="text" name="num_diners"↵
 id="num_diners" value="1"></p>
                <p>
                        <label>Gratuity</label>
                        <select id="gratuity" name="gratuity">
                                <option value="1.0">None</option>
```

```
                    <option value="1.10">10%</option>
                    <option value="1.15" selected="1.15">15%</option>
                    <option value="1.18">18%</option>
                    <option value="1.20">20%</option>
                </select>
        </p>
        <p><input type="text" name="result" id="result"></p>
        <p><input type="submit" value="Calc"></p>
        <p><a href="#" id="clear">Clear</a></p>
    </form>
    </div>
</body>
</html>
```

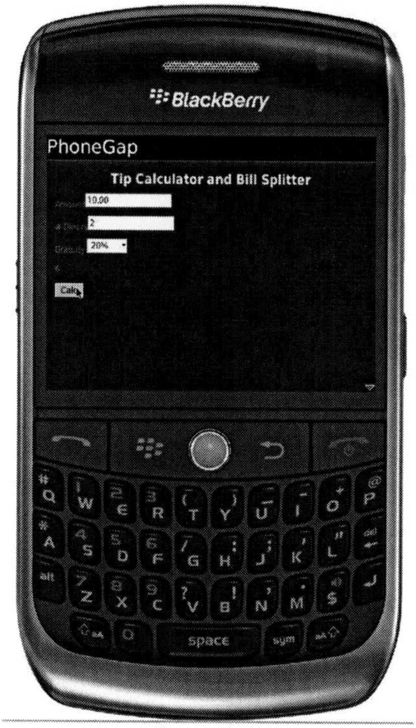

Figure 8–11. *Tip calculator in PhoneGap BlackBerry*

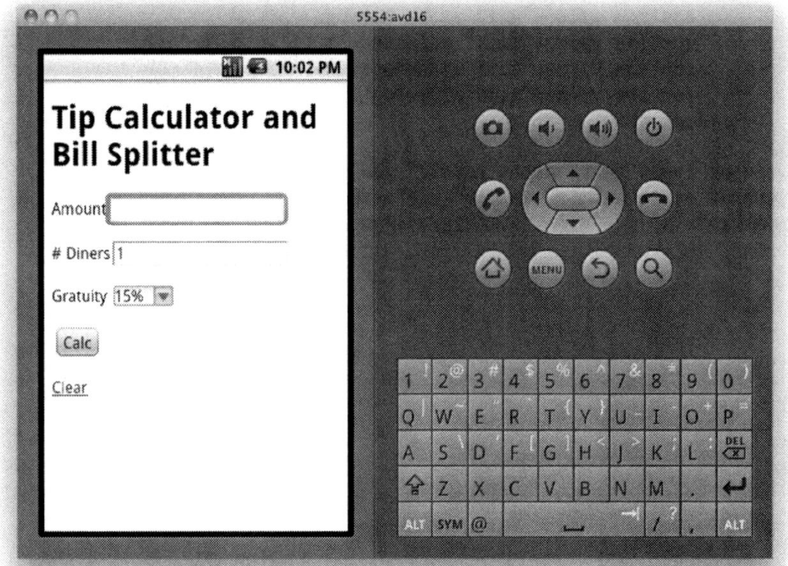

Figure 8–12. *Tip calculator in PhoneGap Simulator*

Contacts Example

For the next example, we will demonstrate using native device APIs that are made available by PhoneGap. Smartphones all have a built-in Personal Information Management (PIM) contacts applications that allows users to store phone numbers and addresses. Smartphone platforms allow applications to access those contacts through APIs that differ per platform, but generally offer the same capabilities.

In this section, we will step through writing a PhoneGap application that will allow you to show and edit native PIM contacts using PhoneGap's APIs on iPhone. This example also uses jQTouch for styling and, because of that, will only work on the iPhone. Please refer to Chapter 12 for more information about jQTouch. Note that the PIM contacts APIs will work on any platform, but it is typical to style applications differently per platform. PhoneGap does not provide any infrastructure to facilitate sharing code across platforms; however, you can use standard mobile web techniques to support the range of platforms you are targeting.

Create a new PhoneGap iPhone project using the steps from the previous examples. Name the project *pg_contacts*. The complete source code to the completed application is available online at: http://github.com/VGraupera/PhoneGap-Contacts-Sample.

Replace the generated *index.html* file in the *www* directory with the following:

```
<!doctype html>
<html>
  <head>
    <script src="jqtouch/jquery.1.3.2.min.js" type="text/javascript" charset=↵
```

```
"utf-8"></script>
    <script src="jqtouch/jqtouch.js" type="text/javascript" charset="utf-8"></script>
    <link rel="stylesheet" href="jqtouch/jqtouch.css" type="text/css" media=↵
"screen" title="no title" charset="utf-8">
    <link rel="stylesheet" href="themes/apple/theme.css" type="text/css" media=↵
"screen" title="no title" charset="utf-8">

    <script type="text/javascript" charset="utf-8" src="phonegap.js"></script>

    <script type="text/javascript">
// initialize jQTouch with defaults
    var jQT = $.jQTouch();

    function getContacts(){
      var fail = function(){};
      var options = {pageSize:10};
      var nameFilter = $("#some_name").val();
      if (nameFilter) {
        options.nameFilter = nameFilter;
      }
      navigator.contacts.getAllContacts(getContacts_callback, fail, options);
    };

    function getContacts_callback(contactsArray)
    {
      var ul = $('#contacts');
      // remove any existing data as we resuse this function to update contact list
      ul.find("li").remove();

      for (var i = 0; i < contactsArray.length; i++) {
        var contact = contactsArray[i];
        var li = $("<li><a href='#'>"+contact.name+'</a></li>');
        li.find('a').bind('click', function(e) {showContact(contact.recordID);});
        ul.append(li);
      }
    };

        function showContact(contactId)
            {
                var options = { allowsEditing: true };
                navigator.contacts.displayContact(contactId, null, options);
    $('a').removeClass('loading active');
                return false;
            }

            function submitForm() {
                var contact = {};

                contact.firstName = $('#first_name').val();
                contact.lastName = $('#last_name').val();

                navigator.contacts.newContact(contact, getContacts, {
                    'gui': false
                });

                jQT.goBack();
                $('#add form').reset();
```

```
                           return false;
                };

       function preventBehavior(e) {
          e.preventDefault();
       };

       PhoneGap.addConstructor(function(){
                           // show initial data
                           getContacts();

                           // hook the add form
                           $('#add form').submit(submitForm);
                           $('#add .whiteButton').click(submitForm);

          $("#some_name").keyup(getContacts);

          document.addEventListener("touchmove", preventBehavior, false);
       });

       </script>
   </head>
   <body>
      <div id="home">
       <div class="toolbar">
          <h1>Contacts</h1>
                           <a class="button add slideup" href="#add">+</a>
       </div>
          <ul class="edit rounded">
             <li><input type="search" name="search" placeholder="Search" id="some_name"⏎
style="border:none; margin:0; padding:0;font-size:16px;"/></li>
          </ul>
          <ul id="contacts" class="edgetoedge">
          </ul>
       </div>
       <div id="add">
          <form>
             <div class="toolbar">
                <h1>New Contact</h1>
                <a href="#" class="cancel back">Cancel</a>
             </div>
             <ul class="edit rounded">
                <li><input type="text" name="first_name" placeholder="First Name"⏎
id="first_name" /></li>
                <li><input type="text" name="last_name" placeholder="Last Name"⏎
id="last_name" /></li>
                <li><input type="text" name="email_address" placeholder="Email Address"⏎
id="email_address" type="email" /></li>
                <li><input type="text" name="business_number" placeholder="Business⏎
Number" id="business_number" type="tel" /></li>

             </ul>
             <a href="#" class="whiteButton" style="margin: 10px">Add</a>
          </form>
       </div>
   </body>
</html>
```

Contact Example Code Explained

We began the example by including jQuery and jQTouch JavaScript libraries and CSS. We used these for convenience and style, but they are not absolutely required. However, the *phonegap.js* we included is required. The following recaps what was done in the remainder of the example:

1. We initialize the jQTouch library. Please refer to the Chapter 12 on jQTouch for complete details.

2. We define a function called getContacts". getContacts uses the navigator.contacts.getAllContacts function provided by the PhoneGap API. getAllContacts takes three arguments the last two of which are optional. We pass in on success and on failure callback functions as the first two arguments. Our on failure callback is a trivial function we define inline called "fail". Our on success callback "getContacts_callback" is described next. Because the total number of contacts on the smartphone can be very large, we limit the results to just ten contacts using the pageSize option. In order to see more than just the first ten contacts on the phone, we pass in a filter parameter in nameFilter if we have one. The value of nameFilter comes from the some_name text input field defined later.

3. Our getContacts_callback clears the list of contacts we have on the screen and recreates it from the array of contacts that are passed in from a successful return of the getAllContacts API. Using JavaScript, we add new <li> rows to our list of contacts and register onClick callbacks for each so that when the user clicks any one of them, showContact will be called for that record ID.

4. showContact uses the navigator.contacts.displayContact API provided by PhoneGap to natively show a contact record. We do not need to create any HTML forms for this. Nice!

5. We define submitForm. This function will be called when we create a new contact and uses the navigator.contacts.newContact API provided by PhoneGap. This function reads the values from our new contact form defined later and also resets the form when we are done.

6. Finally, we call PhoneGap.addConstructor, which adds our initialization function to a queue that ensures it will run and initialize only once PhoneGap has been initialized. Within our initialization function, we get the list of contacts (by default, the first 10) and register handlers for our new contact form search box (see Figure 8–13) described later.

7. Our HTML markup consists of two major parts. The first DIV with id="home" shows the list of contacts. There is a button to add a new

contact, and a search box to trigger refreshing the list of contacts based on what is entered in the box. We bind to the onKeyUp event in the search box so that our search is run live as the user types. The second DIV is a form that is used to enter new contacts. We only include some basic fields here in the example.

Figure 8–13. *The Contacts example code in action*

Camera Example

In this section, we will step through writing an application that will allow you to take pictures using the smartphone camera using PhoneGap APIs on iPhone.

Create a new PhoneGap iPhone project, using the steps from the previous examples. Name the project *pg_camera*. The complete source code to the completed application is available online at: http://github.com/VGraupera/PhoneGap-Photos-Sample.

Replace the generated *index.html* file in the *www* directory with the following:

```
<!DOCTYPE HTML PUBLIC "-//W3C//DTD HTML 4.01//EN"
"http://www.w3.org/TR/html4/strict.dtd">
<html>
  <head>
  <meta name="viewport" content="width=default-width; user-scalable=no" />
  <meta http-equiv="Content-type" content="text/html; charset=utf-8">

  <script src="jqtouch/jquery.1.3.2.min.js" type="text/javascript" charset=↵
```

```
"utf-8"></script>
  <script src="jqtouch/jqtouch.js" type="text/javascript" charset="utf-8"></script>
  <link rel="stylesheet" href="jqtouch/jqtouch.css" type="text/css" media="screen"↵
title="no title" charset="utf-8">
  <link rel="stylesheet" href="themes/apple/theme.css" type="text/css" media="screen"↵
title="no title" charset="utf-8">

  <script type="text/javascript" charset="utf-8" src="phonegap.js"></script>
  <script type="text/javascript" charset="utf-8">
  // initialize jQTouch with defaults
  var jQT = $.jQTouch();

function onBodyLoad()
      {
              document.addEventListener("deviceready",onDeviceReady,false);
      }

function dump_pic(data)
  {
    document.getElementById("test_img").src = "data:image/jpeg;base64," + data;
  }

  function fail() {
    alert('problem');
  };

  function takePicture() {
    navigator.camera.getPicture(dump_pic, fail, { quality: 50 });
  };

  </script>
  </head>
  <body onload="onBodyLoad()">
    <div id="home">
     <div class="toolbar">
        <h1>Pictures</h1>
        <a class="button add" href="#" onClick="takePicture();">+</a>
     </div>
     <img id="test_img" style="width:100%" src="" />
    </div>
  </body>
</html>
```

Camera Example Code Explained

The code is similar but simpler than the *pg_contacts* example. We started by setting up and loading the jQTouch and PhoneGap libraries. Then we define "takePicture," which uses the navigator.camera.getPicture API provided by PhoneGap. This will bring up the native camera interface. You need to run this application on an actual iPhone as you cannot test the camera in this way in the iPhone simulator. Finally, in our success callback dump_pic, we set the src of our img tag to the inline data from the camera. Figure 8–14 shows the end result.

Figure 8–14. *The Camera example code in action*

Chapter 9

Titanium Mobile

This chapter will discuss how to build native applications for the iPhone and Android using Appcelerator's Titanium Mobile platform. Titanium is a commercially supported, open source platform for developing native cross-platform applications using web technologies. Source code is released under the Apache 2 license. Appcelerator, Inc. (`www.appcelerator.com/`), a startup in Mountain View, CA., introduced the platform in December 2008. Appcelerator has announced and will soon be releasing a version of Titanium Mobile that also works for the BlackBerry.

Titanium consists of an SDK that provides the necessary tools, compilers, and APIs for building for the target platform, and a visual environment for managing your Titanium-based projects called Titanium Developer. Titanium Developer provides a nice visual way to build your projects, but to edit them you will need to use your favorite source code editor. Titanium is available for Mac, Linux and Windows. To develop for the iPhone (or iPad), you will need to run it on Mac using the iPhone SDK. Developing for the Android requires the Android SDK and can be done using Mac, Windows, or Linux.

The Titanium API provides a platform-independent API to access native UI components including navigation bars, menus, dialog boxes, and alerts, and native device functionality including the file system, sound, network, and local database. You code in JavaScript that is compiled into native counterparts as part of the build process.

Titanium offers a free community edition that can be used to build and distribute your applications. Developers can upgrade to the Titanium Professional Edition or the Titanium Enterprise Edition that offers additional support and services. The Titanium web site includes basic documentation and training videos. Developers can pay for advanced videos and sign up for training classes on the Appcelerator web site.

Getting Started

You should start by downloading the iPhone SDK and Android SDK if you do not already have them installed. These are not included with Titanium and you will need them to build your application. (See Chapters 3 and 4, respectively, for details on setting up the iPhone and Android. You will not need Eclipse for the Android, but the other dependencies are the same.)

Download and install Titantium from the Appcelerator web site at www.appcelerator.com/. Launch Titanium Developer. Titanium Developer will download the latest Titanium SDK. You will need to sign up for a free account on the Appcelerator Developer Center (see Figure 9–1).

Figure 9–1. *Titanium Developer sign-up process*

Once you have signed in, click the **New Project** icon at the top of the screen. Click **Project Type** and select **Mobile**. Titanium Developer should automatically detect the iPhone and Android SDKs that you have installed. If it doesn't, you can point it to where you have them installed. It will also automatically download the Titanium Mobile SDK if you do not already have it installed.

On the following screen (Figure 9–2), fill in the **Name**, **Application ID**, **Directory**, and **Publisher URL** fields. Titanium Developer will create your project in a subdirectory of the directory you choose with the name of the application.

Click the **Test and Package** tab and then the **Launch** button at the base of the screen. If everything is configured correctly, this will build your application and launch it. By default, Titanium will generate an application with two windows that you can tab between.

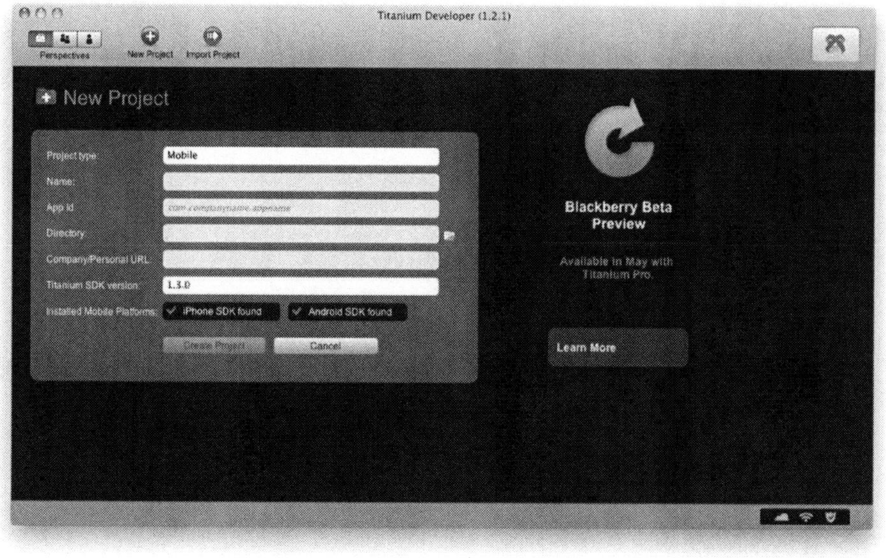

Figure 9–2. *Creating a new project*

Writing Hello World

To change the behavior of the sample application, open and edit the *app.js* file that is found in the Resources directory of your project. Here you will replace the default contents with something simpler shown in Listing 9–1.

Listing 9–1. *Creating a new project*

```
// this sets the background color of the master UIView (when there are no windows/tab
 groups on it)
Titanium.UI.setBackgroundColor('#000');

var win = Titanium.UI.createWindow({backgroundColor:'#fff'});

var myLabel = Titanium.UI.createLabel({
        color:'#999',
        text:'Hello World',
        font:{fontSize:20,fontFamily:'Helvetica Neue'},
        textAlign:'center',
        width:'auto'
});

win.add(myLabel);

win.open({animated:true});
```

Go back to **Test and Package** and click **Launch** again. Figures 9–3 and 9–4 illustrate how Hello World looks on iPhone and Android simulators.

Figure 9–3. *iPhone Hello World*

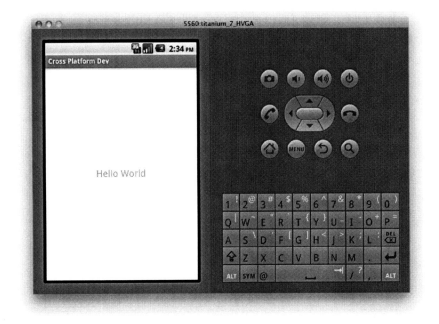

Figure 9–4. *Android Hello World*

Using JavaScript, you create your interface programmatically by creating containers and UI elements as objects and then arranging and connecting them in a hierarchy.

The Titanium API is organized into modules. For example, Titanium.UI is the main UI module responsible for native user-interface components and interaction inside Titanium. Within Titanium.UI you will find classes for Titanium.UI.AlertDialog, Titanium.UI.Button, etc. The iPhone/iPad specific UI capabilities are found within the Titanium.UI.iPhone module and the Android specific UI capabilities are found within the Titanium.UI.Android module.

A complete listing of the modules and classes in the Titanium API are available at the Appcelerator web site. The API is quite extensive. As of version 1.3, it comprises 24 modules with 67 different objects.

Building for Device

The process for building Titanium Mobile applications for iPhone devices is very straightforward. Download your Development Certificate and Provisioning Profile from the Apple iPhone Provisioning Portal. You will need to enter them in the screen titled "Run on Device." Titanium will then build and sign your application, put it into iTunes, and trigger a sync to install it on your device. The only caveat is that you need to do this on a Mac that is configured to sync applications with your iPhone.

Alternately, navigate to the build/iphone subdirectory of your project and open the *.xcodeproj* file. This will launch XCode and you can do **Build and Run**.

Titanium Mobile Device Capabilities

The Titanium platform offers access to a rich collection of native device capabilities including:

- Vibration
- Geolocation & Mapping
- Accelerometer
- Sound
- Photo Gallery (View and Save To)
- Orientation
- Camera. This includes overlays on top of the camera view surface, and Augmented Reality (combines Camera, forward and reverse Geolocation)
- Screenshot
- Shake
- Record Video

- Proximity Events
- Push Notifications

These are all accessed in a platform-independent way using the Titanium SDK from JavaScript. Moreover, the platform also includes wrappers that make it easy to integrate Twitter, Facebook, RSS, and SOAP APIs directly into your application, plus access to sockets, http connections, the native file system, and local database storage.

For complete examples of these device capabilities, please refer to the Titanium Mobile Kitchen Sink Demo (http://github.com/appcelerator/KitchenSink). The Kitchen Sink project (see Figure 9–5) includes a wide variety of the APIs available in Titanium Mobile.

Figure 9–5. *The Kitchen Sink example application*

Camera Example

In this example, you will build a simple full-screen application that will take a picture using the camera. For the iPhone, you will need to test this on a real device as you cannot test taking photos using the simulator.

Create a new Titanium Mobile project and replace the contents of *app.js* with the code shown in Listing 9–2.

Listing 9–2. *Camera example*

```
var tabGroup = Titanium.UI.createTabGroup();
var winMain = Titanium.UI.createWindow({title:'Camera Example', tabBarHidden:true});
var tabMain = Titanium.UI.createTab({title:'', window:winMain});
tabGroup.addTab(tabMain);

var buttonSnap = Titanium.UI.createButton({
title:'Snap',
height:40,
width:145,
top:160,
right:10
});

winMain.rightNavButton=buttonSnap;

buttonSnap.addEventListener('click', function() {
        Titanium.Media.showCamera({

                success:function(event)
                {
                        var cropRect = event.cropRect;
                        var image = event.media;

                        // set image view
                        var imageView = Ti.UI.createImageView({top:0,↵
image:event.media});
                        winMain.add(imageView);
                },
                cancel:function()
                {
                },
                error:function(error)
                {
                        // create alert
                        var a = Titanium.UI.createAlertDialog({title:'Camera'});

                        // set message
                        if (error.code == Titanium.Media.NO_CAMERA)
                        {
                                a.setMessage('Please run this test on device');
                        }
                        else
                        {
                                a.setMessage('Unexpected error: ' + error.code);
                        }

                        // show alert
                        a.show();
                },
                allowImageEditing:true
        });

});

tabGroup.open();
```

In order to get a full-screen window with a Navigation controller at the top, you need to create a tab group and set tabBarHidden to true. Next, you add a button to the right-hand side of navBar and an event handler for the onClick event. This handler brings up the camera, allows you to take a picture, and then creates an image view to see it on the screen (see Figure 9–6). The code for taking the picture is taken from the Kitchen Sink example.

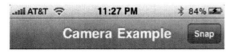

Figure 9–6. *Camera example running on iPhone*

Part **3**

HTML Interfaces

Chapters 10–14 provide examples of how to work with mobile HTML and CSS both with low-level code examples (in Chapters 10 and 14) and diving into three frameworks for creating a native look and feel for iPhone and Android.

Chapter 10

Mobile HTML and CSS

In order to understand how to approach creating HTML and CSS to look and feel like a native mobile interface, we first present common patterns in mobile visual and interaction design as well as highlight specific widgets that are available on different platforms. This chapter also presents specific HTML and CSS code for achieving common effects on WebKit-based browsers. Because, as of this writing, BlackBerry has such severe limitations in browser capabilities, Chapter 14 is dedicated to detailing how to create HTML for the currently available devices. When RIM introduces its new operating systems with a WebKit-based browser, the techniques presented in this chapter may be helpful there as well.

Developers who are new to this approach might wonder why it is relevant to learn about the details of building UI components in HTML and CSS when UI frameworks exist, such as iWebKit, jQTouch, and Sencha Touch, which are presented in the following chapters. There are three key reasons: understanding the fundamentals, size/performance, and branding. First, it is valuable for developers to understand how these frameworks are built in order to use them effectively. All of the frameworks and libraries discussed in this book are open source and in active development. Sometimes the documentation lacks detail and to understand how to achieve desired effects, you need to dive into the source code. Secondly, when you are developing a very simple application, you may not want to absorb the size and performance impact of a full library, in which case the techniques presented in this chapter will help you craft a specific look and feel. Lastly, and most importantly, the trend in visual design for mobile applications is to match the company brand rather than the default look of the operating system. You will likely want to modify the look of any CSS that you work with and before doing so, it is wise to understand the fundamentals.

Platform Overview

This section details what browser is available on each platform and includes a high-level overview of the capabilities and limitations of the platforms.

iOS for iPhone, iPad, iPod Touch

The iOS operating system (for iPhone, iPad, and iPod Touch devices) includes a mobile WebKit-based native browser, which is also available as a UIWebView component that may be embedded in applications. The embedded browser component is as fully featured as the stand-alone browser application. As far as mobile browsers, iOS has one of the most robust browsers with a well-developed CSS3 implementation that allows you to create visual elements that appear like native UI, often without needing to embed graphic images.

The iOS WebKit mobile browser displays web pages in a "view port" of fixed dimensions. You can imagine a view port to be like a window that lets you see into the application. You can touch the window and move what's underneath in and out of view. The browser does this by first rendering the complete web page, then allowing you to move the page up and down under the view port. This is similar to a desktop browser (if you were to ignore the resize control), but the rendering of zooming and panning is much smoother because they are such common operations on the touch devices.

The browser component also offers sophisticated text detection algorithms allowing it to recognize phone numbers, addresses, events, tracking numbers, and e-mail addresses. Other ways to achieve similar functionality would be to add special attributes to the beginning of the href attribute of your link tags (such as mailto: and sms:). The browser will also redirect links to Google Maps and YouTube to their corresponding native applications on the device.

All iPhone devices include a high-resolution touch screen and accelerometer. The new iPhone 4 also adds a gyroscope and retina display, not seen in previous generations. The uniformity of the devices makes it easy to create and test application UI.

Android

The Android operating system also includes a WebKit-based browser and a WebView component, which may be embedded in applications as a fully featured browser component. Android's WebKit-based mobile browser has many of the same features as the iOS mobile browser. It isn't as robust as the Apple implementation and has even less of a CSS2 implementation, but is still a far superior browser when compared to BlackBerry and Windows Mobile.

Such companies as HTC, Motorola, and Google each have devices in the market, most with varying hardware capabilities. This makes it difficult to develop applications that work on Android-based phones. These compatibility issues don't just affect the phone from a hardware perspective; they affect the OS as well. Android is an open source platform that makes it possible for vendors to make changes to the OS. Typically, device vendors create custom branding and a unique design for the main screen of the device, including hardware and software buttons; however, there may be functional changes as well. Common hardware found on most devices include a touch screen, accelerometer, GPS, camera, and wifi.

BlackBerry

Research in Motion (RIM), maker of BlackBerry devices, has announced support for Webkit; however, all currently shipping BlackBerry devices have a proprietary browser with severe limitations (see Chapter 14 for details). There are two browser components found in the OS. The first component has extremely limited HTML and CSS support, and the second has better support for HTML and CSS standards but requires you to use a mouse-like cursor to navigate around the screen even when you are on a non-touch device. Most notably, the browser control that you can embed in your applications does not have an identical feature set to the stand-alone web browser on the device.

BlackBerry has a range of devices with different screen resolutions. The most significant difference between devices is between the track ball and the touch screen. With the BlackBerry Storm, RIM introduced a touch-screen device with soft keyboard. Unfortunately, the low performance of the device and awkward haptics, where the whole screen depresses for click or tap actions, leads to different constraints on different devices when creating applications.

Windows Mobile

Writing applications in HTML and CSS for Windows Mobile is a challenge because it has a browser and browser control that is similar to Internet Explorer 5.5. It can render most basic pages correctly, but has an incomplete implementation of CSS2. Windows Mobile also has a wide variety of devices sold by various hardware vendors, resulting in high device incompatibility. On top of that, some hardware vendors such as HTC have their own proprietary UI for the devices they sell. You can also install third-party UI kit software that will completely change the look on your device, making for an inconsistent user interface.

The Windows Mobile user interface hasn't changed much over the years. There is a button bar on the bottom, which by default has a start menu and a quick launch button. Windows Phone 7 is expected to have a significantly better user experience but, because it is unreleased as of this writing, it is not covered in this book.

Common Patterns

There are common user experience patterns across mobile operating systems, which make a cross-platform approach to implementing the user interface of your application possible.

Screen-Based Approach

The screen-based approach is based on the small form factor of most mobile devices. These small devices have tiny screens, which in turn makes it difficult to display much content at any given time. In the screen-based approach, the application interface is segmented into many views that each have very limited scope. There are several interaction design patterns commonly seen when designing a series of screens to accommodate an interface that doesn't fit in the available screen size:

- *Scroll view:* The simplest approach to accommodating more information than can fit into a single screen is to allow the user to scroll the view, showing only the top portion by default.

- *Scalable view*: Devices with large touch-sensitive screens often use pan and zoom controls to see a large document or view. The pan/zoom approach is most typically seen when displaying a map or a web page.

- *Wizard*: Borrowing a desktop user interface pattern, some mobile applications apply a wizard pattern where the user steps through a series of screens to accomplish a task.

- *Progressive Disclosure*: Often when displaying a large amount of information, it is helpful to divide it by category and sub-categories or even to simply show a list of titles, which lead to the display of an individual item. This generally involves some kind of navigation-based hierarchy system. You will find lists of categories and as you delve into each category you reach a subcategory. As you go into the subcategory, you finally reach your desired content.

Navigation

Because a mobile application typically has many screens, navigational controls are often helpful. Several different approaches to navigation are commonly implemented to help users find different areas of the application. In addition to the navigational paradigms implied by the design pattern details in the Screen-Based previoussection, many devices implement toolbars, tabs, or menus.

Menus

Windows Mobile, BlackBerry, and Android have a standard menu to help their users navigate the application. A menu is a consistent element of every application. These menus usually provide general navigation like "**Home**" or "**Settings**" pages, but also might have actions such as "**Create**" or "**Save**." Menus are typically used like tab bars, in that they include a small number of options for navigation. In many cross-platform iOS-BlackBerry applications, you will see the BlackBerry menu include the same items as the iOS tab bar. Android offers both menu and tab bar, providing flexibility for the application designer.

Tab Bars

Tab bars are found on iOS and Android (see Figures 10–1 and 10–2). These can sit on the top or bottom of the screen. Most platforms also have a maximum number of these that you can show at once. Each tab will hold a fully loaded view for fast context switching. These are generally used to highlight key areas or create segmentation in the application's information architecture.

Figure 10–1. *iOS tab bar*

Figure 10–2. *Android tab bar*

Toolbars

iOS, Android, Blackberry, and Windows Mobile have toolbars (see Figures 10–3 and 10–4). Toolbars sit on the bottom of the screen on iOS and Android, and in custom locations on BlackBerry and Windows Mobile.

Figure 10–3. *iOS toolbar*

Figure 10–4. *Android toolbar*

Navigation Bars

These are similar to toolbars, and usually have navigation-specific items; this can include a title, or left and right navigation buttons (see Figures 10–5 and 10–6). Navigation bars usually sit at the top of the screen.

Figure 10–5. *iOS navigation bar*

Figure 10–6. *Windows Mobile navigation bar*

Button Bars and Context Menus

Like popup menus, in the sense that they can include general navigation, button bars (see Figure 10–7) also can contain screen-specific functions such as "new" or "edit." These bars usually sit on the bottom of the screen like a toolbar.

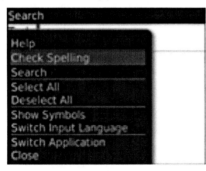

Figure 10–7. *Android button bar*

Blackberry uses context menus (see Figure 10–8)instead of navigation bars to control the flow of the application.

Figure 10–8. *Blackberry context menu*

UI Widgets

UI widgets are native UI controls representing information that is user changeable. They come in many different shapes and colors across each mobile platform. For example, a checkbox and radio button can each be considered a UI widget (See Figure 10–9). They are both standard UI controls that can represent a state that the user selects. The iOS and Android operating systems by far have the most extensive collection of UI widgets compared to the other various platforms.

Figure 10–9. *Check boxes and radio buttons on iOS*

This section of the text will primarily introduce you to the native UIWidgets that can be found in the browser and how to override their functionality to give your application a more consistent native feeling.

Check Boxes

All smartphone mobile platforms provide UI widgets for check boxes to represent boolean or on/off values. All of them have some concept of a check and most have the box that surrounds them. This is the way traditional browsers have implemented checkboxes. Keep in mind here we are talking about native components. To override this functionality in the iOS mobile WebKit browser using CSS, refer to Listing 10–1. This code example assumes you are using a check box image that looks like Figure 10–10. You will need to have an application that implements a UIWebView (refer to Chapter 3).

Listing 10–1. *Checkboxes in CSS3 with WebKit for iOS Look and Feel*

HTML
```
<form action="#">
    <input type="checkbox" name="checkboxiPhone" value="checkboxiPhone" />
</form>
```

CSS

```
form input[type="checkbox"] {
    -WebKit-appearance: none;
    background: url('switch.png') no-repeat center;
    background-position-y: -27px;
    height: 27px;
    width: 94px;
}

form input[type="checkbox"]:checked {
    background-position-y: 0;
}
```

Figure 10–10. *Checkbox image for Listing 10–1*

Listing 10–1 illustrates how to construct an HTML form element that contains a check box. To override the default appearance of the widget you make use of the WebKit CSS3 appearence property. This property can offer default appearences for HTML elements. Setting this property to "none" allows you to remove all default styling of the element. Also, in adding the background image, change its appearence to have a negative offset. This shows the off (or unchecked) version of the element by default. You will also need to set the width to be the width of the image and the height to be only half (on or off). When the check box is checked, now you move the image's y axis to 0 showing the on state of the check box.

Android's implementation of check boxes differs from iOS in that they have offered a more traditional approach (see Figure 10–11). To override this for Android, refer to Listing 10–2 in an Android WebKit browser control.

Figure 10–11. *Check boxes and radio buttons on Android*

Listing 10–2. *Android Check Box Implementation*

```
HTML
<form action="#">
    <input type="checkbox" name="checkboxDroid" value="checkboxDroid" />
</form>
CSS
form input[type="checkbox"] {
    -webkit-appearance: none;
    background: url(btn_check_off.png) no-repeat;
    height: 31px;
    width: 31px;
}
input[type="checkbox"]:checked {
    background: url(btn_check_on.png) no-repeat;
}
```

In this example, you once again have a form that contains an input-type checkbox element. You will need to set -webkit-appearance to "none" and give the element a width and height. In this example, you will simply be switching out the background image to display a checked and unchecked state.

Neither Windows Mobile or BlackBerry devices currently support a CSS3-capable browser. This means there is no way to truly override the default implementation of a check box.

Selection Boxes

iOS and Android platforms both implement a native control for the browser's selection box. Clicking on a select box on either platform will result in a native picker control on iOS (Figure 10–12) and a radio button select modal view on Android (Figure 10–13).

Figure 10–12. *Select box on iOS*

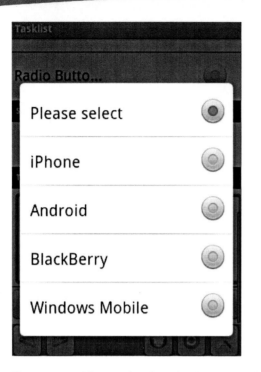

Figure 10–13. *After tapping the select box on Android, will open a list of options for you to select one.*

As previously stated, this functionality is provided for you in the iOS browser control. Any select box the user interacts with will display the selection picker, however, you will still need to style the select box to look more like a native component. By default, this component looks like a standard browser select box (see Listing 10–3).

Listing 10–3. *iOS Select Box Example*

```
HTML
<form action="#">
        <select name="select_box">
            <option selected>Please select</option>
            <option value="apple">iPhone</option>
            <option value="android">Android</option>
            <option value="blackberry">BlackBerry</option>
            <option value="winmo">Windows Mobile</option>
        </select>
</form>

CSS
form select {
  -webkit-appearance: none;
  background: url('select.png') no-repeat right;
  border: 0px;
  width:100%;
  height:40px;
  font-size: medium;
  font-weight: bold;
}
```

In Listing 10–3, you create an HTML form and select box in an iOS mobile WebKit browser. Once again, you will need to override the default appearance using the -webkit-appearance property. Finally, you will add the downward-facing disclosure indicator to the right of the box. This will indicate to the user that this is a select box and something will be happening beneath it. Find an example of the disclosure indicator in Figure 10–14. Android follows a similar pattern, except here we will substitute the background image property for another resource (Refer to Figure 10–15).

Figure 10–14. *iOS downward-facing disclosure indicator*

Figure 10–15. *Android downward-facing disclosure indicator*

Once again, BlackBerry and Windows Mobile do not have this capability and will only show a standard browser select box.

Text Boxes

All smartphone platforms covered in this book have a fairly standard implementation of text boxes. Android, Windows Mobile, and BlackBerry have a label followed by a text box to its right. iOS doesn't use a standard label, but instead employs the HTML5 placeholder attribute of the input type text element. Refer to Figure 10–16 for an example of what this might look like on iOS and Listing 10–4 for an example of using the placeholder attribute in an iOS browser control.

Figure 10–16. *Edit text box on iOS*

Listing 10–4. *HTML Source Code for iOS Placeholder Text Example*

```
<form action="#">
    <input type="text" name=" title" placeholder="Title" />
</form>
```

As shown in Figure 10–17, Android makes use of left-justified labels and right-justified text boxes.

Figure 10–17. *Text Boxes on Android*

Text Areas

Text areas are a standard component between the platforms discussed in this chapter. The biggest difference between them is their background shading and rounded corners on iOS and Android, verses their plan background and square corners on Windows Mobile and Blackberry. iOS has no background shading by default, while Android has a gray gradient; both have rounded corners. You can see an example of an iOS text area in Listing 10–5 and Figure 10–18.

Listing 10–5. *iOS Implementation of a Text Area*

```
HTML
<form action="#">
    <textarea name="thing[text_area]" rows="5" cols="30" >Some great text</textarea>
</form>
CSS
form textarea {
        -webkit-appearance: none;
        border: 1px solid #878787;
        -webkit-border-radius: 8px;
        font-size: medium;
        width:280px;
        line-height:20px;
        background-color:white;
}
```

Figure 10–18. *iOS text area*

In Figure 10–18, you will first remove the default webkit styling applied to the text area. You will then add a one pixel gray border around the outside and make the border radius eight pixels. Set the font size, width, and line-height to the values shown in the example.

Android's implementation is very similar to iOS except that it will have background color. Refer to Listing 10–6 for the implementation and Figure 10–19 for the resulting image.

Listing 10–6. *Android Text Area Implementation*

```
HTML
<form action="#">
            <textarea name="thing[text_area]" rows="5" cols="30" >Some Great↵
 Text</textarea>
</form>
CSS
form textarea {
    -webkit-appearance: none;
    background: -webkit-gradient(linear, left top, left bottom, color-stop(0.0125,↵
#d6d7d6),color-stop(0.25, #efefef),color-stop(0.95, #f7f7f7),color-stop(1.0, #f7f3f7));
    border: 1px solid #d6d7d6;
    -webkit-border-radius: 4px;
    margin: 10px 0 2px 10px;
    font-size: 0.9em;
    padding: 5px 0 2px 2px;
    box-shadow:0 -1px 3px #000000;
}
```

Some Great Text

Figure 10–19. *Android text area*

In Listing 10–6, you will first need to remove the default webkit styling from the text area. Then you will need to add a webkit background gradient and light gray border; the borders are not as round as iOS at four pixels. Apply the default text styling, external margin, and padding, then finish with a slight shadow to give the text area depth.

Radio Buttons

Radio buttons allow you to choose one item in a list of options. BlackBerry and Windows Mobile use a standard radio-button implementation that shows an empty circle when not selected and a filled circle when it has been selected. Android uses the same implementation as BlackBerry and Windows Mobile, but instead of the entire circle being filled, only the center of the circle is filled. iOS has the concept of radio buttons, but Apple suggests using pickers (such as date pickers) instead in their Human Interface Guidelines. If you truly want to use a radio button on iOS, they have a slightly different concept from the other platforms. They choose to use left-bound labels and right-bound check marks to indicate which option has been selected in the list. Refer to Figure 10–20 for an example of an iOS radio button.

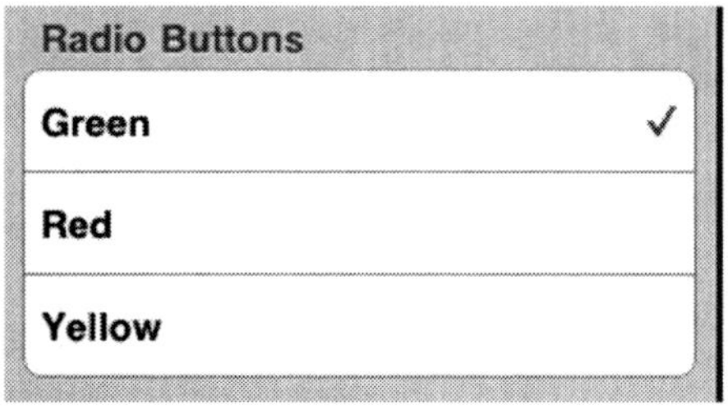

Radio Buttons

Green   ✓

Red

Yellow

Figure 10–20. *iOS radio buttons*

To create this button, you will have to do a couple CSS tricks. Your end goal will be to have the label inside the radio button and the check mark to appear on the right, as shown in Figure 10–20. First, you will need to restyle the radio button by removing its default appearance. By default, you will want the radio button to be unselected. When the radio button has been selected, you will then use the background position attributes to place your background image all the way to the right and 50 percent down the cell. To get the check mark slightly located to the right, you will need to add some transparent right margin to the image. By making the position relative of the radio button, you are able to give it a higher z-index then the label and have it shown above it. You will want the radio button to take up 100 percent of the width and height of the cell so that it is clickable. See Listing 10–7.

Listing 10–7. *iOS Radio Button Implementation*

```
HTML
<form action="#">
    <label for="thing[radio_button]">Radio Button1</label>
    <input type="radio" name="thing[radio_button]" value="radio1"/>
</form>
CSS
form input[type="radio"] {
   -webkit-appearance: none;
   position: relative;
   display:block;
   width:100%;
   height: 40px;
   line-height:40px;
   margin:0;
   -webkit-border-radius: 8px;
}

form input[type="radio"]:checked {
    background: url('radiobutton.png') no-repeat;
    background-position-x: 100%;
    background-position-y: 50%;
}

form label {
    float: left;
    display:block;
    color: black;
    line-height: 40px;
    padding: 0;
```

```
    margin: 0 20px 0 10px;
    width: 40%;
    overflow: hidden;
    text-overflow: ellipsis;
    white-space: nowrap;
    font-weight:bold;
}
```

Creating radio buttons on Android (Figure 10–21 and Listing 10–8)is not that different from Windows Mobile and Blackberry and will use the same HTML as on iOS. The biggest difference is on iOS you can select the entire cell to activate it. On Android, Windows Mobile, and BlackBerry you will only be able to select the radio button itself and not the entire cell. This approach doesn't work very well for touch screen devices.

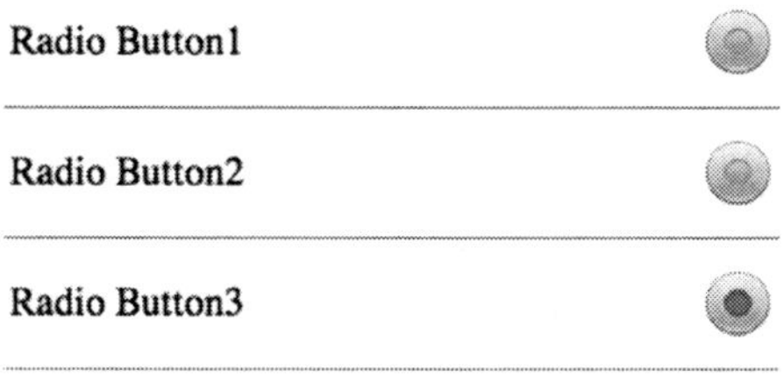

Radio Button1   ◉

Radio Button2   ◉

Radio Button3   ◉

Figure 10–21. *Android radio button implementation*

Listing 10–8. *iOS Radio Button Implementation*

```
HTML
<form action="#">
    <label for="thing[radio_button]">Radio Button1</label>
    <input type="radio" name="thing[radio_button]" value="radio1"/>
</form>
CSS
form input[type="radio"] {
    background: url(btn_radio_off.png) no-repeat right;
    -webkit-appearance: none;
    -webkit-box-sizing: border-box;
    height: 64px;
    width: 32px;
    float:right;
    margin: 0 5px 0 0;
}

form input[type="radio"]:checked {
    background: url(btn_radio_on.png) no-repeat right;
}
```

Additional Components

In addition to the standard HTML form controls, most smartphone platforms have higher-level widgets for date picker and maps; however, you can't add these using pure HTML. They are available in some cross-platform frameworks, which have native code extensions that you would need to hook into.

WebKit Web Views

Web views on iOS and Android OS work very similarly; this is because they both use a WebKit implementation. Try to think of the web view as more of a window on the page. It lets you see any given portion of the page at any moment, while blocking your view of the rest of the page. The WebKit browser engine renders the entire HTML page and places it behind this window. The window stays static while moving the page beneath it. You slide the page up and down beneath this window like a film reel. Understanding how the web view works is important because it makes some CSS implementations a little more difficult. For instance, both Android and iOS browsers do not handle the 'Display: Fixed;' CSS property correctly. This CSS property normally is used to position something statically on the page and allow other content to move behind it, such as a bottom toolbar on a web page. Both browsers will treat this property correctly at first, but then when you move the page beneath the window, the object will move with the page becoming unfixed to its original location. In the case of the bottom toolbar, the toolbar will end up moving up with the page and if your page is long enough, out of the window entirely.

Creating Lists

Lists are an integral part of mobile operating systems. Lists are the primary conduits through which information is segmented. They also allow for hierarchal-based navigation.

When displaying list elements, mobile web UI will typically use an unordered list (<ul>) and list items (<li>), then use CSS to add styling. Listing 10–9 shows how to create a list with disclosure indicators. See Figure 10–22 for how it looks when the HTML is rendered. Note that this approach will work on iOS, Android, and Windows Mobile (although this specific code has not been compatibility-tested across all of the mobile web browsers). With BlackBerry, it is often easiest to implement table-based layout.

Listing 10–9. *Implementation of List with Disclosure Indicators*

```
<!DOCTYPE html SYSTEM "http://www.w3.org/TR/xhtml1/DTD/xhtml1-transitional.dtd">
<html xmlns="http://www.w3.org/1999/xhtml">
    <head>
        <title>HTML LIST</title>
        <style type="text/css">

            body {
                margin: 0;
            }

            .list {
                border-top: 1px solid #ccc;
            }

            .list ul {
                padding: 0;
                margin: 0;
            }
```

```
            .list li {
                width: 100%;
                height: 75px;
                list-style-type: none;
                }

            .list a {
                display: block;
                text-decoration: none;
                color: #000;
                font-size: 20px;
                height: 100%;
                width: 100%;
                background-color: #eef;
            }

            .list a:active {
                background-color: #cce;
                border-bottom: 1px solid #fff;
                border-top: 1px solid #ccc;
            }

            ul.simple_disclosure_list li {
                border-bottom: 1px solid #ccc;
                border-top: 1px solid #fff;
            }

            ul.simple_disclosure_list li a {
                background-image: url(arrow.png);
                background-repeat: no-repeat;
                background-position: center right;
            }

            ul.simple_disclosure_list li a span.title {
                margin-left: 30px;
                font-weight: bold;
                float: left;
                position: relative;
                top: 40%;
                }
        </style>
    </head>
    <body>
        <div class="list">
            <ul class="simple_disclosure_list">
                <li>
                    <a href="#">
                        <span class="title">Title 1</span>

                    </a>
                </li>
                <li>
                    <a href="#">
                        <span class="title">Title 2</span>

                    </a>
                </li>
```

```
        <li>
            <a href="#">
                <span class="title">Title 3</span>

            </a>
        </li>
    </ul>
</div>

    </body>
</html>
```

Title 1	>
Title 2	>
Title 3	>

Figure 10–22. *Implementation of progressive disclosure*

Building a Navigation Bar

Navigation bars can be found on iOS, Android, and Windows Mobile devices. On iOS and Windows Mobile, a bar is represented by a bar that sits on the top of the page. On Android, a navigation bar is more like a button bar that sits on the bottom of the page. Android's version of a navigation bar is a little more difficult to construct. Earlier, we explained how a web view works on Android and iOS. This is especially important in this case because it will make it a lot more difficult to construct a proper navigation bar on Android. As we explained earlier, the display fixed property doesn't work for attaching the bottom bar to the page. How do you get around this? There are a couple of options and none of them are preferable. Firstly, you could wait for the Android development team to release an update to address this issue. Secondly, you could create a floating toolbar that works similarly to Android's but moves with the page. Neither of these options are ideal. Some developers have created their own scrolling implementation to work around this issue. In particular, the iScroll library from Cubiq (http://cubiq.org/iscroll) provides the capability to allow scrolling and position a toolbar or other widgets at the bottom of the screen.

Listing 10–10 and Figure 10–23 has an implementation of a very basic navigation bar; however, this can be modeled into a replica of the iOS implementation of its navigation bar, if given the proper resources and CSS3 attributes.

Listing 10–10. *Simple Implementation of the iOS Navigation Bar*

```
<!DOCTYPE html SYSTEM "http://www.w3.org/TR/xhtml1/DTD/xhtml1-transitional.dtd">
<html xmlns="http://www.w3.org/1999/xhtml">
    <head>
        <title>Navigation Bar</title>
        <style type="text/css">
            body {
                margin: 0;
            }

            div#navbar {
                height: 40px;
                line-height:40px;
                background-color:gray;
            }

            div#navbar div {
                margin: 0 10px 0 10px;
            }

            div#navbar div a {
                text-decoration:none;
                color:black;
            }

            div#navbar div#navLeft {
                float: left;
            }

            div#navbar div#navRight {
                float:right;
            }

            div#navbar div#navTitle {
                width: 100%;
                height: inherit;
                position: absolute;
                text-align:center;
                margin: 0;
            }

        </style>
    </head>
    <body>
        <div id="navbar">
            <div id="navLeft"><a href="#">Back</a></div>
            <div id="navTitle">Nav Bar</div>
            <div id="navRight"><a href="#">Home</a></div>
        </div>
    </body>
</html>
```

Back	Nav Bar	Home

Figure 10–23. *Simple implementation of the iOS navigation bar*

Listing 10–11 is a simple replica of an Android-like button bar. In this case, we use a table so that when buttons are added or removed, the table takes care of the sizing of its elements. The result is shown in Figure 10–24.

Listing 10–11. *Simple Implementation of the Android Button Bar.*

```
<!DOCTYPE html SYSTEM "http://www.w3.org/TR/xhtml1/DTD/xhtml1-transitional.dtd">
<html xmlns="http://www.w3.org/1999/xhtml">
    <head>
        <title>Navigation Bar</title>
        <style type="text/css">
            body {
                margin: 0;
            }

            div#navbar {
                height: 40px;
                width: 100%;
                line-height:40px;
                background-color:gray;

        display: table;

            }

            div#navbar div {
                display: table-cell;
                text-align:center;
                border: 1px solid blue;
            }

            div#navbar div.row {
                display: table-row;
                margin:0;
                padding: 0;
            }

            div#navbar div a {
                text-decoration:none;
                color:black;
            }

        </style>
    </head>
    <body>
        <div id="navbar">
            <div class="row">
                <div id="navLeft"><a href="#">Back</a></div>
                <div id="navTitle">Nav Bar</div>
                <div id="navRight"><a href="#">Home</a></div>
            </div>
        </div>
    </body>
</html>
```

Figure 10–24. *Simple Android button bar*

iWebKit

The iWebKit framework allows you to create HTML that matches the look and feel of native iPhone applications. As the name implies, iWebKit is customized for browsers based on the open source WebKit engine, specifically iPhone's mobile Safari browser. The iWebKit framework was developed in accordance with the Apple Human Interface Guidelines, outlining application look and feel on the popular iPhone OS.

iWebKit was originally developed to optimize web sites for viewing on a mobile device.[1] However, in mobile applications that use HTML in a web browser control (WebUI view) for some or all of its application interface, it is practical to utilize toolkits originally developed for web UI, including iWebKit. iWebKit can be easily integrated into iPhone applications developed in Objective-C, as well as the iPhone versions of applications developed using the Rhodes and PhoneGap frameworks.

As discussed previously, all of these platforms allow you to produce native iPhone applications that can be distributed through the iTunes App Store. However, WebUIView-based applications do not match the look and feel of native iPhone interfaces. iWebKit provides a quick and easy way to apply styles designed to match native interface design to your user interface.

iWebKit is easy to use: anyone familiar with HTML and CSS can use the framework to quickly create forms, hierarchical lists, and more, all integrated into a light and fast application. iWebKit takes advantage of properties new in CSS3 supported in the mobile Safari browser, such as background gradients, forms, and border properties–including rounded corners that don't require the clunky use of image files.

This chapter provides an overview of the features available in iWebKit and concludes with several examples that illustrate how to integrate iWebKit in each of the cross-platform development environments discussed in this book.

---

[1] Complete documentation for using iWebKit in mobile web sites is available at
http://iwebkit.net.

Working With the iWebKit Framework

The iWebKit framework includes a comprehensive set of stylesheets, icons, javascript, and a test index page that serves as a basic template for any views you may need to add to your application.

You can download iWebKit from the project web site at `http://iwebkit.net/downloads`.[2] In addition to the framework itself, the download includes a demo directory containing samples for all of the features described in this chapter. You can view the demo by opening `index.html` in a WebKit browser (such as Safari or Chrome), then resizing the window so it fits the content. An example later in this chapter shows you how to create a native application from the demo, but if you just can't wait to see what the demo looks like on your iPhone, visit `http://demo.iwebkit.net` from your mobile browser.

Pages that integrate the iWebKit framework are standard HTML pages that include CSS and JavaScript. However, some elements of the page structure will vary depending on which iWebKit elements you opt to use. The sample code in Listing 11–1 illustrates the type of document structure you may expect to see in an application that has integrated iWebKit.

Listing 11–1. *iWebKit Document Structure*

```
<!DOCTYPE html PUBLIC "-//W3C//DTD XHTML 1.0 Strict//EN"
 "http://www.w3.org/TR/xhtml1/DTD/xhtml1-strict.dtd">
<html xmlns="http://www.w3.org/1999/xhtml">
<head>
<meta content="minimum-scale=1.0, width=device-width, maximum-scale=0.6667,
 user-scalable=no" name="viewport" />
<link href="css/style.css" rel="stylesheet" media="screen" type="text/css" />
<script src="javascript/functions.js" type="text/javascript"></script>
<title>Demo App</title>
</head>
<body class="list">
<div id="topbar">
                <div id="title">Demo App</div>
                <div id="bluerightbutton">
                        <a href="#" class="noeffect">New</a>
                </div>
        </div>
<div class="searchbox">
        <form action="" method="get">
        <fieldset>
                <input id="search" placeholder="search" type="text" />
                <input id="submit" type="hidden" />
        </fieldset>
        </form>
</div>
<div id="content">
```

---

[2] The current version at the time of this writing is iWebKit 5.04.

```
        <ul>
            <li class="title">Task Categories</li>
            <li><a class="noeffect" href="#"><span class="name">Work</span><span↵
class="arrow"></span></a></li>
            <li><a class="noeffect" href="#"><span class="name">School</span><span↵
class="arrow"></span></a></li>
            <li><a class="noeffect" href="#"><span class="name">Home</span><span↵
class="arrow"></span></a></li>
        </ul>
</div>
</body>
</html>
```

Figure 11–1. *iWebKit application*

A Few Words of Caution

When using iWebKit, in most cases, your HTML must match the structure found in the following examples in order to achieve the desired appearance in your application. This means that you will typically need to edit existing HTML to create the look that you want. This is in stark contrast with the approach you would likely take if you were creating your own CSS for your HTML application. Unless the discussion surrounding one of the following code examples refers to a tag or applied style as optional, the following code samples reflect the structure that is required.

Also, note that iWebKit uses compressed style sheets and JavaScript files to increase the load speed of the application, which means that the files included in your application will be hard to read and understand. However, the iWebKit download also contains human-readable stylesheets and JavaScript files for debugging and understanding how it works under the covers.

Required Header

Assuming the iWebKit framework has been included in your project's resources directory, you need to include links to the files inside your HTML <head> section of your default HTML document (Listing 11–2).

Listing 11–2. *Required iWebKit Header Links*

```
<head>
<link href="css/style.css" rel="stylesheet" type="text/css" />
<script src="javascript/functions.js" type="text/javascript"></script>
</head>
```

Body

The <body> of an iWebKit document includes a <div> tag styled with the topbar class, followed by a <div> tag styled with the content class. The topbar contains title and navigation information at the top of the screen, while the content section contains your application's lists, forms, and custom screens. Several other styles are available for <div> tags that are children of the <body> tag: searchbox, duobutton, tributton, and footer.

To include a searchbox on your page like the one that follows, add an iWebKit form containing a div styled with the searchbox class as a child of the <body> tag. As an example, you can see a text field formatted to resemble the native iPhone search box in the example form code in Listing 11–1.

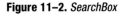

Figure 11–2. *SearchBox*

If you are retrofitting an existing application with iWebKit, or if you are using a cross-platform framework to generate your application HTML, you will need to manually modify your HTML to include the appropriate classes on container tags. In the Rhodes framework, which stores repeated code in a layout, you will need to move the <body> tag into the page since iWebKit typically requires different classes for different <body> tags. Alternately, you could include a JavaScript function that will place the class on the <body> when the page is rendered.

Organizing Data with Lists

Lists are one of the most frequently used components in iPhone applications, as they provide a simple way to layout various types of information, and can optionally provide hierarchical organization to allow for sub-lists and navigation. iWebKit provides several different formatting options for lists in your application. You can choose to style your list using the classic style, with support for images and comments; a list in the classic iTunes style, containing album covers, artist, title, and rating information; an App Store list with ratings and prices; an iTunes style list with ratings and album covers; an iPod/music list that shows a numbered list of songs with times.

In iWebKit forms, as with a lot of mobile web UI, `<ul>` and `<li>` tags are used quite differently than you would typically see on the Web. When considering the small amount of screen real estate available on a mobile device, it makes sense that a single column would take up the entire width of the screen. For this reason, it makes sense to use unordered lists to vertically organize your content instead of divs and other containers.

Additionally, in order to utilize the custom iWebKit list styles, you need to ensure that you have properly declared the list type in the required location. Most list classes require you to apply a class to the `<body>` tag or the `<ul>` tag, and some list items require styles as well. You can see an overview of available list types and corresponding body classes in Table 11–1.

Use the following code samples as your guide to make sure you've got all the right classes in all the right locations.

Table 11–1. *iWebKit List Types and <body> Tag Class*

List Type	Body Class	Example
Classic	`list`	List Group / List Item > / List Item With Image Comment >
App Store	`applist`	List Group / List Item > / List Item With Image Comment >
iTunes Music	`musiclist`	List Group / List Item > / List Item With Image Comment >

List Type	Body Class	Example
iTunes Classic	n/a	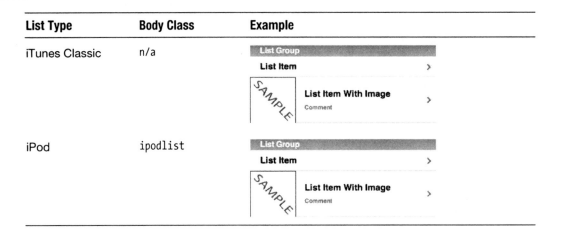
iPod	ipodlist	

Classic Lists

There are two main ways to format content in a Classic list:

- *Simple format*: list items without a class display text (Figure 11–3 and Listing 11–3)

- *Pretty format*: list items with the withimage class include an image, main text and comment text (Figure 11–4 and Listing 11–4)

In addition to the simple and pretty formatting available for content cells, you can include one or more *Title* cells in a list to logically group the items in your list. For example, in a corporate directory application, you may wish to display employees grouped by their department. Each department would then have a Title cell at the top of the group and employees in that department would be listed alphabetically below. All of these options require you to use unordered lists <ul> and list item <li> tags inside your document's content <div> tag.

Technically, it is possible to mix-and-match all three types of list items within a list; however, mixing different types of list items would create a non-standard UI and could negatively affect usability, as it will impede the user's ability to visually parse the data contained in the list. However, if your use case requires items to be displayed with multiple formatting types on the same page, you should consider using a Title cell to separate your list into groups.

Figure 11–3. *Classic list—simple Format*

Listing 11–3. *Classic List—Simple Format*

```
<body class="list">
<div id="content">
        <ul>
                <li class="title">Title Bar</li>
                <li><a class="noeffect" href="#">
                        <span class="name">List Item</span>
                        <span class="arrow"></span></a>
                </li>
                <li><a class="noeffect" href="#">
                        <span class="name">List Item</span>
                        <span class="arrow"></span></a>
                </li>

                <li><a class="noeffect" href="#">
                        <span class="name">List Item</span>
                        <span class="arrow"></span></a>
                </li>
        </ul>
</div>
</body>
```

Figure 11–4. *Classic list—pretty format*

Listing 11–4. *Classic Lists with Images in iWebkit*

```
<body class="list">
<div id="content">
        <ul>
                <li class="title">Title Bar</li>
                <li class="withimage">
                                <a class="noeffect" href="#">
                                        <img alt="Sample" src="sample_image-1.jpg" />
                                        <span class="name">List Item with Image</span>
                                        <span class="comment">Comment</span>
                                        <span class="arrow"></span>
                                </a>
                </li>
                <li class="withimage">
                                <a class="noeffect" href="#">
                                        <img alt="Sample" src="sample_image-1.jpg" />
                                        <span class="name">List Item with Image</span>
                                        <span class="comment">Comment</span>
```

```
                                                <span class="arrow"></span>
                                </a>
                </li>
                <li class="withimage">
                                <a class="noeffect" href="#">
                                                <img alt="Sample" src="sample_image-1.jpg" />
                                                <span class="name">List Item with Image</span>
                                                <span class="comment">Comment</span>
                                                <span class="arrow"></span>
                                </a>
                </li>

        </ul>
</div>
</body>
```

iTunes Classic Style Lists

iTunes Classic-style lists are like classic lists, except in a iTunes Classic-style list, the list item doesn't expand to the full width of the screen. Additionally, the top and bottom cells in each iTunes Classic-style list will have rounded corners.

Figure 11–5. *iTunes classic-style list with title and sample list item*

To include any of the options available to the cells in an App-store style list, simply add a <span> tag styled with the appropriate class inside the list item's <a> tag (Listing 11–5).

Listing 11–5. *Store List Item*

```
<li>
        <a class="noeffect" href="#">
                <span class="image" style="background-image:↵
                url(/public/img.jpg)"></span>
                <span class="comment">This is a Comment</span>
                <span class="name">Cell Title</span>
                <span class="stars4"></span>
                <span class="starcomment">100 Ratings</span>
                <span class="arrow"></span>
                <span class="price">$1.99</span>
        </a>
</li>
```

You can also display a title above your store list by including a <span> tag styled with the graytitle class immediately above the <ul class="pageitem"> tag.

Although the iTunes Classic-style list type does not require a class to be added to the <body> tag, you must include a pageitem class on the <ul> tag, as shown in Listing 11–6.

Listing 11–6. *Store List Example*

```
<body>
<div id="content">
<span class="graytitle">Store lists</span>
<ul class="pageitem">
        <li class="store">
                <a class="noeffect" href="#">
                        <span class="image" style="background-image:↵
 url('images/sample.png')"></span>
                        <span class="comment">Comment</span>
                        <span class="name">Sample Title</span>
                        <span class="stars5"></span>
                        <span class="starcomment">151 Ratings</span>
                        <span class="arrow"></span>
                </a>
        </li>
</ul>
</div>
</body>
```

App Store-style Lists

App Store-style lists support background images, star rating comments, the number of ratings, and price of the product.

Figure 11–6. *App store list items*

App Store-style lists also optionally include inline ads at the top of the lists. To include ads at the top of the list, create a list item styled with the doublead class. Each doublead list item has space for two ad links. Note that the ads are fixed in width and height, will not resize if only a single ad is included, and the topmost list item may make the page feel unbalanced.

To include background images for your links, simply apply an inline style to the <a> tag. Listing 11–7 illustrates how to create the top ad element for an App Store-style list.

Listing 11–7. *Double Ad Link*

```
<ul>
        <li id="doublead">
                <a href="http://iwebkit.mobi" style="background-image: ⏎
                    url('pics/ad1.png')"></a>
                <a href="http://iwebkit.mobi" style="background-image: ⏎
                    url('pics/ad2.png')"></a>
        </li>
</ul>
```

App Store-style list items are structured in the same way as regular Store-list style items. See Listing 11–8 for a stand-alone example.

Listing 11–8. *App Store Style List Example*

```
<body class="applist">
<div id="content">
        <ul>
                <li id="doublead">
        <a href="http://iwebkit.mobi" style="background-image: url('pics/ad1.png')"></a>
        <a href="http://iwebkit.mobi" style="background-image: url('pics/ad2.png')"></a>
                </li>
                <li>
                <a class="noeffect" href="http://itunes.apple.com/us/app/⏎
bejeweled-2/id284832142?mt=8">
                        <span class="image" style="background-image: ⏎
 url('/images/bejeweled.jpg')"></span>
                        <span class="comment">Games</span>
                        <span class="name">Bejeweled 2</span>
                        <span class="stars5"></span>
                        <span class="starcomment">16924 Ratings</span>
                        <span class="arrow"></span><span class="price">$2.99</span>
                </a>
                </li>
                <li>
                <a class="noeffect" href="#">
                        <span class="image" style="background-image: ⏎
 url('images/sample.png')"></span>
                        <span class="comment">Comment</span>
                        <span class="name">Sample Title</span>
                        <span class="stars5"></span>
                        <span class="starcomment">151 Ratings</span>
                        <span class="arrow"></span>
                </a>
                </li>
        </ul>
</div>
</body>
```

iTunes style-lists

iTunes-style lists are simple lists that can display a number, title, and time comment. The background of the cells in this class alternate between light and dark gray (see Figure 11–7 and Listing 11–9).

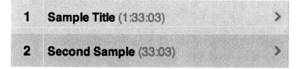

Figure 11–7. *iTunes-style list with alternating table cells*

Listing 11–9. *iTunes List Item Example*

```
<body class="musiclist">
<div id="content">
<ul>
        <li>
                <a class="noeffect" href="#">
                <span class="number">1</span>
                <span class="name">Sample Title</span>
                <span class="time">(1:33:03)</span>
                <span class="arrow"></span></a>
        </li>
        <li>
                <a class="noeffect" href="#">
                <span class="number">1</span>
                <span class="name">Second Sample</span>
                <span class="time">(33:03)</span>
                <span class="arrow"></span></a>
        </li>
</ul>
</div>
</body>
```

iPod-style lists

iPod-style lists use the same basic structure as the other lists, but are designed with play icons to visually indicate when music is playing (Figure 11–8).

Figure 11–8. *iPod list selected and non-selected cell*

To play music using an iPod list, each list item should contain a link to a JavaScript call that plays the music and toggles the pause/play icon.[3]

To include an iPod-style list, the <body> tag must be styled with the ipodlist class.

As with the iTunes-style lists, you are responsible for defining the track numbers for the items in your list within the <span class="number"> tag. Track numbers can be generated dynamically with JavaScript, or you can hard-code the desired value inside the <span class="number">.

Additionally, each list item must have a child that includes a <span> tag styled with the auto class (see Listing 11–10). This container serves as a placeholder for the location where the play button will be displayed when the user selects the cell.

Listing 11–10. *iWebKit iPod List Example*

```
<body class="ipodlist">
<div id="content">
<ul>
        <li>
                <a class="noeffect" href="javascript:document.sample.Play();">
                        <span class="number">1</span>
                        <span class="auto"></span>
                        <span class="name">Sample Song</span>
                        <span class="time">4:11</span>
                </a>
        </li>
</ul>
</div>
</body>
```

Navigation

Since most applications include more than just a single view, you'll most likely want to include a navigation bar in your iWebKit application (Figure 11–9). To add the navigation bar, include a div tag with the topbar class as a child of the <body> tag.

Figure 11–9. *Sample Navigation Bar*

You can embed up to three <div> tags in the topbar that allow users to navigate through your application. Most applications include the page title and an element that allows the user to move left/backward. It is less common to see elements that allow the user to move forward, as forward navigation is typically accomplished by interacting with a list item or other page content.

---

[3] iWebKit's default JavaScript does not include functions to play streaming music. You need to include your own custom JavaScript. However, the demo does include a sample JavaScript that implements some of this functionality for you to use as a guide.

Standard UI conventions dictate the home button should be located on the left side of the top bar.

Table 11–2. *iWebKit Top Bar Navigation Elements*

Element		Sample Code
Title		`<div id="title">This is a Title</div>`

Home Button		`<div id="leftnav">`
		   `<a href="index.html"><img alt="home" src="images/home.png" /></a>`
		`</div>`

Left Navigation		`<div id="leftnav"><a href="#">Left Nav Button</a></div>`
Right Navigation		`<div id="rightnav"><a href="#">Right Nav Button</a></div>`
Left Button		`<div id="leftbutton"><a href="#">Left Button</a></div>`
Right Button		`<div id="rightbutton"><a href="#">Right Button</a></div>`
Blue Button – Right		`<div id="bluerightbutton"><a href="#" class="noeffect">Blue Right Button</a> </div>`
Blue Button – Left		`<div id="blueleftbutton"><a href="#" class="noeffect">Blue Left Button</a> </div>`

Forms

Forms can be styled using page items that group your form elements together. Use a standard `<form>` and `<fieldset>` tags to create the form, as shown in Figure 11–10 and Listing 11–11.

Figure 11–10. *The iWebKit 5 Demo Application*

Listing 11–11. *Example iWebKit Form*

```
<!DOCTYPE html PUBLIC "-//W3C//DTD XHTML 1.0 Strict//EN"↵
 "http://www.w3.org/TR/xhtml1/DTD/xhtml1-strict.dtd">
<html xmlns="http://www.w3.org/1999/xhtml">
<head>
<meta content="minimum-scale=1.0, width=device-width, maximum-scale=0.6667,↵
 user-scalable=no" name="viewport" />
<link href="css/style.css" rel="stylesheet" media="screen" type="text/css" />
<script src="javascript/functions.js" type="text/javascript"></script>
<title>iWebKit Demo - Easy form elements!</title>
</head>
<body>
<div id="topbar">
                <div id="title">iWebKit 5 Demo</div>
</div>
<div class="searchbox">
        <form action="" method="get">
                <fieldset>
                                        <input id="search" placeholder="search"↵
 type="text" />
                                <input id="submit" type="hidden" />
```

```
                                    </fieldset>
            </form>
</div>
<div id="content">
        <form method="post">

                <fieldset>
                <ul class="pageitem">
                        <li class="bigfield"><input placeholder="Username" type="text"↵
/></li>
                        <li class="bigfield"><input placeholder="Password"↵
type="password" /></li>
                </ul>
                <ul class="pageitem">
                        <li class="textbox">
                                <span class="header">Insert text</span>
                                <textarea name="TextArea" rows="4"></textarea>
                        </li>
                </ul>
                </fieldset>
        </form>
</div>
</body>
</html>
```

iWebKit provides pre-styled login fields, input fields for names and telephone numbers, radio buttons, selection boxes, text area, and input buttons. A list of the interface components and code required to include those items in your view can be found in Table 11–3.

Table 11–3. *List Item Classes[4]*

List Item Class		Description
Bigfield	`<input type="text">`	**Big Field Example** Big Field Creates a text field spanning the entire available horizontal width, often used for Username and Password fields.
smallfield	`<input type="text">` `<input type="tel">`	**Narrow Field Example with text and telephone input fields** **Title** — enter text **Phone number** — Telephone Dial Pad Small fields or narrow fields display labels inside the field. The input field takes up half the width of the cell and is right justified.

---

[4] Note: `<input type="tel">` is a custom field on the iPhone that displays a popup dial pad when selected.

List Item Class		Description
checkbox	`<input type="checkbox">`	On the iPhone, check Boxes look like On/Off switches.
		The labels are left-justified and the "On/Off switch" is right-justified.
radiobutton	`<input type="radio">`	
		Radio Buttons fields have a label. When clicked, they create a custom checkmark that is right-justified.
Select	`<select>`	
		Selection Boxes have a left-justified label with a right-justified down arrow. When clicked, they reveal an iPhone UIselection box.

List Item Class		Description
Textbox	`<input>`	 Creates a textbox that takes up the majority of the vertical and horizontal space on the screen. Apply to HTML form input element.

In forms, as with a lot of mobile web UIs, you use `<ul>` and `<li>` tags quite differently than you would typically see on the Web. To create a group, create an unordered list styled with the pageitem class. To embed form elements in the group, wrap each item in a list item tag styled with the appropriate class as shown in Listing 11–12.

Listing 11–12. *iWebKit Example Form*

```
<form method="post">
        <fieldset>
                <ul class="pageitem">
                        <li class="bigfield"><input placeholder="Big Field" type=↩
"text" /></li>
<li class="smallfield"><input placeholder="enter text" type="text" /></li>
                        <li class="checkbox">
                                <span class="name">Title</span>
                                <input name="Checkbox Name" type="checkbox" />
                        </li>

                </ul>
        </fieldset>
</form>
```

Labeling Field Sets

Add labels to your field sets by adding a `<span class="graytitle">` tag as the first child of the `<fieldset>` tag (Listing 11–13).

Listing 11–13. *Fieldset Title Example*

```
<form method="post">
        <fieldset>
                <span class="graytitle">Fieldset Title</span>
        </fieldset>
</form>
```

Fieldset Title

Figure 11–11. *iWebKit fieldset title example*

Landscape Mode

iWebKit also offers landscape and portrait modes for all screens. As the orientation of the device changes, the onscreen layout of the elements adapts to the new orientation.

Note that while the layout modification is handled by iWebKit's CSS, the UIWebView is responsible for managing the rotation of content contained within. In order to prevent rotation from occurring, you will need to modify your view programatically in Xcode.

Phone Integration

iWebKit offers several simple ways to trigger device functionality and launch other applications. Table 11–4 shows how to format links so the associated application launches on the device when a user follows the link.

Table 11–4. *Integrating with iPhone Functionality*

Application	Link to...	Url Format
New email	`mailto:[emailaddress]`	`<a class="noeffect" href="mailto:example@example.com">`
iTunes Store	URL for item in the iTunes store	`<a class="noeffect" href="http://itunes.apple.com/us/album/the-e-n-d-the-energy-never-dies/id318390146"/>`
Appstore	URL for item in the Appstore	`<a class="noeffect" href="http://www.itunes.com/app/CameraBag"/>`
SMS	`sms:[phonenumber]`	`<a class="noeffect" href="sms:12125551212"/>`
Phone Launches a dialogue that asks if you would like to call the number provided	`tel:[phonenumber]`	`<a class="noeffect" href="tel:408-555-5555"/>`
Youtube	URL for a YouTube video	`<a class="noeffect" href="http://www.youtube.com/watch?v=DWmQEvOoF08"/>`
Google Maps	GoogleMaps query url, e.g. http://maps.google.com?q=New+York,+NY	`<a class="noeffect" href="http://maps.google.com?q=New+York,+NY"/>`

If you're familiar with the GoogleMaps API, you may wish to note that there is no need to include an API key in your request.

Integrating iWebKit in Mobile Applications

In this section, you'll see how to integrate iWebKit into your UIWebView-based mobile applications to match what users expect to see in an iPhone application. The following sections walk you through integrating iWebKit in applications built in Xcode using Objective-C, as well as applications built using the Rhodes and PhoneGap frameworks. These examples build on the foundation provided in earlier chapters, so if it's been awhile, take a minute to refresh your memory before continuing on.

Creating a Native iPhone Application with iWebKit in Objective C

Use the instructions in Chapter 2 to create a new native UIWebView-based application.

To include iWebKit in an application, you need to place a copy of the iWebKit framework in your iPhone project directory. In this example, you will build an app using the iWebKit feature demo.

In the root directory of the iWebKit Framework you downloaded earlier, find the folder entitled *Demo*. Drag the contents of the Demo folder into the *Resource* folder in Xcode. A dialogue box should prompt you for import handling of these files into your project: check the **Copy items into destination group's folder (if needed)** check box, and select **Create Folder References for any added folders**. The **Create Folder References** option will preserve your directory structure in Xcode and on the device, as opposed to the soft folders Xcode normally uses that do not preserve your directory structure.

The **Xcode groups** option creates groups to help you organize your files during development. Note, though, that groups do not translate to directories when building: in your compiled application, all files will be found at the root level.

Verify your prompt looks like Figure 11–12 and click the **Add** button to continue.

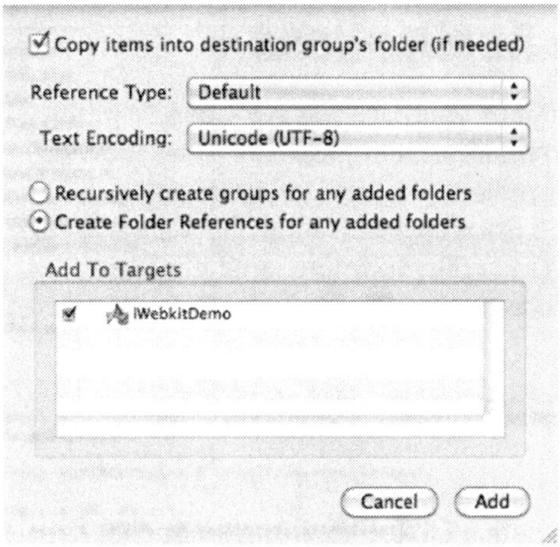

Figure 11–12. *Xcode file copy prompt*

Then, to test-drive all the functionality available in iWebKit, implement the code from Listing 11–14 in your viewDidLoad method.

Listing 11–14. *viewDidLoad Method*

```
- (void)viewDidLoad {

    // String representation of the URL
    NSString *urlAddress = [[NSBundle mainBundle] pathForResource:@"index"↵
ofType:@"html"];

    //Create an URL object.
    NSURL *url = [NSURL fileURLWithPath:urlAddress];

    //URL Request Object
    NSURLRequest *requestObj = [NSURLRequest requestWithURL:url];

    //Load the request in the UIWebView.
    [webView loadRequest:requestObj];
}
```

Follow the instructions in Chapter 2 to build and test your application shown in Figure 11–13.

Figure 11–13. *iWebkit demo in UIWebViewSetting up Rhodes for iWebKit*

Create an Application

Setting up Rhodes to use iWebKit is a simple process. The first thing you will need to do is generate an application (Listing 11–15).

Listing 11–15. *viewDidLoad Method*

```
> rhogen app iWebKit

Generating with app generator:
    [ADDED]   iWebKit/rhoconfig.txt
    [ADDED]   iWebKit/build.yml
    [ADDED]   iWebKit/app/application.rb
    [ADDED]   iWebKit/app/index.erb
    [ADDED]   iWebKit/app/layout.erb
    [ADDED]   iWebKit/app/loading.html
    [ADDED]   iWebKit/Rakefile
    [ADDED]   iWebKit/app/helpers
    [ADDED]   iWebKit/icon
    [ADDED]   iWebKit/app/Settings
    [ADDED]   iWebKit/public
```

Rhodes generates default CSS, JavaScript and HTML. Although you can delete the default Rhodes CSS, make sure to leave the JavaScript intact. Some features depend on the included JavaScript to function.

Copy the *Framework* folder from the iWebKit root directory to the public directory of your Rhodes application. If you wish, you can rename the *Framework* folder to "iWebKit" or something that compliments your workflow. The *Framework* folder will contain everything you need to build an application.

Add iWebKit Framework to Application Layout Template

iWebKit/app/layout.erb contains the basic header and layout for your application. This file will contain references to all the CSS files for each target device. To guarantee the Framework works as intended, you will need to remove all global references to the autogenerated stylesheets from the header of your application.

Additionally, in the header, you will see a series of conditional statements. These statements define which HTML, CSS and JavaScript files are loaded at runtime. In this case, you should modify the "APPLE" stanza to match Listing 11–16.

Listing 11–16. *iWebKit Layout.erb*

```
<% if System::get_property('platform') == 'APPLE' %>
  <meta name="viewport" content="width=device-width; initial-scale=1.0;↵
 maximum-scale=1.0; user-scalable=0;"/>

  <!-- iWebkit CSS and JavaScript -->
  <link href="/public/Framework/css/style.css" rel="stylesheet" media="screen"↵
type="text/css" />
  <script src="/public/Framework/javascript/functions.js"↵
type="text/javascript"></script>

  <!-- Rhodes JavaScript -->
  <script src="/public/js/jquery-1.2.6.min.js"></script>
  <script src="/public/js/rho.js"></script>
  <script src="/public/js/application.js"></script>
<% end %>
```

iWebkit expects its resources to be in the /images folder. However, in this scenario iWebkit will be unable to find them in their default locations. To resolve this issue, you should update the path to any resources referenced in the iWebKit CSS.

Build an application as you normally would, using the Rhodes generators. Refer to the previous code examples to drop iWebKit components into your application.

The autogenerated HTML included in your Rhodes application is not compatible with the iWebKit framework. To utilize the iWebKit components in a view, you will need to replace the autogenerated HTML with its iWebKit equivalent. If you are using one of the iWebKit list styles anywhere in your application, make sure to remove the <body> tag from your *iWebKit/app/layout.erb* and place it as the outermost parent tag in every view of your application.

For inspiration, refer to the code examples earlier in this chapter.

To test your application, build it as described in Chapter 6, *Your First Rhodes App.*

Setting up PhoneGap for iWebKit

Using iWebKit with PhoneGap is very simple.

To create a new PhoneGap for iPhone project, see Chapter 8 for complete details. You will need to be using XCode. Copy the contents of the iWebKit demo directory into the www folder in your PhoneGap project, replacing the existing *index.html*. Target the iPhone simulator and then choose **Build and Run**.

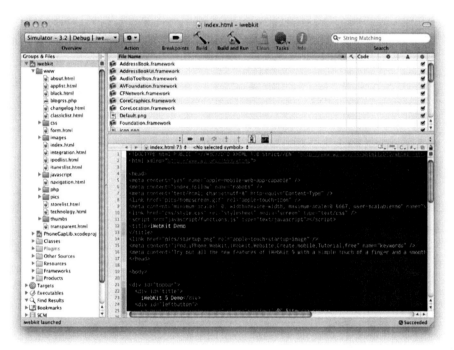

Figure 11–14. *iWebKit example in PhoneGap project*

Figure 11–15. *iWebKit demo app running in PhoneGap*

Chapter 12

Animated UI with jQTouch

jQTouch is a jQuery plug-in for mobile web development originally developed for the iPhone and iPod Touch.[1] jQTouch enables animated transitions, swipe detection, and themes for HTML-based web applications based on features in WebKit. The most exciting and interesting feature of jQTouch is that it allows you to quickly make HTML pages look like a native iPhone application.

jQTouch enables you to quickly develop applications that take advantage of common UI patterns, leveraging the JavaScript skills many developers already have. jQTouch is actively under development. With its simple and clean API, jQTouch is gaining in popularity.

While you can use jQTouch in hosted mobile applications and access it on a device with a web browser, you can also use it in native applications produced by several cross-platform frameworks. To use jQTouch in a native application, you would include it in a browser control, as discussed in Part 1, or leverage a cross-platform framework, such as Rhodes or PhoneGap (Chapters 6 and 8), that enable the use of HTML UI in a native application. The visual themes and styling of jQTouch are suitable for any WebKit-based mobile browser; however, its animated transitions only work on iOS, as of this writing.

In this chapter, we will cover how to use jQTouch in your device's web browser, as well as with the frameworks Rhodes and PhoneGap. The information presented is based on jQTouch 1.0 beta ,2 which is the current version at the time of this writing.

In order to work effectively with jQTouch, you will need to be proficient in JavaScript, CSS, and HTML. In particular, you should be comfortable with how AJAX applications work, in making asynchronous requests, and modifying the Document Object Model (DOM) of the HTML page based on the response.

---

[1] jQTouch is an open source project initially developed for mobile web applications by David Kaneda, and is free to use under an MIT license. You can find more information about jQTouch at http://www.jqtouch.com

Getting Started with jQTouch

jQTouch is a source code library that includes Javascript and CSS. It requires (and includes) the popular JavaScript library, jQuery. In order to use jQTouch to control the look and feel of your application, it requires that you structure your HTML in a specific way and that you follow some specific patterns that are not clearly documented. This section explains those patterns and the assumptions that jQuery makes about how your code will work. In this chapter, we will use the terms "Application" and "Screen" as follows:

- *Screen*: what the user sees from page to page. Each screen is assumed to be a DIV element that is a child of the HTML body.

- *Application*: the HTML page that includes the jQTouch JavaScript and CSS, as well as all of the screens (some of which may be dynamically loaded).

Starting a new application that uses jQTouch is straightforward; however, modifying an existing application is tricky because your application needs to work within the constraints of jQTouch. These constraints will be made clear through the examples in this chapter.

- You never leave the single page of the application.

- URLs must have full paths (or be relative to the root of your web app).

- Each screen isn't a full web page; instead, it is a DIV that is an immediate child of the application body.

- Make sure you don't use IDs, except to identify screens.

Running Example Code

When you download the jQTouch source code,[2] you will find several sample applications that you can examine for an overview of all the features in jQTouch. While you can view the examples in any browser, to view the animations, you should run the jQTouch examples using the iPhone simulator or in the WebKit-based desktop browser of your choice to see the animations.

To load these examples in your iPhone simulator, right click on any of the *index.html* files in the demo folders using the Finder and select **Open With ➤ iPhone Simulator.app**. This will load the HTML, CSS, and JavaScript into the browser on your iPhone simulator so you can explore the examples and see what they would look like on an iPhone. To view the same page on an iOS device, you must host the web page on a web server that can be accessed via HTTP.

---

[2] Source code and additional documentation is available at http://code.google.com/p/jqtouch

Creating a Simple jQTouch Application

The user will go to a page that is the jQTouch application. This page includes jQuery, jQTouch JavaScript, jQtouch CSS, and a theme to skin the application with. While you don't need to (and shouldn't) modify the jQTouch CSS file, it is helpful to understand that the jQTouch CSS file contains the transition classes (such as slide, pop, and so forth) and defines the WebKit animations for each transition. Typically, you will use the jQTouch styles by annotating your HTML with the jQTouch classes. You can, of course, create your own styles that extend or modify jQTouch styles and you would typically place those in your own CSS file loaded after the jQTouch CSS file.

The application begins with one or more screens already preloaded. In other words, the source code to your application (your main HTML page) may declare one or more DIVs as children of the body, which will each act as a screen. If a screen isn't already marked as current (by declaring the HTML attribute *class="current"*), jQTouch will interpret the first DIV in the BODY tag as the first screen. Only the current screen is visible. Each screen is assumed to be a single DIV element. Preloaded screens should have IDs already assigned to them so they can be transitioned to via links in the document that contain internal anchors that represent the screen IDs.

Listing 12–1 shows a starter application for jQTouch. The jQTouch libraries must be included and you must also initialize the jQTouch library. If you are already using jQTouch in your project, be sure to include the jQuery file included in your downloaded jQTouch source to avoid a version mismatch. To get started, copy the jQTouch and themes directories to the root of your web application (or simply experiment at the root of the folder created when you unzip the jQTouch download).

As is common practice, this example initializes jQTouch in a script tag in the HTML header. (Optional initialization parameters are discussed later in this chapter.) This example uses a toolbar, which is an optional component, but commonly used in most mobile applications. To get started, copy the jQTouch and themes directories to the root of your web application with apple theme.

Listing 12–1. *Starter*

```
<html xmlns="http://www.w3.org/1999/xhtml">
    <head>
        <script src="jqtouch/jquery.1.3.2.min.js" type="text/javascript"></script>
        <script src="jqtouch/jqtouch.js" type="text/javascript"></script>
        <link rel="stylesheet" href="jqtouch/jqtouch.css" type="text/css"/>
        <link rel="stylesheet" href="themes/apple/theme.css" type="text/css"/>
        <script>
            var jqt = $.jQTouch();
        </script>
    </head>
    <body>
        <div id="page-home">
            <div class="toolbar">
                <h1>Home</h1>
            </div>
```

Figure 12–1 shows what this example looks like running in the Safari desktop browser, which is recommended for quick iterative development.

Figure 12–1. *Starter application with apple theme*

jQTouch ships with an alternate "jqt" theme. You can change the full look of your application simply by specifying an alternate theme, as shown in Listing 12–2. Figure 12–2 shows what this example looks like running in the Safari desktop browser with the jqt theme.

Listing 12–2. *Including the jqt Theme*

```
<link rel="stylesheet" href="themes/jqt/theme.css" type="text/css"/>
```

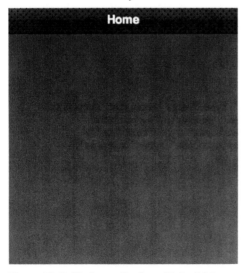

Figure 12–2. *Starter application with the jqt theme*

A theme is a directory made up of a CSS file and images. The jqt theme[3] will give your application a jQTouch skin and is used by most of the jQTouch demos. The apple theme[4] simulates a native iPhone UIKit interface. The behavior of the application remains the same across themes, only the look is changed.

Adding Screens

Next we'll add a few screens to the same example to illustrate how jQTouch modifies the DOM to achieve its transition effects (see Listing 12–3).

Listing 12–3. *Example Application with Three Screens and Links Between Them*

```html
<html xmlns="http://www.w3.org/1999/xhtml">
    <head>
        <script src="jqtouch/jquery.1.3.2.min.js" type="text/javascript"></script>
        <script src="jqtouch/jqtouch.js" type="text/javascript"></script>
        <link rel="stylesheet" href="jqtouch/jqtouch.css" type="text/css"/>
        <link rel="stylesheet" href="themes/apple/theme.css" type="text/css"/>
        <script>
            var jqt = $.jQTouch();
        </script>
    </head>
    <body>
        <div id="page-home">
            <div class="toolbar">
                <h1>Home</h1>
            </div>
            <ul>
                <li class="arrow"><a href="#page-1" class="slide">Go to page 1</a></li>
                <li class="arrow"><a href="#page-2" class="cube">Go to page 2</a></li>
            </ul>
        </div>
        <div id="page-1">
            <div class="toolbar">
                <h1>Page 1</h1>
                <a class="back" href="#">Back</a>
            </div>
            <ul>
                <li class="arrow"><a href="#page-home" class="pop">Go home</a></li>
                <li class="arrow"><a href="#page-2" class="cube">Go to page 2</a></li>
            </ul>
        </div>
        <div id="page-2">
            <div class="toolbar">
                <h1>Page 2</h1>
                <a class="cancel" href="#">Cancel</a>
            </div>
            <ul>
                <li class="arrow"><a href="#page-home" class="pop">Go home</a></li>
```

---

[3] Found in *themes/jqt/theme.min.css*.

[4] Found in *themes/apple/theme.min.css*.

```
                    <li class="arrow"><a href="#page-1" class="slide">Go to page 1</a></li>
            </ul>
        </div>
    </body>
</html>
```

To understand what is happening with your application, you will want to open the Safari Inspector, as shown in Figure 12–3. To do so, select **Show Web Inspector** under the **Develop** menu. (If you don't see a **Develop** menu, open Safari Preferences and on the **Advanced** tab, select **Show Develop menu in menu bar**.)

Note how the code is different once it is loaded. In particular, look closely at how the screens **page-home**, **page-1**, and **page-2** are modified at runtime. On initial load of the application, jQTouch modified the DOM and now the **page-home** div has class=*"current"*. When you click a link, you will see an animated transition to the next screen, then you will see that a different DIV will have class = *"current"* and the **page-home** DIV will not.

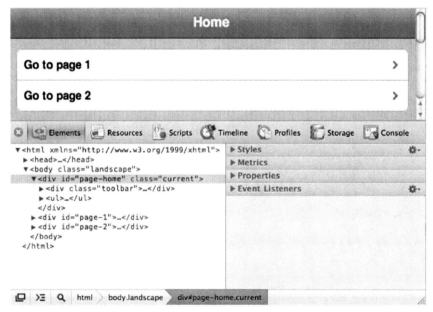

Figure 12–3. *Safari Web Inspector showing the first page as current*

Loading Additional Screens with Ajax

For jQTouch transitions to work, screens must already be in the DOM. jQTouch handles this for you with Ajax requests as long as your application conforms to its (undocumented) expectations.

In order to achieve the visual effects of animated page transitions, screens that are not present in the initial application HTML page must be fetched with Ajax requests. jQTouch detects which links are internal by inspecting the HREF of the link. The screen is assumed to have been loaded if the HREF is an internal anchor, such as *#screen-1*. If the HREF is a path, it will make an Ajax request to the URL the link is pointing to and optimistically include whatever HTML snippet it receives. The returned content must be one or more DIV elements, where each DIV element represents a screen.

> **NOTE:** It is an HTML error to include a full document inside of another document. If a full HTML page is returned by your web service, then your application will not work. Specifically, the screen will appear blank. Also, if your web service returns an HTML element other than a DIV, jQTouch styles may not apply correctly.

The content of the Ajax request is appended to the document and each of the links is assigned an id (such as **page-1**, **page-2**, and so forth). If one of the screens has a "current" class, jQTouch will transition to that screen after the external content has been inserted. If you only have one DIV in the response or structure the response so that the first DIV is the desired target page, then specifying a "current" class is not required–jQTouch will make that assumption and annotate the DOM accordingly when the response is received. The other change that jQTouch makes to the DOM is that the HREF of the link that initiated the Ajax request is modified to include an anchor reference to the ID of the new "current" screen. Listing 12–4 show a sample snippet from a jQTouch application where the initial load is a single screen. Listing 12–5 shows the AJAX response, which simply includes a snippet of HTML with a single DIV, not a whole HTML page. Listing 12–6 shows the modified application page.

Listing 12–4. *Application Body Before /beatles Link is Clicked*

```
<body>
<div id="page-1" class="current">
    <a href="/beatles">Get Beatles</a>
</div>
</body>
```

Listing 12–5. *AJAX Response*

```
<div>
    <ul>
        <li>John</li>
        <li>Paul</li>
        <li>George</li>
        <li>Ringo</li>
    </ul>
</div>
```

Listing 12–6. *Application Body After the Link Was Clicked*

```
<body>
<div id="page-1">
    <ul>
        <li><a href="#page-2">Get Beatles</a></li>
    </ul>
</div>

<div id="page-2" class="current">
    <ul>
        <li>John</li>
```

```
        <li>Paul</li>
        <li>George</li>
        <li>Ringo</li>
    </ul>
</div>
</body>
```

The new screen has been inserted into the DOM with an ID and class. The HREF that was originally *"/beatles"* is now *"#page-2"* and therefore, if the user were to click that link again, no server request would be made.

> **WARNING:** All paths must be full URLs or relative to the root of your application.

Your entire application will end up being a single page. Relative paths in this context don't make sense. Because of this architecture, all links must be full URLs or relative to the root of your application.

To navigate away from the application, include a *target="_webapp"* to your link, as shown in Listing 12–7.

Listing 12–7. *Linking Away from Your Application.*

```
<a href="http://www.thewho.com" target="_webapp">The Who</a>
```

Cancel, Back, and Browser History

You can reverse a link animation by including a back or cancel class to your links. Those links are then styled as buttons and will appear as top-left buttons in the application. See Listing 12–8 for an example of how a Back button is placed within a page. Figure 12–4 shows the page with the apple theme.

Listing 12–8. *Back Button Inside a Toolbar on a Page*

```
        <div id="page-1">
            <div class="toolbar">
                <h1>Page 1</h1>
                <a class="back" href="#">Back</a>
            </div>
            <ul>
                <li class="arrow"><a href="#page-home" class="pop">Go home</a></li>
                <li class="arrow"><a href="#page-2" class="cube">Go to page 2</a></li>
            </ul>
        </div>
```

Figure 12–4. *Page with Back button, rendered with apple theme*

jQTouch doesn't interact well with the browser history. Back simply pops the previous page off an internal stack–there is no implementation of Forward. Consider hiding the browser Back and Forward buttons and instead embed back and cancel in your application. Forward will then be just a function of clicking buttons and links within the application.

Other Buttons

Buttons normally appear on the top-right. To define a button, just add the button class:

```
<a href="/home" class="button">Home</a>
```

If you want to force a button left, add both the button and leftButton class:

```
<a href="/home" class="button leftButton">Home on the left</a>
```

jQTouch Initialization Options

jQTouch must be initialized by calling $.jQTouch(), as shown in Listing 12-9. jQTouch returns an object with public that enables you to interact with it via JavaScript:

- ▨ getOrientation
- ▨ goBack
- ▨ goTo

If you want to invoke any of these public methods programmatically, you can save the jQTouch instance in a variable, otherwise ignore it.

You can also pass options to the initialize function.[5]

Listing 12–9. *Initializing jQTouch with Options*

```
$.jQTouch({
        icon: 'jqtouch.png',
        statusBar: 'black-translucent',
        preloadImages: [
            'themes/jqt/img/chevron_white.png',
            'themes/jqt/img/bg_row_select.gif',
            'themes/jqt/img/back_button_clicked.png',
            'themes/jqt/img/button_clicked.png'
            ]
    });
```

The jQTouch initialization options are listed in Table12–1.

---

[5] You can find a full listing of options in Appendix A, jQTouch Options.

Table 12–1. *jQTouch Initialization Options*

Value	Default	Meaning
addGlossToIcon	TRUE	Set to false to prevent automatic glossy button effect on icon.
backSelector	.back, .cancel, .goback'	A CSS selector for Back links/buttons. When clicked, the page history goes back one, automatically reversing whichever entrance animation was used.
cacheGetRequests	TRUE	Automatically caches GET requests, so subsequent clicks reference the already loaded data.
cubeSelector	.cube'	Link selector for a cube animation.
dissolveSelector	.dissolve'	Link selector for a dissolve animation.
fadeSelector	.fade'	Link selector for a fade animation.
fixedViewport	TRUE	Removes the user's ability to scale the page. Ensures the site behaves more like an application.
flipSelector	.flip'	Link selector for a 3-D flip animation.
formSelector	form'	Sets which forms are automatically submitted via Ajax.
fullScreen	TRUE	The web site will become a full-screen application when saved to a user's home screen. Set to false to disable.
fullScreenClass	fullscreen'	Adds a class to the <body> when running in full-screen mode, to allow for easy detection and styling. Set to false to disable.
icon	FALSE	Sets the home screen icon for the application. To use, pass a string path for a 57x57px PNG. Example: icon: 'images/appicon.png'
initializeTouch	a, .touch'	Selector for items that are automatically given expanded touch events. This makes ordinary links more responsive and provides trigger events such as swipe.
popSelector	'.pop'	Link selector for a pop animation.
preloadImages	FALSE	Pass an array of image paths to load them before page loads. Example: ['images/link_over.png', 'images/link_select.png']

Value	Default	Meaning
slideSelector	'body > * > ul li a'	Link selector for the default slide-left transition. By default, applies to all links within an unordered list. Accepts any jQuery-capable selector 'li > a, a:not(.dontslide)', and so forth.
slideupSelector	.slideup'	Link selector for a slide up animation.
startupScreen	null	Pass a string path to a 320px × 460px startup screen for full-screen apps. Use a 320px × 480px image if you set 'statusBar' to black-translucent.
statusBar	'default'	Styles the status bar when running as a full-screen app. Other options are black and black-translucent.
submitSelector	'.submit'	Selector that, when clicked, will submit its parent form (and close keyboard if open).
swapSelector	'.swap'	Link selector for 3-D swap animation.
useAnimations	true	Set to false to disable all animations.

[source: http://code.google.com/p/jqtouch/wiki/InitOptions]

Basic Views

As seen in the examples so far, jQTouch applications consist of a single HTML file, used to create the individual views in your the application. You can create additional views by creating new DIVs as children of the body. .

The following is an example excerpt from an application with two views:

```
<body>
  <div id="jqt">
    <div id="index">
      <div class="toolbar">
        <h1>My Application</h1>
        <a class="button flip" href="#about">About</a>
      </div>
      <p>Hello I am the index page</p>
    </div>

    <div id="about">
      <div class="toolbar">
        <h1>About</h1>
        <a class="back" href="#">Back</a>
      </div>
      <p>Hello I am the about page</p>
    </div>
  </div>
</body>
```

jQTouch also supports organizing your application into separate HTML files. You can use the _webapp_ target to break up sections of your application and then refer to them as you would an external link. In that case, your link should reference the new file's name and anchor tag, if appropriate (for example, `<a class="button flip" target="_webapp" href="/about_us.html#about">About</a>`).

Customizing Your jQTouch Applications Animations

Specify the transition you wish to apply to a link by adding a CSS class to the link. jQTouch includes eight default page animations: slide, slideup, dissolve, fade, flip, pop, swap, and cube.[6] When the user presses the Back button, jQTouch automatically handles reversing the animation for a natural transition.

Navigation Bar (aka the Toolbar)

jQTouch includes a special CSS class called *toolbar* that will turn a DIV into an element resembling an iPhone Navigation Bar at the top of the screen (see Figure 12–5). The jQTouch toolbar is simply a style generated from the jQTouch CSS, and shouldn't be confused with the toolbar element available in native Objective-C-based applications.

```
<div class="toolbar">
    <h1>My Application</h1>
    <a class="button flip" href="#about">About</a>
</div>
```

Figure 12–5. *Navigation bar*

Tables or Lists

In jQTouch, you can create lists that appear almost identical to those found in native iPhone applications (see Figure 12–6). Create an unordered list *<ul>* and apply one of the following classes to the *ul* element: *edgetoedge*, *plastic*, or *metal* to style your list. Then you can add items to your list as you normally would, using the *<li>* tag.

```
<div id="jqt">
  <div id="index">
    <div class="toolbar">

<h1>Tables</h1>

    </div>
    <ul class="edgetoedge">
```

---

[6] In the event those eight animations just aren't enough, the jQTouch documentation includes details on how to add your own custom animations.

```
        <li>Hydrogen</li>
        <li>Helium</li>
        <li>Lithium</li>
      </ul>
    </div>
  </div>
```

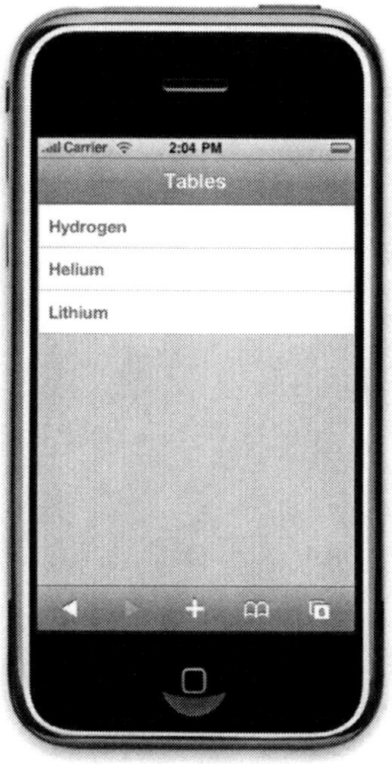

Figure 12–6. *List*

To round the corners of your lists, apply the *"rounded"* class to the unordered list (Figure 12–7).

```
<div id="jqt">
  <div id="index">
    <div class="toolbar">

  <h1>Tables</h1>

    </div>
    <ul class="rounded">
      <li>Hydrogen</li>
      <li>Helium</li>
      <li>Lithium</li>
    </ul>
  </div>
</div>
```

Figure 12–7. *List with rounded corners*

To add a standard disclosure indicator to an item in your list, add the class *"arrow"* to the list item *<li>* element.

```
<div id="jqt">
  <div id="index">
    <div class="toolbar">
      <h1>Email</h1>
    </div>
    <ul class="edgetoedge">
      <li class="arrow"><a href="#">dev@example.com</a><small↩
class="counter">3</small></li>
      <li class="arrow"><a href="#">marketing@example.com</a><small↩
class="counter">221</small></li>
      <li class="arrow"><a href="#">webmaster@example.com</a><small↩
class="counter">37</small></li>
    </ul>
  </div>
</div>
```

Finally, you can add numbers to the right-hand sides of your elements (see Figure 12–8) by including a SMALL element with *class="counter"*. Note: the body of the *li* has to be an anchor tag for this to display correctly. This style is used in the Apple Mail application, for example.

Figure 12–8. *List with disclosure indicator and numbers added*

Customizing Your Views with Themes

jQTouch comes with two default themes. The first theme we've already seen matches native iPhone UI controls. The second is similar to the first, but the color scheme is dominated by black (see Figure 12–9). You can change between them by including a different *theme.css* file. You can create your own themes as well. To modify or add to the existing styles, you can add your own CSS by including additional files or defining additional styles in the HTML head after including the theme.

```
using <link rel="stylesheet" href="themes/jqt/theme.css" type="text/css"↵
 media="screen" title="no title" charset="utf-8">
```

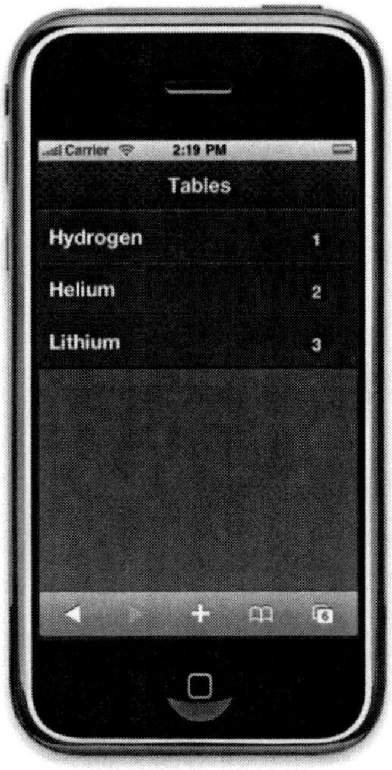

Figure 12–9. *Changing themes*

There are additional features you might use to customize a stand-alone jQTouch mobile web app, but we recommend using Rhodes or PhoneGap's methods to customize such features as application icons, caching, and geolocation.

Integration with Rhodes

In Rhodes 2.1,[7] jQTouch integration is built-in. By default, the iOS- and Android-generated code includes animated transitions. The jQTouch library that ships with Rhodes has been modified to be compatible with Android.[8]

Integration with PhoneGap

To use jQTouch features in a PhoneGap application, copy the *jQTouch/* and *themes/* directories into the *www* directory of your PhoneGap app.

---

[7] Rhodes 2.1 is in beta, as of this writing

[8] Since both Rhodes and jQTouch are MIT Licensed. These can be expected to roll back into the jQTouch project.

In your application's *index.html* file, replace any the default CSS and JavaScript in the HEAD section with the following:

```
<link rel="stylesheet" href="jqtouch/jqtouch.min.css" type="text/css" media="screen"↩
title="no title" charset="utf-8">
<link rel="stylesheet" href="themes/apple/theme.min.css" type="text/css"↩
media="screen" title="no title" charset="utf-8">

<script src="jqtouch/jquery.1.3.2.min.js" type="text/javascript" charset=↩
"utf-8"></script>
<script src="jqtouch/jqtouch.min.js" type="text/javascript" charset="utf-8"></script>

<script>
  var jQT = $.jQTouch();
</script>
```

Chapter 13

Sencha Touch

Sencha Touch (www.sencha.com/products/touch) is a JavaScript framework for creating web applications targeted to touch-based devices. Sencha Touch is the flagship product of Sencha (formerly Ext JS), a Palo Alto, Calif. company launched in 2007 that makes application frameworks. Sencha Touch combines ExtJS, jQTouch and Raphaël. Unlike jQTouch, Sencha Touch is not dependent on jQuery and is compatible with both the iPhone and Android. Sencha Touch is distributed under the GPL v3 open source license. As of this writing, it is in beta and not available for commercial distribution; however, it is expected to have a commercial license upon final release.

Sencha Touch allows your web applications to have a consistent look and feel across both the iPhone and Android. It does not strive for a native look in most cases, but rather has created a blend of widgets that don't look like any specific operating system (with the exception of some iPhone-looking toolbars.)

Sencha Touch is powered by HTML5 and CSS3. Unlike the iWebKit and jQTouch, the Sencha Touch API is pure JavaScript. Developers need to be fairly experienced at JavaScript to take advantage of the Sencha Touch framework. Due to Sencha's recent release, still in beta at the time of this writing, this chapter focuses on providing a foundation in the Sencha style of UI layout and programming and does not provide full recipes for how to develop applications.

Getting Started

In Sencha Touch, you write all of your application code in JavaScript. Focused on the WebKit-based mobile browsers of iOS and Android, you will get the best results when developing if you do your testing on the Safari desktop browser before testing it in the simulator. As with all mobile development, be sure to test on target devices, not just the simulator, before releasing your mobile application.

When implementing the visual design and client-side interaction and testing on your desktop, you can simply open an HTML file in Safari. However, when integrating the interface into your web application, you will make AJAX requests that require your HTML file be hosted in a web server (for example, accessed via "http://…" rather than "file:///…"). Also, to run in a simulator, you will need to access your application via your web server (which can run on your local machine, but you will need to access it as a web server over the network).

There is no requirement for how you organize your files; however, to follow the code in this chapter, your starter application directory should look like Figure 13–1 (the complete list of files is provided in Table 13–1). In all of Sencha's own demos, the application JavaScript file is called *index.js* and they keep it at the root of the application directory as a sibling of *index.html*; however, this chapter follows the convention of having subfolders for JavaScript and CSS, which is a common convention in web application development.

For development, we include *ext-touch-debug.js* but you will switch to *ext-touch.js* for deployment. The debug version helps you detect and troubleshoot errors, as well as isolate issues in your application code by seeing exactly where in the library errors occur. We include the *debug-with-comments.js* for convenient reference.

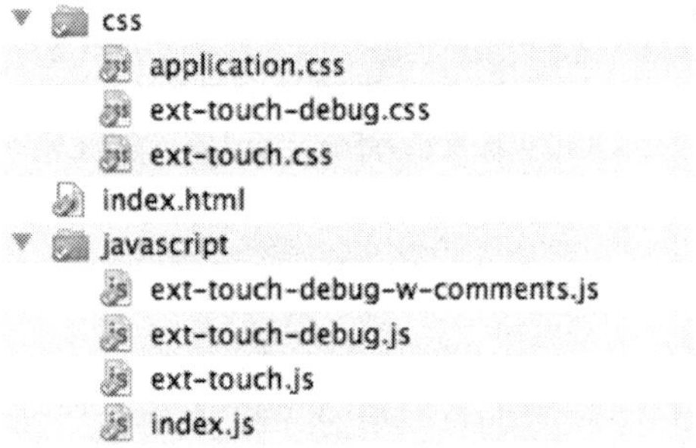

```
▼ 📁 css
      📄 application.css
      📄 ext-touch-debug.css
      📄 ext-touch.css
   📄 index.html
▼ 📁 javascript
      📄 ext-touch-debug-w-comments.js
      📄 ext-touch-debug.js
      📄 ext-touch.js
      📄 index.js
```

Figure 13–1. *A typical directory structure for a Sencha application*

There are a number of standard files that are included in a Sencha application tree. These are listed in Table 13–1 along with an explanation of their purpose.

Table 13–1. *Standard Files in a Sencha Touch Application*

File	Purpose
index.html	the entry-point of your application. You may have multiple HTML files; however, a single HTML file will typically represent many "pages" in your application (or multiple screens on a mobile device).
index.js	for your application code
application.css	for your application CSS
ext-touch.js	Sencha JavaScript library. During development you will want to use *ext-touch-debug.js* instead.
ext-touch.css	Sencha CSS library that is required to go with the JavaScript library.

To get started with your application, you need to create an *index.html* file with the content shown in Listing 13–1.

Listing 13–1. *A Typical index.html File for a Sencha Application*

```
<!DOCTYPE html>
<html>
<head>
    <meta http-equiv="Content-Type" content="text/html; charset=utf-8"/>
    <title>My Application</title>
        <link rel="stylesheet" href="css/ext-touch.css" type="text/css"/>
        <link rel="stylesheet" href="css/application.css" type="text/css"/>
        <script type="text/javascript" src="javascript/ext-touch-debug.js"></script>
        <script type="text/javascript" src="javascript/index.js"></script>
</head>
<body/>
</html>
```

Create subfolders "javascript" and "css." Place the Sencha Touch library files in appropriate folders and create blank files for *index.js* and *application.js*.

Next, you need to fill in the boilerplate JavaScript in *index.js* as shown in Listing 13–2. The Ext.setup method sets up a page for use on a touch-enabled device. It allows you to set various startup properties and behaviors for your application. All of your application code needs to be wrapped in a function called by the Sencha framework. Your application code is declared as an anonymous function and assigned to the "onReady" property.

Listing 13–2. *The Minimum JavaScript You Need to Start Coding in index.js*

```
Ext.setup({
    onReady: function()
        // your code goes here
    }
});
```

The setup method optionally allows for properties that control how the application starts up and appears on the device. A more typical boilerplate wrapper for a Sencha application is shown in Listing 13–3.

Listing 13–3. *The Typical Sencha Setup Properties Used in index.js*

```
Ext.setup({

  tabletStartupScreen: 'tablet_startup.png',

    phoneStartupScreen: 'phone_startup.png',
    icon: 'icon.png',
    glossOnIcon: true,
    onReady: function() {
            // your code goes here
});
```

The key properties of the setup method are listed and described in Table 13–2.

Table 13–2. *The Properties of the Setup Method*

File	Purpose
Icon (String)	specifies the name of the application's default icon file, such as "*icon.png*." This will apply to both tablet and phones (or you can specify tabletIcon or phoneIcon if you want different icons for different types of devices). The image should be 72×72 and will be used as the application icon when saving the app to the device's home screen.
GlossOnIcon (Boolean)	specifies whether you want the gloss effect to be applied to the default icon (for iOS only)
fullscreen (Boolean)	sets an appropriate meta tag for iOS devices to run in full-screen mode.
tabletStartupScreen (String)	specifies the name of an image to be used as a splash screen for iPad. The image must be 768×1004 and in portrait orientation.
phoneStartupScreen (String)	specifies the name of an image to be used on an iPhone or iPod touch. The image must be 320×460 and in portrait orientation.
statusBarStyle (String)	sets the status bar style for fullscreen iPhone OS web apps. Valid options are • default • black • black-translucent
preloadImages (Array)	specifies a list of urls of images to be loaded. This is useful for applications with several screens where preloading the images gives a smoother user experience than having them load on demand over a potentially slow network.
onReady (Function)	runs the specified function when the page is loaded and it is safe to interact with the HTML DOM (Document Object Model).
scope (Object)	A frequently used property in Sencha Touch that allows you to set the execution context (the value of "this") of a particular function. In this case you can set the execution context of the onReady function. If not set, the function will execute in the context of the "window" object.

Adding HTML Text with a Panel

Sencha applications are created dynamically using procedural code to create UI objects, in contrast to declarative UI frameworks that use markup in XML or HTML to create interface elements. Coding in Sencha Touch feels similar to traditional UI frameworks such as the Microsoft Foundation Classes (MFC) or Java Swing. You will add UI components to a "panel" and specify a layout to visually organize an application screen.

You will start with a panel, which is a fairly generic container for application layout. In this example, you'll use the fullscreen config option to make the panel fill the screen.

Add a panel with some text in it by modifying *index.js* to include the code in Listing 13–4. When you open the *index.html* file in Safari, you should see the text shown in Figure 13–2. Note that the panel has no visual appearance.

Listing 13–4. *Adding a Panel With Text in it*

```
Ext.setup({
        onReady: function() {
            new Ext.Panel({
                id: 'mainscreen',
                html: 'This is some text in a panel. <br /><small>This is↩
smaller text.</small>',
                fullscreen: true
            });
        }
});
```

> **NOTE:** When testing in Safari, you will want to display the error console. Often when there are JavaScript errors all you will see is a blank page. To display the error console, you will need to enable the **Developer** menu and select **Show Error Console.** (To enable the **Developer** menu, open **Preferences**, select the **Advanced** panel and check **Show Develop menu in menu bar.**)

This is some text in a panel.
This is smaller text.

Figure 13–2. *Text in a panel*

If you **View Source** in Safari, you will still see the HTML as shown back in Listing 13–1. However, if you **Show Web Inspector** under the **Develop** menu and open all of the DOM elements, you will see that Sencha Touch has dynamically added elements to the DOM to display the text (see Figure 13–3).

```
▼ <html>
  ▼ <head id="ext-gen1006">
      <meta http-equiv="Content-Type" content="text/html; charset=utf-8">
      <title> My Application </title>
      <link rel="stylesheet" href="css/ext-touch.css" type="text/css">
      <link rel="stylesheet" href="css/application.css" type="text/css">
      <script type="text/javascript" src="javascript/ext-touch-debug.js">
      <script type="text/javascript" src="javascript/index.js">
      <meta id="ext-gen1001" name="viewport" content="width=device-width, user-scalable=no, initial-scale=1.0, maximum-scale=1.0;">
      <meta id="ext-gen1002" name="apple-mobile-web-app-capable" content="yes">
  </head>
  ▼ <body>
    ▼ <div id="mainscreen" class="x-panel x-fullscreen x-landscape" style="width: 1303px; height: 516px; ">
      ▼ <div class="x-panel-body" id="ext-gen1008" style="left: 0px; top: 0px; width: 1303px; height: 516px; ">
          "This is some text in a panel. "
          <br>
          <small>This is smaller text. </small>
      </div>
    </div>
  </body>
</html>
```

Figure 13–3. *Sencha modifies the HTML DOM at runtime to display text in a panel.*

While everything in Sencha Touch is implemented with procedural JavaScript, the components are typically created using configuration. The panel is a "container" and any container may be configured with a list of "items" that may be a single component, or an array of child components. The components are then spatially arranged according to a specified layout. Listings 13–5 and 13–6 show two variants of container configuration values.

Listing 13–5. *A Container May Be Configured With a Single Item and a Layout*

```
// specifying a single item
items: {...},
layout: 'fit',
…
```

Listing 13–6. *A Container May Be Configured With an Array of Items and a Layout*

```
// specifying multiple items
items: [{...}, {...}],
layout: 'hbox',
…
```

Each item may be an instance of a component or a component configuration with specified "xtype." Table 13–3 provides a list of visual and non-visual component xtypes.

Table 13–3. *xtypes*

Visual Component xtypes	Non-visual component xtypes
button	component: super class of all components
slider	container: a non-visual component that has a list of items and a layout that specifies how to arrange its items
toolbar	dataview, datapanel: can be bound to a data store for rendering dynamic data
tabpanel	panel: typically used for layout, a panel can have its own CSS style ("baseCls") and can detect orientation when in fullscreen mode
checkbox	spacer: used for layout
select	form: allows for layout in a typical manner for a form
field	component: super class of all components
fieldset	container: a non-visual component that has a list of items and a layout that specifies how to arrange its items
numberfield	dataview, datapanel: can be bound to a data store for rendering dynamic data

Visual Component xtypes	Non-visual component xtypes
textarea	panel: typically used for layout, a panel can have its own CSS style ("baseCls") and can detect orientation when in fullscreen mode
Radio	spacer: used for layout
Textfield	form: allows for layout in a typical manner for a form

Adding Components

Next you'll add some user interface components to the application. In this case, you want a toolbar across the top with three buttons that will navigate between screens. It is easiest to understand (and debug) if you add one component at a time and test the application. You'll start by adding a "splitbutton," which is a component that has a list of buttons as child items. Modify your code as shown in Listing 13–7 and the application should appear as shown in Figure 13–4.

Listing 13–7. *A Container May Be Configured With an Array of Items and a Layout*

```
Ext.setup({
        onReady: function() {
            var buttonsGroup = {
              xtype: 'splitbutton',
              items: [{
                  text: 'One',
                  active: true
              },
              {
                text: 'Two'
              },
              {
                text: 'Three'
              }]
          };

          new Ext.Panel({
              id: 'mainscreen',
              html: 'This is some text in a panel. <br /><small>This is
smaller text.</small>',
              fullscreen: true,
              items: buttonsGroup
          });

    }
});
```

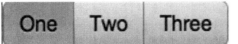

This is some text in a panel.

This is smaller text.

Figure 13–4. *A simple button bar added to the panel.*

Creating Interactivity

To illustrate how to make the application interactive and respond when someone clicks a button, the examples in this section show how to simply change text and then how to swap which panel is shown. These examples provide a guide to fundamental concepts in Sencha Touch that should provide insight on implementing any interactivity. Note that this specific example of panel hiding/showing is more easily achieved with an Ext.TabPanel, but the general coding techniques will give you a feel for what it is like to develop web UI with Sencha Touch.

As shown in Listing 13–8, you can define a handler for any button. The handler is just a JavaScript function that is passed a reference to the button and the event that triggered the call. Ext.getCmp('mainscreen') will get a reference to the component with the id 'mainscreen' (the panel component with text in it). Then "update(txt)" will set the HTML of the component to the text in the local variable "txt."

Listing 13–8. *A Handler May Be Associated With a Button*

```
Ext.setup({
    onReady: function() {
        var tapHandler = function(button, event) {
            var txt = "User tapped the '" + button.text + "' button.";
            Ext.getCmp('mainscreen').update(txt);
        };
        var buttonsGroup = {
          xtype: 'splitbutton',
          items: [{
              text: 'One',
              active: true,
              handler: tapHandler
          },
          { text: 'Two',
            handler: tapHandler
          },
          { text: 'Three',
            handler: tapHandler
          }]
        };

        new Ext.Panel({
            id: 'mainscreen',
            html: 'This is some text in a panel. <br /><small>This is⏎
 smaller text.</small>',
            fullscreen: true,
```

```
            items: buttonsGroup
        });


    }
});
```

A more meaningful action would be to create multiple panels where selecting one of the buttons displays a corresponding panel. It is also typical to arrange the buttons in a toolbar, which can be done by nesting the splitButton component in a toolbar component. The code that combines these features can be seen in Listing 13–9. Portrait and Landscape views are shown in Figures 13–5 and 13–6, respectively.

Listing 13–9. *Interface Elements to Display Multiple Screens Selected by a "splitButton"*

```
Ext.setup({
      onReady: function() {
          var tapHandler = function(button, event) {
              var txt = "User tapped the '" + button.id + "' button.";
              panel_id = 'panel' + button.id
              Ext.getCmp('panelone').hide();
              Ext.getCmp('paneltwo').hide();
              Ext.getCmp('panelthree').hide();

              Ext.getCmp(panel_id).show();
          };

           var buttonsGroup = {
            xtype: 'splitbutton',
            items: [{
                id: 'one',
                text: 'One',
                handler: tapHandler,
                active: true
            },
            {
              id: 'two',
              handler: tapHandler,
              text: 'Two'
            },
            {
               id: 'three',
               handler: tapHandler,
               text: 'Three'
            }]
          };

          var panelOne = {
              id: 'panelone',
              xtype: 'panel',
              html: 'This is some text in a panel. <br /><small>This is
    smaller text.</small>',

          };
          var panelTwo = {
              id: 'paneltwo',
              xtype: 'panel',
```

```
                        html: 'Here is the second panel',
                        hidden: true
                   };
                var panelThree = {
                        id: 'panelthree',
                        xtype: 'panel',
                        html: 'This is number 3',
                        hidden: true
                   };

                var mytoolbar = {
                    xtype: 'toolbar',
                    ui:    'dark',
                    items: buttonsGroup,
                    dock: 'top',
                    layout: { pack: 'center' }
                }

                new Ext.Panel({
                    id: 'mainscreen',
                    items: [mytoolbar, panelOne, panelTwo, panelThree],
                    fullscreen: true
                });


         }
    });
```

Figure 13–5. *SplitButton in a toolbar (portrait)*

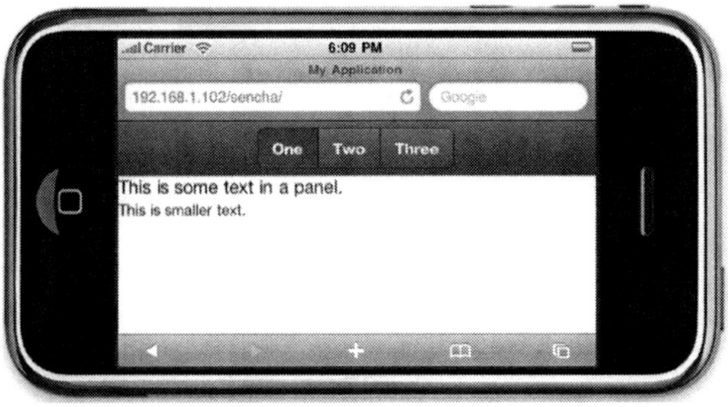

Figure 13–6. *SplitButton in a toolbar (landscape)*

Chapter 14

BlackBerry HTML UI

The BlackBerry platform was one of the earliest smartphone platforms to gain widespread adoption in the business- and gadget-loving communities. Developed by Research in Motion (RIM), it remains one of the leaders in market share for devices in the United States; however, the BlackBerry is outpaced by iPhone and Android sales in terms of market growth.

Support for the BlackBerry is included in both the Rhomobile and PhoneGap platforms. However, the limited capabilities of the embedded web UI control limit the degree of creativity and flexibility you can include in designing the layout and visual design of your application. Quite possibly the greatest limitation for developing native applications for the BlackBerry using HTML for UI lies not within these development environments, but within the BlackBerry platform itself.

Note that for mobile web applications, the BlackBerry has an added limitation: all network traffic for BlackBerry devices is routed through a central gateway. In the case of enterprise data transfer, it's routed through the BlackBerry MDS Connection Service; for web traffic, it's routed through the BlackBerry Internet service. Both services aim to minimize bandwidth usage by optimizing content for the requesting device's rendering capabilities, transcoding incompatible content, and only transferring data not currently in the device's local cache. Instead of allowing the developer to optimize content as desired, RIM applies a transformation to the HTML, adding to the challenges presented by the rendering limitations of the browser. However, when building a native application with a cross-platform framework, the HTML UI is delivered as part of the app and therefore bypasses the gateway transformation.

RIM recommends that your content be designed to meet the needs of users with the first-generation browser (4.2). Whether you are developing web applications or native applications with web UI controls for the BlackBerry, the number of users who will be using a first-generation BlackBerry browser to access content is currently much larger than the number of users with second-generation browsers.

RIM recently demoed a new WebKit-based browser with full support for HTML5, modern JavaScript, and improved CSS support. While at the time of this writing there is no stated timeline for release and no word on which devices will support the WebKit-based browser, this yields hope for improved support for future generations of BlackBerry devices.

The remainder of the sections in this chapter detail the features and limitations often encountered when building applications that make use of web UI controls for BlackBerry devices.

BlackBerry Browser UI Controls

Developing for the BlackBerry web UI requires a disciplined approach to work within the limitations of the target browser.

There are two separate browser-rendering engines included on the BlackBerry platform

- **browser.field** (available since ~v3.8 with most recent changes made in v4.5); The level of content support provided by this browser is limited to:

    - Document Object Model (DOM) L1 (read only access to the DOM).

    - Partial support for HTML, JavaScript and CSS. Content rendered using this browser field will look similar to content rendered by the BlackBerry browser on a 4.5 device.

    - Interaction model supports quick traversal of form fields with trackpad, trackwheel or trackball.

- **browser.field2.BrowserField** RIM's second rendering engine for the BlackBerry was introduced with the BlackBerry Bold (version 4.6 handheld software). This browser field greatly improved the capabilities of the BlackBerry browser; however, the interaction model was changed significantly by adding:

    - Support for industry standards such as HTML 4.01, JavaScript 1.5, CSS 2.1.

    - Support for DOM L2 (read/write) and XmlHttpRequest (AJAX). However, modern Javascript frameworks, such as JQuery and XUI, are not supported.

    - Interaction model for control of the pointer require spatial motion that is similar to a mouse on a computer screen or touch interface. This negatively affects usability when using the trackpad, trackwheel or trackball.

The differences between browser.field (4.2) and browser.field2 (4.6) are reviewed in detail. Note that PhoneGap automatically includes the 4.6 control and only supports 4.6 or later devices. By default, Rhodes applications use the 4.2 browser control, but a configuration option allows you to use the 4.6 control. Rhodes supports BlackBerry OS versions 4.2 and above.

BlackBerry 4.2 Browser Control

Targeting the 4.2 browser control allows your application to reach a wider audience and allows your user interface to conform to the conventions users have come to expect from other BlackBerry applications.

CSS

Although the BlackBerry documentation leads you to believe you can use CSS, it buries the fact that it lacks the ability to position divs and style lists in fact, there isn't support for float, left, right, or any other modern positioning tag available in the 4.2 browser. For this reason, if you plan on building a single cross-platform application that also targets BlackBerry 4.2, table-based layouts are your best option.

The following tables were adapted from the BlackBerry Browser Version 4.2 Content Developer Guide.[1]

```
background styles
Background
background-color
background-image
background-repeat
```

```
font styles
Color
Font
font-family
font-size
font-style
font-weight
```

		border styles	
border	border-color	Border-style	border-width
border-bottom	border-bottom-color	Border-bottom-style	border-bottom-width
border-left	border-left-color	Border-left-style	border-left-width
border-right	border-right-color	Border-right-style	border-right-width
border-top	border-top-color	Border-top-style	border-top-width

---

[1] http://docs.blackberry.com/en/developers/deliverables/1143/browser_devguide.pdf

	font styles	Text-align	text-decoration	background-color	background styles
a	X	x	x	X	
body	X	x	x	X	X
div	X	x	x	X	
head	X	x	x	X	
img	X	x	x	X	
p	X	x	x	X	
span	X	x	x	X	
title	X	x	x	X	
frame	X	x	x	X	
frameset	X	x	x	X	
legend	X	x	x	X	
blink	X	x	x	X	
marquee	X	x	x	X	

	Font styles	background-color
blockquote	X	x
h1 - h6	X	x
pre	X	x
sub	X	x
sup	X	x
b	X	x
big	X	x
center	X	x
cite	X	x
code	X	x
dfn	X	x
i	X	x
em	X	x
font	X	x
kbd	X	x
s	X	x
samp	X	x
small	X	x
strike	X	x
strong	X	x
tt	X	x
u	X	x
var	X	X

	Font styles	border styles	text-align	text-decoration	background-color	height	width
form	X		X	x	x		
fieldset	X		X	x	x		
textarea	X	X		x	x		
input	X	X		x	x		
select	X	X		x	x		
optgroup	X		X	x	x		
option	X		X	x	x		
button	X	X		x	x	x	x
input type="button"	X	X		x	x	x	x
input type="submit"	X	X		x	x	x	x
input type="reset"	X	X		x	x	x	x
input type="text"	X	X		x	x		
img		X				x	x

	background-color	Font styles	text-align	text-decoration
ol	X	x	X	X
ul	X	x	X	X
li	X	x	X	X
dd	X	x	X	X
dt	X	x	X	X
*dir**	X	x	X	X
*menu**	X	x	X	X

A complete guide to supported tags can be found in the BlackBerry Browser Version 4.2 Content Developer Guide.

Fonts

There are three font families supported in the BlackBerry browser: Arial, Courier, and an oddly pixelated version of Helvetica (see Figure 14–1). The code for these fonts is provided in Listing 14–1. You can use custom font sizes in the stylesheet, but any font styles not included in the previous list of supported CSS must be applied through inline tags such as <b>, <em>, and so forth.

Arial **bold**
Arial 12pt **bold**

Courier **bold**

Courier 12pt **bold**

Helvetica **bold**

Helvetica 12pt **bold**

Figure 14–1. *The three fonts are shown in their default and 12px sizes.*

Listing 14–1. *The Code For the Font Text in Figure 14–1*

```
.arial {
 font-family: "Arial";
}
.arial12 {
 font-family: "Arial";    font-size: 12px;
}
.c {
 font-family: "Courier";
}
.c12 {
 font-family: "Courier"; font-size: 12px;
}
.helv {
 font-family: "Helvetica";
}
.helv12 {
 font-family: "Helvetica"; font-size: 12px;
}


<p>no font</o>
<div class="arial">
       <p>Arial <b>bold</b></p>
</div>
<div class="arial12">
       <p>Arial 12pt <b>bold</b></p>
</div>
<div class="c">
       <p>Courier <b>bold</b></p>
</div>
```

```
<div class="c12">
        <p>Courier 12pt <b>bold</b></p>
</div>
<div class="helv">
        <p>Helvetica <b>bold</b></p>
</div>
<div class="helv12">
        <p>Helvetica 12pt <b>bold</b></p>
</div>
```

Frames

The browser supports the `<frameset>` and `<frame>` elements, but does it not support inline frames (the `<iframe>` element). Instead, frames will be rendered vertically in a single column. See page 42 of the BlackBerry Browser Version 4.2 Content Developer Guide for more information if you wish to use frames in your application.

JavaScript

Regardless of the specific JavaScript capabilities, the most notable limitation is that the BlackBerry 4.2 browser will not allow you to modify the DOM. The browser supports JavaScript 1.0, 1.1, 1.2, 1.3, and small subsets of JavaScript 1.4 and 1.5. Additionally, a custom location function is supported on devices running BlackBerry Device Software Version 4.1 or later, but will likely be integrated into the cross-platform solution you have selected. However, when working directly with JavaScript on the BlackBerry, there are a few issues you may wish to note.

- In BlackBerry Device Software version 4.5 or earlier, if the BlackBerry Browser encounters any script that produces common dynamic HTML effects, the browser executes without error but produces no visual effect. JavaScript that is not supported simply produces an error, and unless the error is handled to satisfaction within the script, the script will be prevented from executing any further.

- On the BlackBerry Browser, users can turn JavaScript support on or off. Perhaps more importantly, JavaScript support can also be turned off through a centralized IT policy, leading to confusion in user expectations about what they should see on the screen.

In translation: Make sure your JavaScript degrades gracefully. Again, refer to your copy of the BlackBerry Browser Version 4.2 Content Developer Guide to determine if a particular feature you are interested in is available in the embedded browser.

Rhodes Tip for Dynamic Layout

If you need to layout a screen dynamically and you can divide the screen into table cells that are a percentage of the width or height, then you can use simple width and height attributes that specify a percentage. If you need to calculate width and height based on specific values, then it normally would not be possible to create a dynamic layout for the BlackBerry 4.2 browser. In Rhodes, however, you can do a calculation in the ERb (Embedded Ruby) HTML file.

This technique is demonstrated in Listings 14–2 and 14–3. The sample application (illustrated in Figure 14–2) has a layout for two images that can't be calculated based on a percentage of the screen width. To work around the browser limitation, this example includes a layout (in Listing 14–2) that dynamically determines the size of the outer and inner margin by calculating the size based on screen width and the width of the two images. This can be accomplished using Rhodes because the HTML page is processed, evaluating the Ruby code inside <%= %> before it is rendered in the browser control.

Figure 14–2. *In this layout, note that to create even spaces around the images, the screen cannot use percentages for table widths.*

Listing 14–2. *This Code in layout.erb Dynamically Generates the Width of the Table Cells When the Page is Rendered, So That it Will Be Laid Out Proportionally On Different Screen Sizes*

```
<% if System::get_property('platform') == 'Blackberry' %>
  <link href="/public/css/blackberry.css" type="text/css" rel="stylesheet"/>

  <style type="text/css">
    #start td.space {
    width: <%= (System.get_screen_width - 333)/3 %>px;
```

```
      }

      #start td.blurb {
      width: <%= (System.get_screen_width - 333)/3 +333 %>px;
      }

      #start td.sf1 {
        text-align: center;
        width: 133px;
      }
      #start td.sf2 {
        text-align: center;
        width: 200px;
      }

   </style>

<% else %>
   <link href="/public/css/xhtml.css" type="text/css" rel="stylesheet"/>
<% end %>
```

Listing 14–3. *The Elements Can Be Laid Out in a Table in the Page With the Table Sizes Controlled By the CSS Specified in layout.erb Shown in Listing 14–2*

```
<table id="start">
      <tr height="40"/>
      <tr>
   <td class="space"/>
   <td class="sf1"><img src="/public/images/sf1.png"></td>
   <td class="space"/>
   <td class="sf2"><img src="/public/images/sf2.png"></td>
   <td class="space"/>

  </tr>
  <tr>
    <td class="space"/>
    <td class="sf1">Day Trips</td>
    <td class="space"/>
    <td class="sf2">Night Life</td>
    <td class="space"/>

    </tr>

    <tr>
    <td class="space"/>
    <td class="blurb">Explore San Francisco.  Choose "day trips" or "night life" to find
fun things to do in and around San Francisco.</td>
    <td class="space"/>
    </tr>
</table>
```

BlackBerry 4.6 Browser Control

The BlackBerry 4.6 browser control is significantly easier for development than the 4.2 browser, since you can modify the DOM and you do have access to more CSS. While the 4.6 browser technically supports the latest standards (HTML 4.01, CSS 2.1, and DOM Level 2), in reality, modern desktop and other mobile browsers have moved forward. As of this writing, most popular JavaScript frameworks (jQuery, XUI, etc.) do not work on any BlackBerry web browser. The 4.6 browser also brings with it an awkward usability issue: in the 4.2 browser, the user can easily navigate form fields and links by a brief gesture with the trackball which jumps from field to field; however, the new browser requires that you navigate just as you would with a mouse or a touch screen by rolling the pointer around the screen which ends up being a slow and awkward experience with the trackball or trackpad.

Display and User Interaction

BlackBerry produces a wide variety of devices but along with choice and variety inevitably comes complexity. Blackberry devices are known to have at least 11 different listed screen resolutions, with variation ranging from 132×65 up to 360×480 (see Table 14–1).

Additionally, the range of pointer accuracy on BlackBerry devices is vast—from the precision of the Bold or Curve where the trackball lets you roll from element to element, to the tactile frustrations of the Storm where you need to leave wide spaces around your UI elements in order to give people any hope of hitting them. The usability of your application will not be apparent in the simulator, even if you try it on simulators that target different devices. It is easy to create a layout which looks and feels like an effective design in the simulator and then completely fails to allow someone to enter text or click a button on a specific device. For these reasons, it is critical that you test on the device early (and often) on actual devices for all of your target platforms.

Table 14–1. *BlackBerry Screen Resolutions*

Listed resolution	Model numbers	Brands
132 × 65	950	
160 × 160	857, 957	
240 × 160	7520	
240 × 240	7730, 7750, 7780	
240 × 260	7100, 7130, 8100, 8120, 8130	Pearl
240 × 320	8130, 8220	Pearl Flip

Listed resolution	Model numbers	Brands
320 × 240	8830, 8300, 8310, 8320, 8330, 8700, 8703e, 8707, 8800,8820	Curve
324 × 352		Charm
480 × 320	9000	Bold
480 × 360	8900	Curve
360 × 480	9500, 9530	Storm

Development Environment

One final complication: The native BlackBerry development environment is currently only fully accessible in Windows development environments. If you're developing your applications on a map and want to test your BlackBerry builds (which you should do early and often), you'll need to track down a development system running Windows XP or Vista. Windows 7 is not supported at the time of this writing. However, it is possible to develop on Macintosh hardware using a virtual machine, such as VMWare or Parallels.

Cascading Style Sheets

Cascading Style Sheets (CSS) define how HTML elements are displayed. Styling can happen in a few different places. The most common place for CSS is an external style sheet (which is a file with a *.css* extension). You place a <link> between your HTML <head> tags like Listing A–1.

Listing A–1. *HTML header - External Stylesheet*

```
<head>
    <link href="stylesheet.css" rel="stylesheet" type="text/css">
</head>
```

> **NOTE:** You can use relative or absolute paths to your style sheets for the href attribute of <link>.

You can also place a <style> tag in the <head> portion of your HTML document and define your CSS there (Listing A–2); this is called an *internal style sheet*.

Listing A–2. *HTML Header - Internal Stylesheet*

```
<head>
    <style type="text/css">
        …
    </style>
</head>
```

Finally you can add a style attribute to any HTML element and define your styles there; this is called an *inline style* (Listing A–3).

Listing A–3. *Inline Style*

```
<div style="width:50px;height:50px;">…</div>
```

The Cascading in Style Sheets

When an HTML element has multiple styles defined on it, the one with the highest priority will be chosen and override the rest. An inline style (a style defined on the HTML element) has the highest priority and will override any other CSS defined. Next is an internal style sheet (one defined in the header of your HTML document), then external style sheets (you reference these with a link tag in the header of your HTML document, which are typically declared before the internal style sheets). Finally, browser default options are at the bottom of the list, and will have the lowest priority.

- Inline styles
- Internal/external style sheets (last one defined determines style)
- Browser defaults

Note that overwriting happens only if the specificity of the selectors is the same. So, for example, let's say you have a style that applies to p elements in a div, and then later on you have a style that applies to all p elements.

p elements inside a div will get the first style, because the most specific style wins, even if there's a more general one later.

Style declarations aren't monolithic. When something gets "overridden," what's really happening is that any declarations that are the same level of specificity and the same property are overridden, but all the other properties remain.

So, for example, let's say you have something similar to Listing A–4.

Listing A–4. *Paragraph tag with color*

```
div p { /* applies to p elements inside a div */
 color: blue;
}
```

And then later on, you have Listing A–5.

Listing A–5. *Paragraph Tag with color and text decoration*

```
p { /* applies to all p elements */
 color: black;
 text-decoration: underline;
}
```

<p> elements in a div will be blue and underlined and all other <p> elements will be black. The more-specific declaration has a color so that overrides the general color, even though it is defined first. Because it doesn't say anything about text-decoration, that style is determined from the more-general set.

CSS Syntax

A typical CSS statement looks like this:

```
SELECTOR {DECLARATION[PROPERTY: VALUE];DECLARATION[PROPERTY:VALUE]; }
```

For example, consider Listing A–6.

Listing A–6. *Header 1 tag with color*

```
h1 { color: #FFFFFF; }

Selector-> h1
Declaration-> color: #FFFFFF;
Property-> color
Value-> #FFFFFF
```

CSS declarations always end with a semicolon, and curly brackets surround declaration groups.

> **NOTE:** Do not leave spaces between property values and units.
>
> Incorrect top: 20 px;
>
> Correct top: 20px;

Comments

A CSS comment begins with "/*", and ends with "*/", like Listing A–7.

Listing A–7. *Comments*

```
/* This is a comment */

/*
This is a
multiline
comment
*/
```

Identifying Elements with ID and Class

ID defines a special and unique case for an element (this means that it can only be used once per document). These should be treated like global variables and used sparingly. In CSS, an ID is declared with a pound sign (#) followed by a unique name, such as #unique_box in Listing A–8.

Listing A–8. *CSS ID Example*

```
<html>
    <head>
        <style type="text/css">
            #unique_box {
                width: 50px;
                height: 50px;
                background-color: blue;
            }
        </style>
    </head>
    <body>
        <div id="unique_box"></div>
```

```
    </body>
</html>
```

In CSS, if you follow a class declaration with a selector, you can define specific declarations for that element.

CSS classes define a special non-unique case for elements. Classes should be used when multiple elements require the same styling. CSS classes are declared with a period (.) followed by a unique name, such as .box in Listing A–9.

Listing A–9. *CSS Class Example*

```
<html>
    <head>
        <style type="text/css">
            .box {
                width: 50px;
                height: 50px;
            }
        </style>
    </head>
    <body>
        <div class="box"></div>
        <div class="box"></div>
        <div class="box"></div>
    </body>
</html>
```

In CSS, if you follow a class declaration with a selector, you can define specific declarations for that element. Where ".box" is the class, "p" is the selector, and "color: green;" is the declaration (Listing A–10).

Listing A–10. *Apply a class to a <p> tag*

```
.box p {
    color: green;
}
```

Common Patterns

Generally, you won't be writing CSS that applies to all <p> elements, or all <a> elements. You will write CSS that applies only to certain elements based on how they are placed relative to other elements. For example, you might have a specific style for all <p> elements inside any <div> with class 'bounding-box.'

Examples of nesting selectors include Listing A–11 and examples of grouping selectors include listing A–12.

Listing A–11. *Examples of nesting selectors*

```
div p { /* all p elements that are inside a div */
 color: green;
}

div p.box { /* all p elements with class box that are inside a div */
 color: black;
```

```
}

div.main-text p.box { /* all p elements with class box that are inside
a div with class main-text */
 color: blue;
}
```

Listing A–12. *Examples of grouping selectors*

```
/* all p and h1 elements inside the div with class main-text */
div.main-text p, div.main-text h1 {
  color: black;
}
```

Common CSS Attributes (Display: block verses inline)

The display property controls how an element is displayed. It does this with two properties called block and inline. The block property tells the element to take up the full width available and forces line breaks in text. The inline property tells the element to take up just as much width as necessary and doesn't force line breaks.

> **NOTE:** "display: none;" will hide an element, making it invisible.

These HTML elements have a display: block; by default:

```
<p>, <h1>…<h4>, <div>
```

These HTML elements have a display: inline; by default:

```
<a>, <span>
```

Visibility has two values, visible or hidden, to control whether an element is visible or not. [visibility: hidden;]

Margin clears the area outside of the container. Margin takes four values in a clockwise rotation: MARGIN TOP RIGHT BOTTOM LEFT. Each value must be defined in pixels, pt, em, or % (Listing A–13).

> **NOTE:** Negatives values are allowed, so that you may overlap content.

Listing A–13. *Margin Example*

```
margin-left: VALUE;
margin-right: VALUE;
margin-top: VALUE;
margin-bottom: VALUE;
```

Padding clears the area inside the container (Listing A–14). Padding takes four values in a clockwise rotation: PADDING TOP RIGHT BOTTOM LEFT. Each value must be defined in pixels, pt, em, or %. [p { padding: 0px 10px 0px 10px;}]

Listing A–14. *Padding Example*

```
padding-left: VALUE;
padding-right: VALUE;
padding-top: VALUE;
padding-bottom: VALUE;
```

Background controls the background color or image of an HTML element (Listing A–15). It has options BACKGROUND: COLOR IMAGE REPEAT ATTACHMENT POSITION. [body { background: #00ff00 url('image.png') no-repeat fixed top; }]

Listing A–15. *Background Example*

```
background-color: VALUE;
background-image: VALUE;
background-repeat: VALUE;
background-attachment: VALUE;
background-position: VALUE;
```

Color controls text color. Colors can be defined by name [color: red;], RGB [color: rgb(255,0,0);], or hex representation. [color: #ff0000;].

Text-align is used to set the horizontal alignment of text. [p {text-align: center;}]

Text-decoration allows you to over-line, under-line, line-through, or blink text. The blink option will flash the text and hide it at a fixed rate. It is not supported in IE, Safari, or Chrome. It is most commonly used to remove the decoration for link elements. [a { text-decoration: none; }]

Text-transform is used to turn everything into uppercase or lowercase letters, or capitalize the first letter of each word (Listing A–16). [h1 { text-transform: uppercase; }]

Float specifies how elements lay out relative to each other. Elements can be told to move as far left or right as they can, allowing other elements to wrap around them. Floating <div>(s) or <img>(s) is common.

Listing A–16. *Float Example*<html>

```
    <head>
       <style type="text/css">
          img {
             float: right;
          }
       </style>
    </head>
    <body>
```

<p> This text is only here to show wrapping around the image. You will see that the text will continue to flow on the left around the image on the right. You will also see that the image has floated as far right as possible (Listing A–17).

Listing A–17. *Text wrapping and images*

```
<img src="image.jpg" width="50" height="50" alt="some image" /></p>
   </body>
</html>
```

> **TIP:** Elements after the floated element(s) will continue to wrap. To avoid this, use the clear property on the elements you do not want floated (Listing A–18). Values of clear are: left, right, both, none, inherit.

Listing A–18. *Clear Example*

```
.foo {
   clear: both;
}
```

Index

A

<a> tag, 190–191
Action menu, File System Editor, 78
Activate for BlackBerry option, 137
ActiveSync window, Visual Studio 2008, 79
adb devices utility, 49
Add a New Item context menu item, Visual Studio 2008, 75
Add Devices button, iPhone Developer Program Portal, 30
Add New Project dialog box, Visual Studio 2008, 77
Add New Smart Device Project wizard, Visual Studio 2008, 67–68
Add or Remove Programs screen, Visual Studio 2008, 77
Add Project Output Group dialog box, File System Editor, 78
addGlossToIcon option, 216
AdHoc application, 31
ADT (Android Development Tools), 36, 136
ADT Layout Editor, 41
ADT plug-in, 41
Advanced panel, 229
Advanced tab, 212
Ajax, adding screens with jQTouch, 212–214
anchor tag, 218
Android
    building for Android device, 48–49
    development for
        building application, 39–46
        with Eclipse, 36–38
        embedding WebView in application, 46–48
    digitally signing application, 50
    HTML and CSS support on, 164
    overview, 35
    PhoneGap, open source framework for, 136
    and Rhodes
        debugging on, 101
        running application on, 94
Android Development Tools (ADT), 36, 136
Android Market, 50
Android SDK and AVD Manager, 37
Android Virtual Device (AVD), 37
Android WebKit browser control, 170
/android/framework/assets/www directory, 140
Any iPhone OS Device option, Xcode, 32–33
.apk file, 50
app folder, 90, 96–97
App IDs, iPhone Developer Program Portal, 31
App Store style, list styles with iWebKit, 191–192
App World, BlackBerry, 63–64
Appearance section, Visual Studio 2008, 70, 73
app.js file, 155, 158
Apple Mail application, 220
Application Folder, 78
Application ID field, Titanium, 154
Application tab, 49
application.css file, 226
application.js file, 227
application.rb file, 91, 121, 129
applications
    adding to CAB Projects, 78
    building and testing, 58
    creating shortcuts, 78
    distributing, 80
    embedding Web View in, 75
    layout template, adding iWebKit framework to, 204
    marketplace, 2–4
applist class, 187
app/Product/index.erb page, 97
apps
    building. See also base functionality; interfaces, creating

adding WebBrowser controls, 75
create Xcode project, 19
creating HTML pages, 75
creating Smart Device Projects, 67
deploying and testing, 72
embedding Web View in
    applications, 75
loading HTML in WebBrowser
    controls, 76
overview, 18
installing on devices
    creating provisioning profiles, 32
    finding device IDs, 31
    install provisioning profiles, 32
    installing and running on devices,
      32–33
    manually setting up iPhone
      provisioning, 30
    using development provisioning
      assistant, 29–30
packaging and distributing
    adding applications to CAB Projects,
      78
    adding CAB Projects to solutions, 77
    adding Registry entries, 78
    building and deploying CAB files, 78–
      79
    creating application shortcuts, 78
    customizing product names, 77
    installing CAB files, 79
    overview, 76
app/Settings/setting.yml file, 116
Appstore application, 200
arrow class, 220
Ask, Julie, 4
Associated Attributes for Backend
      Credentials section, RhoHub, 126
Attribute Inspector, Interface Builder, 23
attributes, for CSS, 251–253
Attributes Inspector, Interface Builder, 28
authenticate method, in RhoSync, 121
authentication, in RhoSync, 116–117
Authenticode Signature option, Solution
      Explorer, 79
auto class, 194
AVD (Android Virtual Device), 37

■ B

Back button, 214–215, 218
back class, 214

background
    attribute, 252
    image property, 173
    position attributes, 176
backSelector option, 216
base functionality
    adding buttons to views, 69
    creating click event handlers, 71–72
    customizing buttons, 70
    overview, 68
basic views, in jQTouch, 217–218
BasicEditField class, 60
/beatles HREF, 214
/beatles link, 213
Behavior section, Visual Studio 2008, 76
Berries button, 86
BES (BlackBerry Enterprise Server), 52
Bigfield class, 197
BlackBerry
    applications, building and testing, 58
    BlackBerry Browser Field
      BlackBerry App World, 63–64
      building for BlackBerry devices, 62–
        63
      over the air (OTA) distribution, 63
      overview, 61
    browser-rendering engine 4.2
      CSS in, 237–239
      dynamic layout in with Rhodes, 242–
        243
      fonts for, 239–241
      frames in, 241
      JavaScript support in, 241
    browser-rendering engine 4.6, 244
    code, 57–60
    creating Eclipse project, 53–55
    creating interfaces, 55–57
    development environment for, 245
    HTML and CSS support on, 165
    Java Development, 52–53
    labels, text fields, and buttons, 58–60
    and limitations of target browser, 236
    overview, 235
    PhoneGap, open source framework for,
      137
    platform of, 51–52
    and Rhodes
      debugging on, 101
      running application on, 94–95
    screen resolutions for, 244–245
    user interaction on, 244–245

BlackBerry Enterprise Server (BES), 52
BlackBerry JDE Plug-in, 137
BlackBerry menu, Eclipse, 55
BlackBerry Project option, Eclipse, 54
BlackBerry Signature Tool, 62
BlackBerry Workspace, Eclipse, 55
blackberry/framework/ directory, 137, 140
Blue Button - Left element, 195
Blue Button - Right element, 195
body, with iWebKit, 186
<body> tag, 186–187, 190, 194, 204, 216
browser.field (4.2) engine, 236
BrowserField class, 61
browser-rendering engine 4.2, for
        BlackBerry
    CSS in, 237–239
    dynamic layout in with Rhodes, 242–243
    fonts for, 239–241
    frames in, 241
    JavaScript support in, 241
browser-rendering engine 4.6, for
        BlackBerry, 244
Build and Go option, Xcode, 26, 33
Build and Run as Android Application menu
        option, 136
Build and Run command, Xcode, 157
Build and Run option, 135, 142, 205
Build page, Solution Explorer, 79
Build tab, Xcode, 33
Build Target list, 40
build.yml file, 90, 93
Button Bar, Android, 182
button bars, HTML and CSS support for,
        168
Button class, 44, 215
Button control, 44
button xtype, 230
buttons
    adding to views, 69
    customizing, 70
    layout of, 22–23
    overview, 58–60
    on screens with jQTouch, 215

■C
CAB files, 78–79
CAB Projects
    adding applications to, 78
    adding to solutions, 77

CABProject Property Pages dialog box,
        Solution Explorer, 77
CABProject\Debug folder, 79
cacheGetRequests option, 216
Camera example
    in PhoneGap, 150–152
    Rhodes application framework, 106–108
    Titanium Mobile, 158–160
cancel and back, adding screens with
        jQTouch, 214–215
cancel class, 214
Cascading Style Sheets. *See* CSS
Certificate box, Solution Explorer, 79
Certificates option, iPhone Developer
        Program Portal, 30
check boxes, HTML and CSS support for,
        169–171
checkbox class, 198, 230
Choose button, 135
class, identifying elements in CSS with, 250
class attribute, 209, 220
Class menu item, Eclipse, 55
classic style, list styles with iWebKit, 188–
        190
Classic type, 187
clean.bat file, 101
click event handlers, creating, 71–72
Click Select from Store button, Solution
        Explorer, 79
close/back action, 111
code, 25, 57–60
Code Signing Identity, Xcode, 33
color attribute, 252
comments, in CSS, 249
components
    adding in Sencha Touch, 231
    xtype, 230
com.xplatform.helloworld package, 55
Configure BlackBerry Workspace, Eclipse,
        55
connecting code to views, 26
Connection Inspector, Interface Builder, 28
contact_controller.rb file, 104
Contact/index.erb page, 105
Contacts example
    in PhoneGap, 146–150
    Rhodes application framework, 103–106
Contacts/app/Contact/index.erb page, 105
Contacts/app/Photo/index.erb page, 107
Contacts/app/Photo/photo_controller.rb file,
        107

container xtype, 230
content <div> tag, 188
content class, 186
ContentView control, 47
context menus, HTML and CSS support for, 168
controller code, writing, 23–25
controls, WebBrowser, 75–76
Copy items into destination group's folder (if needed) check box, 201
Copy to Output Directory field, solution browser, 75
create, read, update, and delete (CRUD), 96
Create Application button, RhoHub, 123
Create Folder References for any added folders check box, 201
Create Folder References option, 201
create method, in RhoSync, 119
Create New Object page, RhoHub, 123
Create Object button, RhoHub, 123
create_hash argument, 119
cross-platform development, 9–10
cross-platform frameworks, 5–6, 10–13
CRUD (create, read, update, and delete), 96
CSS (Cascading Style Sheets)
    applying to elements, based on placement, 250
    attributes for, 251–253
    on BlackBerry, browser-rendering engine 4.2, 237–239
    comments in, 249
    identifying elements, 249–250
    priority of styles in, 247–248
    syntax for, 248–249
css folder, 227
cubeSelector option, 216
current_user method, 116
current_user.login method, 116

D

Dashboard, RhoHub, 125
data storage format, in RhoSync, 114
database (Rhom), for Rhodes, 86–87
datapanel xtype, 230
dataview xtype, 230
dealloc method, 25
Debug\HelloWorld.cab, 77
debug-with-comments.js file, 226
delete method, in RhoSync, 120
Demo folder, 201

Design section, Visual Studio 2008, 70
Design view, Visual Studio 2008, 68
Developer menu, 229
Developer Portals Device registration page, 31
development
    architecture, for Rhodes, 84–85
    environment, for BlackBerry, 245
    provisioning assistant, 29–30
Device Application template, Visual Studio 2008, 67
device capabilities, in Titanium Mobile, 157–158
Device Chooser dialog box, 49
Device Emulator Manager menu item, Visual Studio 2008, 76, 79
devices
    capabilities with Rhodes, 101–102
    IDs, finding, 31
    iPhone Developer Program Portal, 30
digitally signing application for Android, 50
Directory field, Titanium, 154
display: none attribute, 251
dissolveSelector option, 216
<div> tag, 186, 194, 250
DOM (Document Object Model), 207, 236
doublead class, 191
Downloads folder, 58
downward-facing disclosure indicator, 173
dump_pic callback, 152

E

Eclipse
    creating Eclipse project, 53–55
    development for Android with, 36–38
edgetoedge class, 218
Edit Text item, 43
Editor screen, RhoHub, 126
Editor tab, RhoHub, 126
EditText control, 45
EditText item, 42–43
elements, in CSS, 249–250
Embedded Ruby (ERB), 84, 242
enterEventDispatcher( ) method, 57
Entity-Attribute-Value (EVA), 114
ERB (Embedded Ruby), 84, 242
EVA (Entity-Attribute-Value), 114
event handlers
    click, 71
    creating, 72

example applications
    Rhodes application framework
        Camera, 106–108
        Contacts, 103–106
        Geolocation, 108–111
    RhoSync, product inventory, 122–130
    Titanium Mobile, Camera, 158–160
Ext.getCmp('mainscreen') call, 232
Ext.setup method, 227
Ext.TabPanel class, 232
ext-touch.css file, 226
ext-touch-debug.js file, 226
ext-touch.js file, 226

F

fadeSelector option, 216
fail callback, 149
field xtype, 230
fieldChanged method, 60
FieldChangeListener method, 60
fieldset xtype, 230
<fieldset> tag, 196, 199
File menu
    Registry Editor, 78
    Visual Studio 2008, 67, 77
File System context menu item, Solution
    Explorer, 78
File System Editor, 78
File System on Target Machine, File System
    Editor, 78
files, CAB, 78–79
fixedViewport option, 216
flipSelector option, 216
float attribute, 252
fonts, on BlackBerry, 239–241
Force https://... option, Android SDK and
    AVD Manager, 37
Force https://... sources to be fetched using
    http://... check box, 109
form xtype, 230–231
<form> tag, 196
Form1.cs Design view, Visual Studio 2008,
    73
Form1.cs file, 71
forms, with iWebKit, 196–199
formSelector option, 216
Forward button, 215
<frame> element, 241
frames, on BlackBerry, 241
<frameset> element, 241

Framework folder, 204
frameworks, cross-platform, 5–6, 10–13
fullscreen (Boolean) property, 228
fullscreen config option, 229
fullScreen option, 216
fullScreenClass option, 216

G

geo fix command, 108
GeoLocation class, 110
Geolocation example, Rhodes application
    framework, 108–111
GET requests, 216
getContacts function, 149
getContacts_callback, 149
glossOnIcon (Boolean) property, 228
Google Maps application, 200
graytitle class, 190
greetingLabel, Interface Builder, 25, 60
greetingLabel IBOutlet, 24
greetingLabel property, 24
greetings text, aligning, 22
Groups & Files section, Xcode, 32–33

H

Hammerschmidt, Christoph, 3
HEAD section, 223
<head> tag, 186, 247
headers, required for iWebKit, 186
Hello BlackBerry Application, 59
Hello iPhone! button, Interface Builder, 25
Hello World application
    in PhoneGap, 139–140
    Titanium Mobile, 155–157
Hello World project, 54
HelloiPhone file, 32
HelloiPhone project, 19
HelloiPhoneViewController implementation
    declaration, 24
HelloiPhoneViewController.h file, 23
HelloiPhoneViewController.m file, 24
HelloiPhoneViewController.xib file, 20, 25
Hello.java class, 40–41, 44, 46
helloMessage string, 24
HelloWorld application, 58
HelloWorld class, 55, 57
HelloWorld.java file, 56
HelloWorldScreen class, 57

HelloWorldScreen constructor, 57
/helpers folder, 91
HKEY_CURRENT_USER, Registry Editor, 78
Home Button element, 195
home screen, iPhone Developer Program
        Portal, 30
href attribute, 247
HTML
    on Android, 164
    on BlackBerry, 165
    button bars, 168
    check boxes, 169–171
    context menus, 168
    on iOS, 164
    lists, 178–180
    loading in WebBrowser controls, 76
    menus, 166
    navigation bars, 168–180
    overview, 163
    pages, creating, 75
    radio buttons, 175–177
    screen-based considerations, 165–166
    selection boxes, 171–173
    tab bars, 167
    text areas, 174–175
    text boxes, 173–174
    toolbars, 167
    UI widgets, 169
    and WebKit web views, 178–182
    on Windows Mobile, 165

■I

IBAction keyword, 23–24
IBOutlet keyword, 23
Icon (String) property, 228
icon/ folder, 90
icon option, 216
ID
    finding, 31
    identifying elements in CSS with, 249–
        250
IDE (integrated development environment),
        52
<iframe> element, 241
/images folder, 204
<img> tag, 97, 152
Import 'Button' (android.widget) option, 44
Import wizard, Solution Explorer, 79
index.erb file, 91
index.erb page, 97, 107

index.html file, 138–139, 142–143, 146, 150,
        184, 205, 223, 226
index.html web page, 140
index.js file, 226–227, 229
initialization options, for jQTouch, 215–223
initialize method, in RhoSync, 116
initializeTouch option, 216
inline style, 247
inline tags, 239
<input type="checkbox">, 198
<input type="radio"> tag, 198
<input type="tel"> tag, 197
<input type="text"> tag, 197
<input> tag, 199
Install selected button, 109
Installed Components, Eclipse, 55
Installer Package, 134
interactivity, in Sencha Touch, 232
interfaces, creating
    add UI elements, 21
    adding UI elements, 21
    aligning text greetings, 22
    buttons and text field layouts, 22–23
    connecting code to views, 25–26
    overview, 20
    simple user application, 55–57
    Web View, 26–28
    writing controller code, 23–25
internal style sheet, 247
Inventory application, 123
iOS, HTML and CSS support on, 164
iPhone Developer Program Portal, 30
iPhone OS Application option, Xcode, 19, 26
iPhone Simulator menu, 101
iPhone Simulator.app, 208
/iphone/PhoneGap-based Application/www
        directory, 140
iPhones
    building apps, 18–28. See also
        interfaces, creating
    development of, 18
    installing apps on devices
        creating provisioning profiles, 32
        finding device IDs, 31
        install provisioning profiles, 32
        installing and running on devices,
            32–33
        manually setting up provisioning, 30
        using development provisioning
            assistant, 29–30

PhoneGap, open source framework for, 134–135
and Rhodes
    debugging on, 100–101
    running application on, 93
Xcode, 17
iphone/www directory, 142
iPod style, list styles with iWebKit, 193–194
ipodlist class, 188, 194
iScroll library, Cubiq, 180
iTunes, 190–191, 193
iWebDemo project, 26
iWebDemoViewController.xib file, 26
iWebKit
    body, 186
    forms with, 196–199
    headers required, 186
    and HTML structure, 185–186
    integrating in mobile applications
        adding framework to application
            layout template, 204
        native iPhone application, 201–202
        with Rhodes, 203–204
        setting up PhoneGap for, 205
    and landscape mode, 200
    lists with
        App Store style, 191–192
        classic, 188–190
        iPod style, 193–194
        iTunes classic style, 190–191
        iTunes style, 193
        overview, 187
    navigation with, 194–195
    overview, 183–184
    phone integration in, 200
iWebKit/app/layout.erb file, 204
iWebkitDemoViewController.h file, 26
iWebkitDemoViewController.m file, 27–28
iWebkitDemoViewController.xib file, 28

J

Jarsigner tool, 50
Java Development, 52–53
Java Development Kit (JDK), 52
Java Runtime Environment (JRE), 52
JavaScript, support for on BlackBerry, 241
javascript folder, 227
JDK (Java Development Kit), 52
jqt theme, 210–211
jQTouch
    adding screens
        with Ajax, 212–214
        buttons on, 215
        cancel and back, 214–215
        overview, 211
    basic views, 217–218
    creating simple application, 209–211
    customizing application animations, 218
    initialization options for, 215–223
    integration
        with PhoneGap, 222–223
        with Rhodes, 222
    lists, 218–220
    overview, 207
    running example code, 208
    themes in, 221–222
    toolbars, 218
jquery.js file, 142–143
JRE (Java Runtime Environment), 52

K

Kaneda, David, 207
Kawamoto, Dawn, 3
Keychain Access, 30
Keytool tool, 50
Kim, Gary, 4
Kitchen Sink application, Titanium, 158

L

Label element, Interface Builder, 22
LabelField class, 57, 60
labels, text fields, and buttons, 58–60
landscape mode, and iWebKit, 200
Landscape view, 233
Launch Assistant, iPhone Developer
        Program Portal, 30
Launch button, Titanium, 154–155
Layout Editor, 41, 43
Layout menu, Interface Builder, 22
Layout tab, 41
layout.erb file, 91, 204, 242–243
Left Button element, 195
Left Navigation element, 195
leftButton class, 215
<li> tag, 149, 178, 187–188, 199, 218, 220
Library menu item, Interface Builder, 20
Library window, Interface Builder, 20–21, 26
<link> tag, 247

list class, 187
lists
    HTML and CSS support for, 178–180
    with iWebKit
        App Store style, 191–192
        classic, 188–190
        iPod style, 193–194
        iTunes classic style, 190–191
        iTunes style, 193
        overview, 187
    in jQTouch, 218–220
loading.html file, 91
Login screen, 130

M

main method, 57
MainScreen class, 57
main.xml panel, 41
make command, 134
Manage Certificates option, Solution
        Explorer, 79
Manage tab, iPhone Developer Program
        Portal, 30
manifest.xml file, 49
map_example/app/Person/person_controller
        .rb file, 110
MapView class, 110
margin attribute, 251
Market application, 50
Menu button, 42
menus, HTML and CSS support for, 166
metal class, 218
MFC (Microsoft Foundation Classes), 228
Min SDK Version box, 40
mobile applications, 6–10
models, generating in Rhodes, 95–98
Model-View-Controller (MVC), 18, 83–84, 95
musiclist class, 187
MVC (Model-View-Controller), 18, 83–84, 95
MyCompany, Registry Editor, 78

N

Name field, Titanium, 154
Name value, Registry Editor, 78
nameFilter parameter, 149
Native Development Kit (NDK), 36, 39
native picker control, iOS, 171

native UI elements, and runtime
        architecture, 86
navigation
    bars, HTML and CSS support for, 168–
        180
    with iWebKit, 194–195
navigator.camera.getPicture function, 152
navigator.contacts.displayContact function,
        149
navigator.contacts.getAllContacts function,
        149
navigator.contacts.newContact function,
        149
NDK (Native Development Kit), 36, 39
New App ID button, iPhone Developer
        Program Portal, 31
New email application, 200
New Key option, Registry Editor, 78
new person form, 109
New Project dialog box, Eclipse, 53
New Project icon, Titanium, 154
New Project menu item, Visual Studio 2008,
        77
New Project window, Visual Studio 2008, 67
New Referencing Outlet, Interface Builder,
        26
new.erb page, 110
Nielson, Jacob, 6
NSURLRequest, Xcode, 28
numberfield xtype, 230

O

OAV (object-attribute-value), 114
Object Relational Manager (ORM), 84
object-attribute-value (OAV), 114
OHA (Open Handset Alliance), 35
onClick callbacks, 149
onClick event, 45, 160
onClick method, 45
onCreate method, 40, 44–45
onKeyUp event, 150
onReady (Function) property, 228
onReady property, 227
Open Handset Alliance (OHA), 35
Options menu, 130
Organizer window, Xcode, 31, 33
ORM (Object Relational Manager), 84
OTA (over the air) distribution, 63
Other Project Types, Visual Studio 2008, 77
Outline tab, 43

Output file name field, Solution Explorer, 77
over the air (OTA) distribution, 63

P

p elements, 248
<p> tag, 248, 252
Package menu item, Eclipse, 55
padding attribute, 251
page-home div, 212
pageitem class, 190, 199
pages, HTML, 75
pageSize option, 149
/palm/framework/www directory, 140
panel xtype, 230–231
pause/play icon, 194
Perez, Bryan, 6
Personal Information Management (PIM),
        103, 146
PersonController class, 110
pg_camera project, 150
pg_contacts project, 146, 152
Phone application, 200
PhoneGap
    camera example, 150–152
    contacts example, 146–150
    Hello World application in, 139–140
    overview, 131–133
    PhoneGap simulator for, 138
    setting up for
        Android, 136
        BlackBerry, 137
        iPhone, 134–135
        iWebKit, 205
    tip calculator example, 141–145
PhoneGap Simulator, 138, 146
PhoneGap.addConstructor function, 149
phonegap/android directory, 136
PhoneGap-based Application option,
        Xcode, 134
phonegap/blackberry/framework/src/www/
        directory, 144
phonegap/iphone folder, 134
phonegap.jdp file, 137
phonegap.js file, 149
PhoneGapLib library, 134
PhoneGapLibInstaller.pkg file, 134
phoneStartupScreen (String) property, 228
photo_controller.rb file, 107
PIM (Personal Information Management),
        103, 146

Placeholder attribute
    HTML5, 173
    Interface Builder, 23
plastic class, 218
platform, 51–52
popSelector option, 216
Portrait view, 233
preloadImages (Array) property, 228
preloadImages option, 216
Pretty format, 188
Product edit page, 100
product inventory example, in RhoSync
    debugging source adapters, 130
    generating RhoSync application, 128
    implementing source adapter, 126
    overview, 122–125
    setting up RhoSync server, 129
    testing application, 130
    testing source adapter, 126–130
product names, customizing, 77
product_controller.rb file, 96
product_spec.rb file, 128
ProductName field, Visual Studio 2008, 77
product.rb file, 96, 126, 128
product.rb source adapter, 126
Products link, 97
Program Portal, 31
Programs Folder, File System Editor, 78
Progressive Disclosure, 166
Project creation dialog box, Eclipse, 54
Project drop-down list, File System Editor,
        78
Project Type field, Titanium, 154
Project Types pane, Visual Studio 2008, 67,
        77
projects, Eclipse, 53–55
Properties context menu item, Solution
        Explorer, 77–78
Properties pane, Visual Studio 2008, 70, 73
Properties panel, 43
Properties section, solution browser, 75
Properties tab, 43, 76
Properties Window
    Registry Editor, 78
    Visual Studio 2008, 77
property grid, Visual Studio 2008, 77
provisioning
    manually setting up, 30
    profiles, creating, 32
public/ folder, 90

public void fieldChanged(Field field, int context) method, 60
Publisher URL field, Titanium, 154
pushScreen( ) method, 57
puts @result.inspect statement, 130

Q

query method, in RhoSync, 117–118

R

radio buttons
    HTML and CSS support for, 175–177
    select modal view, Android, 171
Radio xtype, 231
radiobutton class, 198
Rails. See Ruby on Rails, and Rhodes
rake clean:android command, 92
rake clean:bb command, 92
rake clean:iphone command, 92
rake clean:win32 command, 92
rake clean:wm command, 92
rake commands, 92
rake device:android:debug command, 92
rake device:android:production command, 92
rake device:bb:debug command, 92
rake device:bb:production command, 92
rake device:iphone:production command, 92
rake device:wm:production command, 92
rake program, 91
rake run wm:dev command, 92
rake run wm:devcab command, 92
rake run wm:emu command, 92
rake run wm:emucab command, 92
rake run:android command, 92
rake run:android:device command, 92
rake run:bb command, 92, 95
rake run:iphone command, 92–93
rake run:wm:emu command, 95
rake task, 91
rake uninstall:android command, 92
rake uninstall:android:device command, 92
Rakefile file, 90
rake:run command, 98
Received Actions, Interface Builder, 25
Registry entries, adding, 78
Remove context menu item, 42

Request Certificate button, iPhone Developer Program Portal, 30
Research in Motion (RIM), 51, 165, 235
Reset Content and Settings... menu item, iPhone Simulator menu, 101
resignFirstResponder method, 25
res/layout/main.xml file, 40, 42
resources directory, 186
rhoconfig.txt file, 90, 100, 103, 107
Rhodes application framework
    building application, 89–91
    Camera example, 106–108
    Contacts example, 103–106
    database for (Rhom), 86–87
    debugging in
        on Android, 101
        on BlackBerry, 101
        on iPhone, 100–101
    development architecture for, 84–85
    device capabilities with, 101–102
    dynamic layout with, for BlackBerry browser-rendering engine 4.2, 242–243
    example applications
        Camera, 106–108
        Contacts, 103–106
        Geolocation, 108–111
    generating model in, 95–98
    Geolocation example, 108–111
    installing, 88–89
    integrating iWebKit in mobile applications with, 203–204
    overview, 83–84
    and Ruby on Rails, 88
    running application
        on Android, 94
        on BlackBerry, 94–95
        on iPhone, 93
        overview, 91–92
        on Windows Mobile 6, 95
    runtime architecture for, 85–86
    threading in, 87
rhogen app command, 89
rhogen model command, 95, 106
RhoLog.txt file, 100
Rhom, database for Rhodes, 86–87
Rhomobile app directory structure, 88
Rho::RhoContact.find(:all) function, 104–105
RhoSync
    authenticate method, 121
    authentication in, 116–117

create method, 119
data storage format in, 114
delete method, 120
initialize method, 116
methods in
  authenticate, 121
  create, 119
  delete, 120
  initialize, 116
  query, 117–118
  sync, 119
  update, 120
overview, 113
product inventory example
  debugging source adapters, 130
  generating RhoSync application, 128
  implementing source adapter, 126
  overview, 122–125
  setting up RhoSync server, 129
  testing application, 130
  testing source adapter, 126–130
query method, 117–118
source adapters in, 115
sync method, 119
update method, 120
rhosync/lib directory, 128
rhosync/vendor/sync directory, 128
RichTextField class, 57, 61
Right Button element, 195
Right Navigation element, 195
RIM (Research in Motion), 51, 165, 235
R.layout.main parameter, 40
rounded class, 219
Ruby on Rails, and Rhodes, 88
Run menu, 41
Run on Device screen, Titanium, 157
runtime architecture, for Rhodes, 85–86

▪S

SaaS (Software As A Service), 113
SampleWebView.java class, 48
sayHelloToUser method, 24–25
scaffold-generated app, 130
Scalable view, 166
schema.rb file, 88
scope (Object) property, 228
screens
  adding with jQTouch
    with Ajax, 212–214
    buttons on, 215

cancel and back, 214–215
overview, 211
resolutions, for BlackBerry, 244–245
Scroll view, 166
SDK directory, 37
SDK Setup.exe file, 37
SDK tools/ directory, 49
Search box, Interface Builder, 21
searchbox class, 186
Select Certificate window, Solution Explorer, 79
Select class, 198
select xtype, 230
<select> tag, 198
selection boxes, HTML and CSS support for, 171–173
Sencha Touch
  adding components in, 231
  interactivity in, 232
  overview of framework, 227–231
  setting up, 225–227
Sencha Touch library files, 227
Server tab, RhoHub, 126
servers, RhoSync, 129
setChangeListener(this) method, 60
setContentView method, 40
Settings, RhoHub, 125
Settings drop-down menu, Interface Builder, 20
/Settings folder, 91
Settings screen, 90
Setup and Deployment, Visual Studio 2008, 77
shortcuts, applications, 78
Show Develop menu in menu bar option, 212, 229
Show Error Console menu option, 229
Show Records option, RhoHub, 126
Show Web Inspector option, 229
showContact function, 149
Simple format, 188
Simple Tip Calculator Application for BlackBerry, 144
Simulator option, 135
slider xtype, 230
slideSelector option, 217
slideupSelector option, 217
SMALL element, 220
smallfield class, 197
Smart Device Cab project, Solution Explorer, 78

Smart Device CAB Project template, Visual Studio 2008, 77
Smart Device option, Visual Studio 2008, 67
Smart Device Projects, creating, 67
SmartDeviceProject1 project, 72
smartphones
    application marketplace, 2–4
    cross-platform frameworks, 5–6, 10–13
    mobile applications, 6–10
    overview, 1
    web techniques, 10
SMS application, 200
SOFTWARE, Registry Editor, 78
Software As A Service (SaaS), 113
Solution Explorer, 78
source adapters, in RhoSync
    debugging, 130
    implementing, 126
    overview, 115
    testing, 126–130
source class, 114
SourceAdapter class, 114
sources subdirectory, 128
spacer xtype, 230–231
<span class="graytitle"> tag, 199
<span class="number"> tag, 194
<span> tag, 190, 194
spec/sources/ subdirectory, 128
splitbutton component, 231, 233–234
src directory, 40, 44
Start Menu Folder, File System Editor, 78
startupScreen option, 217
stash_result function, 119
statusBar option, 217
statusBarStyle (String) property, 228
<style> tag, 247
Submit button, Visual Studio 2008, 74
submitButton handler, Visual Studio 2008, 74
submitForm function, 149
submitSelector option, 217
super( ) method, 57
swapSelector option, 217
/symbian.wrt/framework/www directory, 140
sync method, in RhoSync, 119
syntax, for CSS, 248–249

■T

tab bars, HTML and CSS support for, 167
tab group, Titanium, 160

tabBarHidden property, Titanium, 160
tabletStartupScreen (String) property, 228
tabpanel xtype, 230
tail -f command, 101
takePicture function, 152
target attribute, 214
Target Machine pane, File System Editor, 78
Targets drop-down, Xcode, 33
Task details page, 99
Tasks list page, 98
Tasks new page, 99
Templates pane, Visual Studio 2008, 67, 77
Terminal.app application, 134
Test & Package tab, Titanium, 154–155
text areas, HTML and CSS support for, 174–175
text boxes, HTML and CSS support for, 173–174
text fields, 22–23, 58–60
text greetings, aligning, 22
Text property, 44
text-align attribute, 252
textarea xtype, 231
Textbox class, 199
text-decoration attribute, 252
Textfield xtype, 231
text-transform attribute, 252
TextView control, 44–45
theme.css file, 221
themes, in jQTouch, 221–222
themes/ directory, 222
themes/apple/theme.min.css file, 211
themes/jqt/theme.min.css file, 211
threading in Rhodes, 87
tip calculator example, in PhoneGap, 141–145
Titanium Mobile
    building applications in, 157
    Camera example, 158–160
    device capabilities in, 157–158
    Hello World application, 155–157
    overview, 153–154
Titanium.UI module, 157
Titanium.UI.AlertDialog class, 157
Titanium.UI.Android module, 157
Titanium.UI.Button class, 157
Titanium.UI.iPhone module, 157
Title element, 195
to_s method, 110, 118
toolbar component, 234
toolbar xtype, 230

toolbars
    HTML and CSS support for, 167
    in jQTouch, 218
toolbox, Visual Studio 2008, 73
Toolbox pane, Visual Studio 2008, 69, 73
Tools menu
    Interface Builder, 20, 22, 25–26
    Visual Studio 2008, 76
topbar class, 186, 194
Touch Up Inside option, Interface Builder,
    25

U

UDIDs (Unique Device Identifiers), 30
UI elements
    adding, 21
    native, and runtime architecture, 86
UI widgets, HTML and CSS support for, 169
UiApplication class, 57, 59
UIWebView, Interface Builder, 27
<ul class="pageitem"> tag, 190
<ul> tag, 178, 187–188, 190, 199, 218
Unique Device Identifiers (UDIDs), 30
update method, in RhoSync, 120
update_hash parameter, 120
update(txt) function, 232
USB Debugging check box, 49
Use Current Location check box, 109–110
useAnimations option, 217
user interaction, for BlackBerry, 244–245
User Templates section, 134
UserInterface class, 59
UserInterfaceScreen class, 60
userNameField class, 24–25, 60
Users tab, RhoHub, 125

V

View context menu item, Solution Explorer,
    78
View Icons and Descriptions setting,
    Interface Builder, 20
View Source option, 229
View window, Interface Builder, 26
View-based Application template, Xcode,
    19, 26
viewDidLoad method, 202–203
views
    adding buttons to, 69

connecting code to, 25–26
Views menu, 42
virtual device properties, Android SDK and
    AVD Manager, 38
visibility attribute, 251

W

W3C (World Wide Web Consortium), 131
Wasserman, Todd, 6
web techniques, 10
Web View
    HTML and CSS support for, 178–182
    Xcode, 26–28, 75
_webapp target, 218
WebBrowser controls
    adding, 75
    loading HTML in, 76
WebBrowser element, Visual Studio 2008,
    76
WebKit web views, HTML and CSS support
    for, 178–182
-webkit-appearance property, 173
WebView, embedding in application, 46–48
WebView.navigate method, 108
Widarsson, Fredrik, 3
width property, 44
Windows Marketplace for Mobile, 76, 80
Windows Mobile
    building apps. See also base
        functionality
        adding WebBrowser controls, 75
        creating HTML pages, 75
        creating Smart Device Projects, 67
        deploying and testing, 72
        embedding Web View in
            applications, 75
        loading HTML in WebBrowser
            controls, 76
    distributing applications, 80
    HTML and CSS support on, 165
    overview, 65
    packaging and distributing apps
        adding applications to CAB Projects,
            78
        adding CAB Projects to solutions, 77
        adding Registry entries, 78
        building and deploying CAB files, 78–
            79
        creating application shortcuts, 78
        customizing product names, 77

installing CAB files, 79
overview, 76
version 6, 95
version 6.5 development, 66
Windows Phone Marketplace, 66
/winmo/www directory, 140
withimage class, 188
Wolfe, Alexander, 4
World Wide Web Consortium (W3C), 131
WWDR (Worldwide Developers Relation), 30

www directory, 139, 146, 150, 205, 222
www/index.html file, 140

 X

Xcode, 17–19
Xcode file copy prompt, 202
Xcode groups option, 200–201
.xcodeproj file, 157

You Need the Companion eBook

Your purchase of this book entitles you to buy the companion PDF-version eBook for only $10. Take the weightless companion with you anywhere.

We believe this Apress title will prove so indispensable that you'll want to carry it with you everywhere, which is why we are offering the companion eBook (in PDF format) for $10 to customers who purchase this book now. Convenient and fully searchable, the PDF version of any content-rich, page-heavy Apress book makes a valuable addition to your programming library. You can easily find and copy code—or perform examples by quickly toggling between instructions and the application. Even simultaneously tackling a donut, diet soda, and complex code becomes simplified with hands-free eBooks!

Once you purchase your book, getting the $10 companion eBook is simple:

❶ Visit **www.apress.com/promo/tendollars/**.

❷ Complete a basic registration form to receive a randomly generated question about this title.

❸ Answer the question correctly in 60 seconds, and you will receive a promotional code to redeem for the $10.00 eBook.

Apress®
THE EXPERT'S VOICE™

233 Spring Street, New York, NY 10013

Offer valid through 06/11.